Racism, Class and the Racialized Outsider

Racism, Class and the Racialized Outsider

Satnam Virdee

University of Glasgow, UK

palgrave
macmillan

First published 2014 by
PALGRAVE MACMILLAN

Palgrave Macmillan in the UK is an imprint of Macmillan Publishers Limited, registered in England, company number 785998, of Houndmills, Basingstoke, Hampshire RG21 6XS.

Palgrave Macmillan in the US is a division of St Martin's Press LLC, 175 Fifth Avenue, New York, NY 10010.

Palgrave Macmillan is the global academic imprint of the above companies and has companies and representatives throughout the world.

Palgrave® and Macmillan® are registered trademarks in the United States, the United Kingdom, Europe and other countries.

ISBN 978–0–230–55163–3 hardback
ISBN 978–0–230–55164–0 paperback

This book is printed on paper suitable for recycling and made from fully managed and sustained forest sources. Logging, pulping and manufacturing processes are expected to conform to the environmental regulations of the country of origin.

A catalogue record for this book is available from the British Library.

A catalog record for this book is available from the Library of Congress.

Printed in China

In loving memory of my grandparents

Contents

Acknowledgements

A book that ranges across two centuries inevitably incurs many debts along the way. I have been extremely fortunate to have benefited from the generous support and advice of a number of friends and colleagues including Laurence Brown, Peter Fairbrother, Ben Gidley, Keith Grint, Rick Halpern, Lynn Jamieson, Steve Jefferys, Rick Kuhn, Sian Moore, Craig Phelan, Liliana Riga, David Renton, Sheila Rowbotham, Evan Smith, John Solomos, Tim Strangleman, Rodolfo D. Torres, Matt Worley, John Wrench and Erik Olin Wright. Special thanks also to all the staff and postgraduates of the Centre for Research on Racism, Ethnicity and Nationalism (CRREN) at the University of Glasgow, in particular Stephen Ashe, Neil Davidson, Bridget Fowler, Robert Gibb, Brendan McGeever and Andrew Smith. I hope those endless hours of argument and debate over copious amounts of tea and coffee proved as enlightening for you as they were for me. I am extremely grateful to Honor Hania – the university librarian – who located references that no one else could, and Mike French – then head of the School of Social and Political Sciences – who helped facilitate the completion of this project by granting me a short period of study leave that took me away from chairing the Sociology Department at just the right time. Emily Salz at Palgrave Macmillan commissioned this book, while Anna Reeve, Lloyd Langman and especially Nicola Cattini have been the perfect editors helping smooth the path to publication. In those fleeting moments of doubt that inevitably arise over the course of writing a book of this kind, it has been the music of Asha Bhosle, Jimmy Cliff and Curtis Mayfield that has inspired me to 'keep on keeping on'. Finally, I thank the members of my family, who have supported me throughout this journey, particularly my parents, parents-in-law, sisters, sister-in-law, brother-in-law and nieces. And most of all, LV and CV who have lived with this book for far too long, and whose love and humour (often at my expense!) helped bring it to completion. I am forever grateful.

The author and publisher would like to thank the copyright holders for permission to reproduce material from the following sources:

De Beauvoir, S. 1976. *The Ethics of Ambiguity*. New York: Citadel Press (reprinted by permission of Kensington Publishing Corp.);

Colley, L. 1986. 'Whose Nation? Class and National Consciousness in Britain 1750–1830', *Past and Present* 113: 1. Oxford: Oxford Journals (reprinted by permission of Oxford University Press);

Thompson, E. P. 1965. 'The Peculiarities of the English', *Socialist Register* 2 (reprinted by permission of the Socialist Register);

Anderson, P. 1964. 'Origins of the Present Crisis', *New Left Review* 1: 23 (reprinted by permission of the New Left Review);

May, R. and Cohen, R. 1974. 'The Interaction Between Race and Colonialism: A Case Study of the Liverpool Race Riots of 1919', *Race and Class* 16: 2. London: Sage Journals (reprinted by permission of the Institute of Race Relations);

Nairn, T. 1970. 'Enoch Powell: The New Right', *New Left Review* 1: 61 (reprinted by permission of the New Left Review);

Sivanandan, A. 1977. 'The Liberation of the Black Intellectual', *Race and Class* 18: 4. London: Sage Journals (reprinted by permission of the Institute of Race Relations);

Widgery, D. 1986. *Beating Time*. London: Vintage (reprinted by permission of The Random House Group Limited and also by kind permission of Juliet Ash);

A speech made by Margaret Thatcher at the Press Conference for American correspondents in London, 25 June 1980 (reprinted by permission of the Margaret Thatcher Foundation).

1

Introduction

We cannot go forward unless we know our yesterdays.
(Alfred Rosmer cited in Tarbuck 1991: 43)

To will oneself free is also to will others free.
(Simone De Beauvoir 1948/1976: 73)

Racism, Class and the Racialized Outsider is a critical analysis of working class efforts to secure economic and social justice and democratize English society. Unlike most studies of the English working class, however, this volume investigates these social and political struggles through 'the prism of race'. Through an insistence 'that race is a central, not peripheral, part of the way things work' (Knowles 2003: 10–11), my intention is to contribute further to unsettling the academic consensus which equates the history and making of the working class in England with the white male worker (see for example Scott 1986; Taylor 1991; Hall 1992). .

From the seventeenth century, England, and then Britain, colonized parts of Ireland, North America, the Caribbean, Africa and Asia, strategically positioning itself at the centre of a plethora of economic and political networks. Military wars, forced population movements and the organization, production and large-scale transfer of goods across the oceans of the world were just some of the key elements that facilitated Britain's rise to power as the undisputed hegemon of the modern world-system. To write 'an insular history of Britain' which didn't consider this Empire, including how it shaped domestic politics, 'is quite inadequate' (Hobsbawm 1968/1990: 19). Since the 1980s, a growing body of postcolonial scholarship has focused its attention precisely on how the Empire impacted at home, particularly the multifarious ways in which it shaped middle-class understandings of the 'other' suggesting that racism was more central to the making of the British nation than hitherto believed (Hall 1992; McClintock 1995; Hall 2002; Hall and Rose 2006).

Studies of how people from the Empire featured in the lives of the English working class and their institutions when they came to this country are comparatively rarer (see for example Fryer 1984; Ramdin 1987; Tabili 1994). While this body of work has made an invaluable contribution in inserting a minority presence in English working class history, they have not succeeded in dislodging those classic 'race-blind' accounts which define the broad contours and signpost the principal co-ordinates of English working class development since the 1780s (see for example Hobsbawm 1964, 1984a, 1984b, 1990; Thompson 1991). That is, even within more recent accounts of the English working class, the discovery of a minority presence represents a kind of 'add-on' which, while deserving of mention, does not fundamentally alter our long-established understanding of the key trends, episodes and events of English working class history (see for example Foster 1977; Joyce 1991; Savage and Miles 1994; Crompton et al. 2000; Devine et al. 2005). Significantly, this 'race-blindness' is mirrored within the contemporary labour movement where the events at Cable Street in 1936 and Grunwick in 1976 remain the only 'official' episodes of racialized minority involvement in working class history that are collectively remembered.

This failing may in part be the result of the continuing Eurocentric presuppositions that underpin many areas of historical sociology, class analysis and social and labour history (van der Linden 2003; Bhambra 2011). However, equally significant in creating this impression may be the focus on producing analyses of singular racialized minority groups across narrow time periods (see for example Tabili 1994) alongside the tendency to disembed and detach such accounts from the narrative of ongoing working class struggles for economic and social justice (see for example Ramdin 1987).

Consequently, those of us who are insistent on investigating the making and unmaking of the working class in England through the prism of race must demonstrate how viewing history through such a lens serves to unsettle long-established understandings of formative episodes such as Chartism in the 1830s and 1840s, the new unionism of the 1880s and 1890s, the formation of the Labour Party and the Communist Party of Great Britain (CPGB) in the early twentieth century and the development and eventual breakdown of the welfare settlement in the second half of the twentieth century. It is for this reason that *Racism, Class and the Racialized Outsider* ranges widely across time from the 1780s and the advent of the Industrial and French Revolutions which heralded the birth of modern society to 1989 and the so-called 'end of history', signalled by the collapse of the state socialist regimes of eastern Europe. Inevitably, there is an opportunity cost implicit in covering such a vast time period in a single volume. Sometimes, for example, the thick description of formative moments in working class history will be sacrificed; what we gain, however, is the development of an innovative argument about the significance of race in English society over the *longue durée*.

The same web of social and economic networks that bound the colonies to England, and then Britain in an unequal relationship, and ensured that everyday foodstuffs such as tea, coffee and sugar would come to form a staple part of our contemporary diet, also brought men and women from all corners of the world to England (Fryer 1984; Visram 2002). Former slaves of African-American and Caribbean descent, Irish Catholic labourers, African and Asian lascars and seamen, along with Jewish migrants escaping the racist pogroms within the Tsarist Empire all made their home in England at different moments in the nineteenth and twentieth centuries, and sometimes earlier.

Significantly, most entered the ranks of the working class in England confirming that it was a multi-ethnic formation long before the *Empire Windrush* docked at Tilbury in Essex in the summer of 1948, carrying 493 passengers from Jamaica. In this sense, *Racism, Class and the Racialized Outsider* is not a historical sociology of a singular nation, but rather an account of how populations from all over the world – from Britain's Empire – shaped the economic and political development of English society. It is a study of the world in England. Further, it is a study not of a singular English working class but an examination of how workers from India, Jamaica and Ireland, alongside those from London, Manchester and elsewhere contributed to the making, unmaking and remaking of the English working class. It brings the working class in all its diversity – black, brown and white; English, Scottish, Irish Catholic, Jewish, Asian and Caribbean – centre stage as an actor in the making of English society, in the making of history, although not always in circumstances of their choosing.

The significance of bringing these social groups together in a single study not only helps to draw out the continuities and discontinuities in the experiences of different racialized minority groups, but also makes an important contribution to produce a more comprehensive account of the place of racism and anti-racism in the working class in England. In particular, *Racism, Class and the Racialized Outsider* focuses on

- the social relations between these minority groups and the English working class, including the part played by the elites and the state in mediating such relations;
- the significance of racism in structuring social relations between different components of the working class in England, as well as the perspectives that informed it; and
- those episodes of class solidarity and anti-racism, including the identification of the principal social actors responsible for their creation, and the ideational perspectives that animated such actions.

As can already be discerned, *Racism, Class and the Racialized Outsider* moves beyond currently dominant conceptualizations of racism as a colour-coded phenomenon, to bring into view other modalities of racism that have been much neglected in sociology, including most notably anti-Irish Catholic racism and anti-Semitism (Holmes 1988; Cesarani 1994; Hickman 1998; Mac an Ghaill 2000). There may be some scholars, particularly in the US, who might question my inclusion of the Irish Catholics as a racialized social group and accuse me of conflating the concept of racism with ethnic conflict. However, such American sociologists conceive racism narrowly as a colour-coded phenomenon (Miles 1982, 1993); that is, race and racism are understood as fundamentally being about colour prejudice and discrimination, whereas ethnicity and ethnic conflict (encompassing religion) are used to refer to forms of social relations and antagonisms based on modes of cultural differentiation. Such an understanding may have theoretical purchase in the US where African slavery was so dominant in distorting and structuring that society. It may also help to understand why migrants of Irish Catholic descent were eventually able to lay claim to whiteness and thus avoid the experience of racialization in the US (see Allen 1994; Ignatiev 1995). However, as we will see in forthcoming chapters, the same was not true of the Irish Catholics in nineteenth-century Britain. Here, they constituted a clearly demarcated racialized minority, members of an allegedly inferior Celtic race that was incompatible with membership of the British nation underpinned at the time by a shared allegiance to Protestantism, and the idea of an Anglo-Saxon race. The nature of racialization against Irish Catholics was remarkably similar to that of 'visible' racialized minorities, comprising a discourse of race and physical representations of the Irish Catholics as simianized, ape-like creatures of ridicule. That is, elements of ethnicity and race entwined in Britain with regard to the Irish Catholics from the middle decades of the nineteenth century in a way that they did not in the US, reinforcing Hall's (1980: 338) important observation that there can be no general theory of racism, only historically specific racisms.

Relatedly, the reader will gather that the overwhelming focus of this study is on developments in the working class in England rather than the working classes in the other two nations of Britain – Scotland and Wales. This has been a deliberate decision determined in large part by the recognition that at key moments, the history of the Scottish and Welsh working class followed a rather different trajectory to that of the working class in England. At the same time, it is also impossible to write a history of the working class in England without recognizing the influential role played particularly by those of Scottish descent in England, as well as within the British working class more broadly. Consequently, in key conjunctures – such as the development of the new unionism, and the formation of the Independent Labour Party (ILP), along with events on Clydeside and the development of the CPGB – the part played by Scottish socialist activists is made transparent. It is clear, for example, that the CPGB would have been a much weaker political force at its inception had it not been for the existence of a 'Little Moscow' in Glasgow. Such coverage of the Scottish contribution to the making of the English working class in no way diminishes the case for a distinctive history of the making of the working class in Scotland, viewed through the prism of race.

The contours of the argument

Racism, Class and the Racialized Outsider advances three main theses. First, the widespread emergence of working class racism is traced to the 1830s and 1840s and the catastrophic defeats that marked the passing of 'the heroic age of the proletariat'. Thereafter, racism was consolidated among an ever-expanding constituency of workers. Facilitated by the rise of Britain as the hegemon of the modern world-system, the elites learnt to rule in a more consensual manner at home. Through the granting of political reforms and the guarantee of relative economic security between the 1850s and 1940s, the British elites ideologically incorporated ever larger components of the working class into the imagined nation as active citizens of the polity. Of course, this strategy would never have worked had it remained a 'top-down' process of working class integration into the nation. The working class were conscious agents in this process. That is, what accompanied this elite process of reform was that slowly but surely those workers to whom such privileges were granted began to imbibe the idea of the British nation underpinned by its notion of a singular people united by race and religion. Subjectively, they too began to embrace a British national identity constructed in opposition to the racialized other, the latter encompassing at various points in our historical timeline, the unrespectable members of the working class, Irish Catholics, Jews, Asians and those of Caribbean and African descent. And in that process, class as a representational form and as a material relation was indelibly nationalized and racialized.

Significantly, what has been neglected in scholarly accounts hitherto is how, by the late nineteenth century, socialist arguments and struggles to secure economic and social justice for the excluded also came to be ideologically located on the terrain of the nation. The idea of the nation operated as a power container, limiting the political imagination of even most of those who were representatives of the exploited and the oppressed. While the conceptions of national belonging that underpinned such socialist nationalisms were undoubtedly broader than those forged by the elites of the time, and in that sense sought to democratize society, they attempted to do so by identifying new racialized others – the refugee Jew, escaping the pogroms from eastern Europe, or Asian and black workers. Indeed, it will be contended that this expanded understanding of national belonging gained growing legitimacy among the working class precisely because it was able to portray elite conceptions of national belonging as unjust due to the exclusion of those, like themselves, who were also British, and thus deserving of fair and equal treatment. Each time the boundary of the nation was extended to encompass ever more members of the working class, it was accompanied and legitimized through the further racialization of nationalism that prevented another more recently arrived social group from being included. And this process of socialist nationalist struggles for social justice and democratization of the polity and their eventual ideological incorporation into the nation was to be repeated throughout much of the twentieth century, mediated by the Labour Party as well as the trade union movement.

The second thesis underpinning *Racism, Class and the Racialized Outsider* is that throughout the period under investigation there were historical moments when the working class suppressed such expressions of racism, and on occasion, actively rejected it. Manifestations of collective action and solidarity between racialized majority and minority fractions of the working class are identified and analysed. Given that such ideologies had not consolidated themselves as a material force within the working class, numerous case studies and vignettes of English and Irish Catholic solidarity are identified during the heroic age of the proletariat, alongside the formative contribution made by individuals of African descent to align such struggles with those against slavery.

It is demonstrated how such working class solidarity across what was to become embedded racialized boundaries became more scarce after the catastrophic defeat of Chartism. Between 1848 and 1968, for example, there were only two moments where parts of the working class and its institutions succeeded briefly in suppressing such racist divisions. The first arose amid the new unionism of the late 1880s and early 1890s, and the industrial revolt of the unrespectable, women and Irish Catholics that would eventually lead to the formation of the Labour Party. A minority of socialists, mainly aligned to the Socialist League of William Morris, Belfort Bax and Eleanor Marx and adhering to the politics of proletarian internationalism, sought to build support on behalf of Jewish migrants engaged in struggles for union organization, often in opposition to the anti-Semitism of socialist nationalists. The second moment occurred during the 1920s and 1930s, when the CPGB – led by some of its Indian, Irish Catholic and Jewish members – attempted to fashion a strategy to challenge English working class attachment to racism and Empire. This book shows that it was only in the aftermath of the world revolution of 1968 – amid decolonization throughout Africa, Asia and the Caribbean; the struggle for civil rights in the US; and black resistance in England itself – that the English working class begin to bifurcate on the question of racism directed in this instance against those of Asian and Caribbean descent. It was in the 1970s amid the organic crisis of British capitalism and the collapsing welfare settlement that the organized labour movement shifted from a position of indifference towards racism to one of actively challenging it, including most notably in support of Asian women workers on strike at Grunwick. Alongside such anti-racist action in the workplace, the attempts by parts of organized labour and youth to fashion anti-racist and anti-fascist social movements of a scale unprecedented in Britain to this day are tracked and evaluated.

Racism, Class and the Racialized Outsider outlines how such suppression of working class racism emerges episodically, in periods of systemic crisis of the capitalist world-system whose effects permeate all spheres of society – the economic, political and ideological/cultural. However, there is no instinctive movement to the political left where workers rush to the flag of solidarity and socialism. It was Walter Benjamin (1940/2006) who first warned socialists in the 1930s of the dangers of assuming the inevitable victory of socialism with his pertinent observation that '[n]othing has corrupted the German working class so much as the notion that it is moving with the current'. Benjamin was attuned to the dangers of teleology and fatalism because he tragically witnessed first-hand the political capitulation of the German Communist Party (KPD) to the Nazis, so powerfully captured by their defeatist slogan 'After Hitler, Us'.

Instead, the explanation advanced in this volume is that systemic change occurs only when those long-established co-ordinates of hegemonic domination, which lock in place key fractions of the working class through a combination of coercion and consent, begin to unravel amid sustained conflict and crisis. It is in the course of re-negotiating the settlement that workers become more amenable to alternative narratives or frames through which to understand their social position and the crisis more generally. That is, they begin to peel away from the political consensus that had held firm and shift to the political left and right. That is why such periods of crisis represent a key moment of potential systemic change, although the outcome can never be predicted in advance but is determined by the relations of force (Gramsci 1971).

The third and final thesis of *Racism, Class and the Racialized Outsider* contends that it is the relative strength of socialist leadership within the working class, in particular socialist internationalist as against socialist nationalist leadership, in such moments of systemic crisis that is crucial in determining the scale and scope of anti-racism that is likely to emerge within the working class. After the defeat of Chartism, such an internationalist current became a minority even among socialists. In fact, from 1848 to 1968 – the highpoint in the strength of British nationalism and scientific racism – this current of leadership, informed by the politics of socialist internationalism, became, with the notable exception of individuals such as William Morris, Belfort Bax, John Maclean, Sylvia Pankhurst, largely the preserve of racialized minorities. Men and women such as Eleanor Marx, James Connolly, Arthur MacManus, Zelda Kahan, Theodore Rothstein and Shapurji Saklatvala were the 'racialized outsiders' who were instrumental in sustaining a current of proletarian internationalism in England. They belonged to racialized minority groups in Britain – Irish Catholic, Jewish and Indian – social groups against whom the dominant conception of British nationalism had been constructed at various points in history. Naturally, their attachment to the British nation was less firm, and their participation in working class struggles gave them a unique capacity to see through the fog of blood, soil and belonging and universalize the militant, yet often particularist, struggles of the working class. In this sense, they acted as a leavening agent, nourishing the struggles of all through their unique perspective on society. This was to come to fruition in the final quarter of the twentieth century, when socialist internationalists, particularly racialized minority socialists, proved to be the conduit through which anti-racist ideas, consciousness and political practice came to be transmitted into the mainstream of the organized labour movement and beyond.

Reading the history of the working class in England against the grain helps to make more transparent the influential contributions made by individuals from different ethnic groups in the formative struggles for economic and social justice, as well as political democratization, waged by the working class between the 1780s and 1980s. By demonstrating the multi-ethnic character of the working class in England from the moment of its inception, racialized minorities can no longer be reduced to the margins of the historical account of its making and unmaking. Additionally, this volume will demonstrate how racism was an influential, structuring force within the working class from as early as the 1830s and 1840s, and by the close of the nineteenth century, racialized minorities were often the foil against whom parts of the English working class legitimated their demands for inclusion in the British nation. Racism had become the modality through which class was lived for key strata within the working class (Hall 1980). At the same time, such racism was on occasion successfully suppressed, and instrumental in developing such collective resistance were socialist internationalists who came from minority groups – the racialized outsiders. Consequently, race was constitutive in the making, unmaking and remaking of the working class in England across two centuries.

Finally, it is hoped that this study makes a small contribution to unsettling those still dominant narratives of the nation, which construe Britain as some kind of ethnically and racially homogeneous society prior to 1948 (see Goodhart 2013). Demonstrating the formative contributions made by individuals from multiple ethnic groups in the making of the working class and modern England from the moment of its inception in the 1780s, will, I hope, encourage black, Asian and white Britons today to not only remember this complex and contradictory history but also to lay claim to an expanded, more democratic conception of the British community – one which finally takes us beyond those narratives of the 'Island Race'.

In *Forging Democracy*, Geoff Eley (2002: 10) draws our attention to the important part played by the working class in democratizing European societies:

> [D]emocracy is not 'given' or 'granted'. It requires *conflict*, namely, coura-geous challenges to authority, risk-taking and reckless exemplary acts, ethical witnessing, violent confrontations, and general crises in which the given sociopolitical order breaks down . . . . [D]emocracy did not arise from natural evolution or economic prosperity. It certainly did not emerge as an inevitable by-product of individualism or the market. It developed because masses of people organised collectively to demand it.

Irish Catholics, Jews, Asians and the African diaspora – not in the colonies but in England itself – made an important contribution to those ongoing efforts of the English working class to fashion a more inclusive and democratic society, sometimes against great odds.

2

Class, Nation and the Racialized Outsider

[C]lass and nation in Britain at this time were not antithetical but two sides of the same historical processes.

(Colley 1986: 100)

A single mistake in extending equality too far may overthrow the existing social order and dissolve the bonds of social order.

(Jeremy Bentham cited in Nairn 1964: 47)

I am a West Indian, a lover of liberty, and would dishonour human nature if I did not show myself a friend to the liberty of others.

(Robert Wedderburn cited in McCalman 1991: 83)

Introduction

In his pivotal work *The Making of the English Working Class* (1963/1991), Edward Palmer Thompson catalogues both the devastating impact of the industrial revolution on labouring lives and how the social struggles that it triggered led to the formation of a distinctive social class; a working class that over the course of such struggles became aware of its own distinctive interests in contradistinction to those of the capitalist class and the political system, known as Old Corruption. As Thompson (1991: 938) put it, it became possible for individual workers to have a sense

of sustained commitment to a movement for their own class objectives, and a confidence which enabled them to stand up against the physical and moral resources of their opponents.

Some of the early leaders of these oppositional movements justified their claims for greater rights and freedoms by ideologically marrying them to a radical patriotism that drew selectively on narratives of a mythical past, the theory of the Norman Yoke and the recovery of the ancient liberties of the free-born Englishman (Thompson 1991: 94–95). Given the consolidation of the modern British state during this period (Tilly 2005), it is perhaps surprising that Thompson has little to say about the evolution of a British national consciousness within the working class, nor the extent to which it shaped the class struggles of the period.

Linda Colley (1996), in her influential volume *Britons*, picking up on this oversight, charges Thompson with neglecting the significance of working class patriotism, and particularly its attachment to British nationalism. According to Colley (1996), central to the formation of a national consciousness across all social classes was the war that raged between Britain and France for almost half the period between 1688 and 1815. The elites 'were obliged, over and over again, to mobilise not just the consent, but increasingly the active co-operation of large numbers of Britons in order to repel this recurrent danger from without' (Colley 1996: 4). And they did so by forging a national identity constructed and informed by a 'strong sense of dissimilarity from those without' (Colley 1996: 18). Hence, the Scots, Welsh and the English first fused together as British around a shared allegiance to Protestantism, in opposition to

> [a] powerful and persistently threatening France [which] became the haunting embodiment of that Catholic Other which Britons had been taught to fear since the Reformation in the sixteenth century. Confronting it encouraged them to bury their internal differences in the struggle for survival, victory and booty.
>
> (Colley 1996: 387)

Colley (1986: 109) is insistent that the working class and labouring poor also embraced this national identification, indeed that it was 'spontaneously generated from below'. Therefore, the process of nation-making wasn't just engineered from above, it was actively worked upon by the working class themselves such that a British nationalism underpinned by a shared religious allegiance to Protestantism 'helped men and women make sense of their lives and gain comfort and dignity in the face of difficulty and dangers. And it was more than prejudice' (Colley 1996: 45). Instead, it

> gave the majority of men and women a sense of their place in history and a sense of worth. It allowed them to feel pride in such advantages as they genuinely did enjoy, and helped them endure when hardship and danger threatened. It gave them identity.
>
> (Colley 1996: 57)

Significantly, there was no inherent antagonism between a consciousness of class and that of nation. Instead, it was the rise of a British national consciousness that made class 'salient' and helped facilitate the advancement of such concerns. That is, working class demands stood a greater chance of success if they 'resorted to nationalist language and activism to advance their claims to wider civic recognition' because 'patriotic vocabulary provided an obvious means to describe and legitimize their endeavours' (Colley 1986: 116).

Colley's work is insightful on a number of different levels, most importantly because she draws our attention to an important layer of working class opinion that saw no necessary conflict between an emergent identification based on class with that based on nation. For Colley, much of the working class resistance of this period was informed by, and remained contained within, the ideological imaginary of British nationalism. Such working class collective action sought not to overthrow the *ancien regime* as Thompson claims, but to reform it, by expanding the boundaries of the imagined nation to accommodate the inclusion of the working class as active citizens. In contrast to Thompson and others who

> have argued that national consciousness in this period was inherently inimical to class consciousness and served merely as an instrument of elite control, there is much to be said for precisely the opposite view.
>
> (Colley 1986: 117)

Surprisingly, given their sophisticated treatment of class and national identifications respectively, neither Thompson nor Colley have very much to say about ethnicity and racism in Britain in this period (Gregg 1998; Hall et al. 2000). Colley's argument, however, associating the formation of class consciousness with a British national consciousness is significant because as Paul Gilroy (1987: 57) reminds us, in Britain, 'statements about nation are invariably statements about "race"'. The danger of ideologically locating demands for greater working class rights and freedoms on the terrain of the nation is that it may simultaneously contribute to the exclusion of others, especially those members of the working class who cannot be imagined as British. While Gilroy is referring specifically to the racialization of British nationalism in the post–Second World War era, can this relationship be traced back to the early nineteenth century, and the 'heroic age of the proletariat?' Was it the case that working class claims were contained within a racialized conception of the British nation?

To investigate these and other questions involves piecing together the presence of racialized minority workers in the formative years of the English working class. This is not as straightforward a task as one might imagine. With British sociologists focusing their energies overwhelmingly on studies of minorities in the post-WWII era (Solomos 2003), it is historians who have shed most light on this period. Influential studies have demonstrated the presence of black people in Britain since the time of Elisabeth I (Fryer 1984), recovered the writings of radical black activists between 1780 and 1850 (McCalman 1991) and told remarkable tales about the establishment of a multi-ethnic proletariat on the high seas (Linebaugh and Rediker 2001).

But even crossing disciplinary boundaries in search of a more comprehensive understanding is insufficient. The dominance of the liberal and radical race relations paradigms (Miles 1984) has further fragmented knowledge. In particular, the overwhelming focus on colour-coded modalities of racism has often rendered invisible the Irish Catholic experience in Britain because of their presumed membership of the white race (Hickman 1995; Mac an Ghaill 2000).

My aim then is to begin the task of re-assembling these fragments of minority history and to re-insert the presence of the racialized minority worker into the early history of the working class in England. This will enable us to explore tentatively, the nature of social relations between English, Irish and black workers in this period, particularly the extent to which these were characterized by conflict, and co-operation. Through this re-assembling, the significance of racism in structuring social relations will be determined alongside a consideration of the part played by minority workers in the radical class struggles of this period. More broadly, the intention is to consider how inserting the presence of the minority worker into the history of the working class in England transforms our traditional understandings of this period.

'The ready made nucleus of degradation and disorder': The Irish Catholic worker and the class struggle

Locked into a colonial relationship to England, and then the British state, and with the peasantry finding themselves increasingly dispossessed of their land due to the continuing consolidation of capitalist agriculture in the country, it is little surprise that parts of the Irish population came to Britain in search of the new work opportunities provided by the take-off of the Industrial Revolution. Initially, migrant workers of both genders found work as agricultural labourers on British farms, replacing English workers who had moved into the newly established factories in the urban conurbations. It is estimated that during this early phase of industrialization in the 1780s, there were 40,000 Irish people resident in Britain (MacRaid 1999).

However, the ever-increasing demand for labour coupled with the appalling conditions faced by most small peasant holders in Ireland meant that this seasonal migration rapidly took on a more permanent form (Thompson 1991: 473). And when growing numbers of English workers began leaving those jobs requiring arduous, unskilled physical labour in the urban areas and moved into the better-paid, skilled jobs in the cotton and textile industries, the demand for unskilled labour in those areas came to be increasingly filled by Irish migrant labour (Miles 1982: 130; Thompson 1991: 473–474). The Irish population in Britain grew rapidly over the next 50 years from 580,000 in 1831 (Colley 1996: 348), to 727,000 (Tuathaigh 1981: 151) over the course of the 1845–1852 famine – during which a million people starved to death

(Hobsbawm 1968; O'Murchadha 2011). Apart from London, the Irish settled in the main industrial cities of the north of England, including Liverpool and Manchester (McDermott 1979). In London, they gained employment in street trading, tailoring and food (Miles 1982), whereas the majority in the North found work as navvies on the canals and railways, as well as labouring jobs in the building trade, docks and the coalfields of Scotland and Wales (McDermott 1979; Thompson 1991).

Given the emphasis Colley places on the strength of British nationalism underpinned by a shared allegiance to Protestantism across all social classes, one might expect considerable resentment, division and conflict within the working class over the arrival of a mainly Catholic population from Ireland. Certainly, such antipathy is not hard to find in a country where absolutist monarchical rule was historically associated with Catholicism, and the threatened return of 'rule from Rome' was an integral component of the national conversation. The most significant of the regular outbursts of anti-Catholic sentiment in Britain – including against English Catholics – occurred in June 1780 in what came to be known as the Gordon riots (Rudé 1956). Government attempts to reduce some of the official discrimination against Catholics, and so draw them into the British armed forces that were severely overstretched fighting wars on different fronts, led to large-scale mobilizations by the Protestant Association. Led by Lord George Gordon – a Londoner born into the Scottish nobility – over 60,000 people marched to the House of Commons to deliver a petition demanding the repeal of the 1778 Papists Act which had removed some of the more obvious manifestations of discrimination against Catholics. While the crowd shouted 'No Popery' others demanded entry into the House of Commons to present their petition. Outside Parliament, a riot erupted, and the 'King and Church Mob' went on a rampage through parts of London attacking Catholic chapels, foreign embassies as well as the residential homes of any Catholics they could find. The following day, Newgate Prison was attacked, and the homes of English Catholics resident in Moorfields and Irish Catholics in Wapping and Spitalfields were ransacked and burnt. It took the army five days to restore order. Two hundred and eighty-five people died in the riots, and 25 individuals were tried and hanged (Rudé 1956).

While conflict between different ethnic components of the working class in this period is undeniable, what has been less remarked upon is the extent to which there emerged a counter tradition of co-operation and solidarity between the English and Irish worker. When the advent of industrial capitalism undermined the moral economy of England (Thompson 2009) triggering massive social and political struggles by English artisans and the labouring poor, the Irish Catholic migrant was a key participant in such struggles.

Overstretched by the wars it was fighting, most notably against France, the Royal Navy had turned to recruiting Irish Catholics. When 16 ships of the Channel fleet refused to sail in April 1797, and mounted a collective mutiny at Spithead in Portsmouth, Irish Catholic workers comprised a key element of the workforce.The English and Irish sailors elected delegates to negotiate with the Admiralty for improved pay and conditions. A detailed study of the mutiny (Coats 2011) reveals little animosity between English and Irish workers during the dispute, and within a month, the Admiralty – fearful of the dispute's capacity to spread in a time of war – conceded to the sailors demands.

The demands of the English and Irish mutineers at Nore in the Thames Estuary in May 1797 were greater than those at Spithead, encompassing additional leave, including the right to shore leave when in port, a pardon for deserters, along with a veto on the appointment of unpopular officers. On this occasion, the leading presence of Irish radicals in the dispute, including members of the United Irishmen – an organization formed in 1791 and committed to Irish freedom and establishing a French-style republic underpinned by the ideals of liberty, equality and fraternity – led the Admiralty to react by enacting a bill to outlaw the mutineers. The dispute was seen as an 'an open revolt against constituted authority', and the Admiralty were insistent about holding out. Over time, divisions grew among the sailors – although not on ethnic lines – about how to proceed, which undermined the mutiny. Later, Richard Parker, President of the Delegates of the Fleet or the 'Floating Republic' as it came to be known was arrested and hanged (Manwaring and Dobree 1935; Thompson 1991).

The corresponding societies that emerged in Britain in the aftermath of the French Revolution played a crucial role in forging 'a new democratic consciousness' (Thompson 1991: 80) by drawing together advocates of all kinds of radical causes, including opposition to the aristocracy, slavery, and by arguing for an extension of rights and freedoms for working people. Rejecting 'any notion of exclusiveness, of politics as the presence of any hereditary elite or property group' (Thompson 1991: 24), these new organizations comprised artisans, shopkeepers, mechanics, general labourers as well as professional men. Their aim was nothing less than to transform 'the mob' 'by education and agitation . . . from 'followers of the camp' to followers of 'the standard of liberty' (Thompson 1991: 109). Here too, Irish Catholics were healthily represented and involved in deliberations on all kinds of questions, including how to secure Irish freedom from the British state (Thale 1983; Thompson 1991: 185).

It was the strength of this current of Jacobinism, and the growth more generally of a culture of political dissent within the working class that helps explain how, sometimes, the class struggles of English and Irish workers could be brought into alignment with the cause of Irish national liberation. The sizeable support for the Irish rebellion of 1798 in England, particularly amongst the radicals in the northern manufacturing districts is a case in point (Thompson 1991: 185). More broadly, Thompson observes that what was striking about this period was 'not the friction but the relative ease with which the Irish were absorbed into working class communities: in those areas where the Irish migrants settled, there was a high degree of inter-marriage' (Foster 1977;

Thompson 1991: 480). Not only were Irish Catholics becoming an integral component of the working class in England in an era when an attachment to British nationalism was allegedly consolidating itself within the English working class, but on occasion they could win some English radicals to the cause of Irish national freedom from British imperial rule. This was a working class that had not yet attached its flag to the mast of the British national interest.

It was inevitable that 'a counter-revolutionary assault backed by the resources of established authority' (Thompson 1991: 123) would follow this increasingly confident demand for an expansion of working class rights and democratic freedoms. Leaders of the corresponding societies were jailed, and the British state concerned at the prospect of newly established trade unions becoming vehicles for radical social change enacted the Combination Acts of 1799 and 1800 prohibiting the right to organize (Pelling 1987: 15). Combinations of two or more workers with the intention of increasing wages or reducing working hours were made illegal, and workers were 'prosecuted in their thousands' (Pelling 1987: 16–20; Morton 1994: 364).

When workers objected to employers replacing unskilled labour with new machinery, they found themselves summarily dismissed and replaced by individuals from the growing reserve army of labour (Pelling 1987: 18). The withdrawal of the right to organize was effectively neutering the power of the working class to collectively resist their harsh conditions of existence. Yet, despite such obstacles, or perhaps because of them, a distinct working class consciousness continued to mature. Groups of workers known as the Luddites responded by systematically destroying machinery and factories understood to be undermining their livelihoods – actions that Hobsbawm (1990: 89) describes as a form of 'collective bargaining by riot'. The presence of the Irish worker can also be detected in these Luddite rebellions with a Catholic priest claiming that they were heavily involved in the rebellions and 'were more prone to take part in trades unions, combinations and secret societies than the English' (cited in Thompson 1991: 484, 652–654). Faced with such workplace resistance, the government was forced to rescind the Combination Acts, eventually introducing a new Combination Law in 1824 that enabled workers to combine again without fear of prosecution (Pelling 1987).

However, this change in the legal status of trade unions did not have the desired effect of dampening down the scale and scope of discontent expressed by significant elements of the working class. Instead, legalization was accompanied by an immediate burst of strike activity (see Morton 1994: 365–366). The Irish Catholic worker was again at the centre of this newly emergent trade unionism. An angry employer stated to a Parliamentary Commission that

> where there is discontent or a disposition to combine or turn-outs among the work people, the Irish are the leaders. They are the most difficult to reason with and convince on the subject of wages and regulations.
>
> (cited in O'Higgins 1961: 89)

And it was during the first few months of legal and militant trade unionism in 1824, that the first national trade union leader emerged in Britain, John Doherty – an Irishman. Doherty began work in the cotton mills of Ireland before crossing the Irish Sea to work in Manchester in 1816 (Tilly 2005: xviii). He 'served his apprenticeship in the days of illegality, when he became a trusted leader of the cotton spinners' (Morton 1994: 366). Alongside establishing a cotton spinners union in the Manchester area, Doherty led strikes against the introduction of new spinning machinery that he contended weakened the operatives' bargaining position. In 1819, he went to prison for two years, convicted of helping start a strike the year before (Tilly 2005: xix).

Doherty was one of the first working class leaders to appreciate how the consolidation of the British national state required that British workers also organize on the same terrain, and that 'British workers' politics' be 'nationalized' (Tilly 2005: xix). However, his proposal for a new form of national political organization couldn't easily be accommodated within the dominant conceptions of British nationalism underpinned by a shared allegiance to Protestantism. Doherty advanced a broader, more democratic non-sectarian arrangement that envisioned English, Scottish as well as migrant Irish Catholic cotton workers in Britain organizing alongside cotton workers in Ireland to demand more rights and freedoms, in opposition to the British state.

In December 1829 on the Isle of Man, he was 'the moving spirit' behind a conference of English, Scottish and Irish textile workers that led to the formation of the Grand General Union of the Operative Spinners of Great Britain and Ireland (Pelling 1987: 26–27; Morton 1994: 366). However, he came to the realization that this initiative of organizing groups of workers into national unions would be incapable of preventing capitalist attempts to divide the working class against itself. And so at a conference held in Manchester in 1830, he established the National Association for the Protection of Labour (NAPL) of which he became secretary (Pelling 1987; Morton 1994). The NAPL was

> the first trades union, or union of trades, as distinct from organisations catering for one section of workers only. It aimed at uniting the whole working class, and did actually reach a membership of 100,000.
>
> (Morton 1994: 366)

It secured substantial support in Lancashire but also Huddersfield, Birmingham and Staffordshire (Pelling 1987: 27). What this vignette of John Doherty suggests then is that despite the prevalence of anti-Irish and anti-Catholic sentiment in Britain, including within parts of the working class, sizeable elements of the organized working class rendered Doherty's 'Irishness' unimportant and chose him as their leader because of his forceful advocacy of working class interests. Dorothy Thompson (1982: 130) is surely correct when she describes John Doherty as 'probably the most important and influential trade unionist in the first half of the century'.

More broadly, the rapid growth in Irish Catholic migration doesn't appear to have generated the level of English working class hostility that one might have expected given Colley's thesis about the growing integration and unification of the population around a shared allegiance to Protestantism. While there was undoubtedly a strand of sectarian conflict within the working class, this chapter has brought to light the relatively less well-reported current of co-operation and solidarity between English and Irish Catholic workers which helps to counter the conventional view of a wholly antagonistic relationship between the migrant Irish and English labour (Miles 1982; Solomos 2003). Instead, Irish Catholic migrants and their descendants emerged as an integral element of the working class movement in England, often playing an important role in the radical industrial and political movements of the period. There was, as Belchem (1985: 89) observes, 'an essential interweaving of English and Irish interests and endeavour, indicative of an all-embracing class loyalty'. In fact, English working class radicalism became so synonymous with the Irish that it often came to be attributed with the 'Irish' temperament (Thompson 1991: 443) since it was a form of class politics that could not easily sit alongside dominant representations of the British nation.

Black radicals as linchpin of the anti-slavery movement

One influential account contends that slavery was abolished in Britain and its colonies because of elite revulsion at its horrors, and because it provided 'a welcome opportunity to reaffirm their libertarian heritage', to 'redeem the nation, as a patriotic act' (Colley 1996: 375) in opposition to the American revolution which had appropriated this mantle of liberty while continuing to practice slavery on its soil. Certainly, American hypocrisy on the matter was an important ingredient in firing the imagination of the emerging abolitionist movement in Britain. It was the prominent abolitionist, Thomas Day, who levelled this charge at Thomas Jefferson – one of the architects of American independence – when he proclaimed

> If there be an object truly ridiculous in nature, it is an American patriot, signing resolutions of independency with the one hand, and with the other brandishing a whip over his affrighted slaves.
>
> (cited in Armitage 2007: 77)

We also know that, as with many of the radical movements of the day, such sentiment was also forged in the dissenting fires of the English non-conformist tradition, of Quakers and Methodists. Abolitionism in this sense comprised several movements – some from above, others from below. In comparison, relatively little consideration has been given to the autonomous actions taken by minorities in pursuit of their freedom, including the slaves themselves, nor the extent to which such action helped shape the anti-slavery movement within Britain itself. We know from the activist-scholar accounts provided by Herbert Aptheker (1943) and C.L.R. James (1938/1991) as well as more recent work by Robin Blackburn (1988) that slave rebellions grew in scale and scope throughout the late eighteenth century as African Americans tried to force the American state to make good on the promise contained within the Declaration of Independence 'that all men are created equal'. Further, in French colonial Saint-Domingue, when African slaves found that the rights of liberty, equality and fraternity developed in the course of the French Revolution were not going to be extended to them, thousands rose up in the Paline du Nord, forcing the French legislature to proclaim belatedly in 1792, the equality of all free people in the French colonies regardless of colour.

In Britain itself, the anti-slavery movement was intellectually and politically nourished by the growing population of freed slaves of African descent. While small numbers of Africans had been resident in the country since the sixteenth century, this population had grown to between 10,000 and 20,000 people by the late eighteenth century (Fryer 1984: 68). It was a freed slave, Olaudah Equiano, who brought firsthand experience of slavery to the attention of the British public. His remarkable autobiography *The Interesting Narrative of the Life of Olaudah Equiano* (1789) – an account of his suffering as a slave, as well as his subsequent life in Britain, rapidly went through several editions and was one of the earliest books promoted by the *Committee for the Abolition of the Slave Trade* (see also Carretta 2005). Equiano was also instrumental in bringing to the attention of Granville Sharp and others, the story of the slave ship Zong, and how in 1781, its captain had thrown 122 sick slaves overboard, with another ten committing suicide in despair. The captain's motivation was clear; because the slaves were considered cargo, the ship's owners were entitled to £30 a head compensation for their loss at sea whereas if the slaves had died on land they would have received no compensation.

Significantly, Equiano was an active member of the London Corresponding Society and a friend of its founder and secretary, Thomas Hardy. We have already noted how the corresponding societies were key meeting places for the exchange of radical ideas about working class freedom and Irish national liberation. And it was through these same networks that ideas of black freedom also circulated and meshed with those other causes. Thomas Hardy declared that the liberty of blacks and whites was indivisible (Fryer 1984: 210) while John Thelwall – Jacobin and fervent abolitionist – fused the struggles against slavery abroad and class exploitation at home with his incendiary statement that '[t]he seed, the root of the oppression is here, and here the cure must begin' (Fryer 1984: 212). It is surely no coincidence that it was the embryonic working class that was most sympathetic to this message. In this dramatic period of social change, conflict and the circulation of revolutionary ideas, the firsthand knowledge of racist oppression offered by Equiano, Ottobah Cugoano, Ignatius Sancho, Phillis Wheatley and countless unknown others,

struck a chord and fused with the disaffection generated by the social conditions experienced by the working class at home. In 1792, the Manchester
petition calling for the abolition of slavery was signed by 20,000 people, more
than 20 per cent of the total population in a city that owed its prosperity to
the slave trade and the production of cotton (Fryer 1984; Blackburn 1988).
As Fryer (1984: 210) observes, 'The unity in struggle of black and white
working people found practical expression on the streets of British provin-
cial centres in the 1790s.' Such solidarity across so-called racial boundaries
horrified the British elite:

> Terrified by the French revolution, horrified by the revolution of black
> slaves on the island of Haiti, the ruling class found the connection between
> domestic radicalism and abolitionism a fearful portent ... Nothing quite like
> it had been known before, and it made the upper classes shudder.
>
> (Fryer 1984: 210–211)

It was against this backdrop of a rising curve of radicalization of the working
poor that another prominent figure of African descent emerged in Britain –
Robert Wedderburn. Born in Jamaica in 1762 to an enslaved African woman
and a Scottish doctor and sugar planter, Wedderburn was – like Equiano before
him – a minority figure, an outsider within the heart of the British Empire, yet
someone who played an influential role in making visible the links between the
suffering and struggles of African slaves abroad and working class struggles at
home (McCalman 1991). His life was shaped by many of the major events of
the period; he had witnessed the brutal violence meted out to slaves, including
his mother and grandmother. He joined the Royal Navy during the American
Revolution and had also been loosely connected to the naval mutiny at Nore in
1797 (Linebaugh and Rediker 2001: 288). He became a follower of Thomas
Spence – a leading English radical from Newcastle – and familiarized himself
with the struggles of working people. Therefore, Wedderburn

> knew the plantation, the ship, the streets, the chapel, the political club, the
> workshop, and the prison as settings of proletarian self-activity ... and was
> [therefore] a strategically central actor in the formation and dissemination
> of revolutionary traditions.
>
> (Linebaugh and Rediker 2001: 288–289)

He discouraged people from submitting petitions against slavery 'for it is
degrading to human nature to petition your oppressors' (Wedderburn cited
in McCalman 1991: 82). In contrast, he emphasized the autonomous activity
of slaves in securing their own freedom because

> the equality of your present station in slavery, is your strength. You all
> feel the injury – you are all capable of making resistance. Your oppressors

know – they dread you – they can foresee their downfall when you determine to obtain your liberty, and possess your natural right – that is freedom.
(cited in McCalman 1991: 87)

By 1813, Wedderburn appears to have joined the Spencean Philanthropists,
a left-wing group inspired by Thomas Spence's writings, and one of the few
organizations to have survived the suppression of the corresponding societies.
Shortly afterwards, he went on to publish six editions of a remarkable magazine called *The Axe Laid to the Root*. Through this magazine and countless
meetings of the Speancean Philanthropists he began to link the plight of the
African slave to the difficulties faced by the English working poor for '[t]he
means to obtain justice is so expensive, that justice cannot be obtained' (cited
in McCalman 1991: 93). This conjoining of the struggles against slavery, and
for social justice for the working poor, found political expression in his calls
for a Jubilee – a free and egalitarian community. According to Wedderburn,
Spence

> knew that the earth was given to the children of men, making no difference
> for colour or character, just or unjust; and that any person calling a piece
> of land his own private property, was a criminal; and though they may sell
> it, or will it to their children, it is only transferring of that which was first
> obtained by force or fraud.
>
> (cited in McCalman 1991: 82)

Wedderburn's increasingly radical politics drew attention from the state. Government spies reported how, at a meeting organized by Wedderburn, the
audience had been asked whether a slave had a right to slay their 'Master'
if they refused them their liberty? The audience – the spies reported – had
voted overwhelmingly in favour. They also logged how Wedderburn drew to
the audience's attention how slaves had been fighting for their freedom for
two decades and 'appealed to Britons who boasted such superior feelings and
principles, whether they were ready to fight now but for a short time for their
liberties' (McCalman 1991: 116).

The indivisibility of the campaigns against exploitation at home and oppression abroad were no more clearly refracted than through the tragic figure
of William Davidson. Born in Jamaica to the Attorney-General of Jamaica,
and a local woman of African descent, Davidson travelled to Britain as a
teenager to study law. Outraged at the massacre of working people in Peterloo
in 1819, he joined the Society of Spencean Philanthropists, and in 1820,
was arrested, along with others, for planning to assassinate members of the
British government in what came to be known as the Cato Street Conspiracy (Thompson 1991). At his trial, Davidson spoke at length about the
radical ideas that had inspired so many working people, including this 'mixed-
race' Englishman, to oppose established authority. In particular, he eloquently
justified his opposition to tyranny with reference to the Magna Carta:

[O]ur history goes on further to say, that when another of their Majesties the Kings of England tried to infringe upon those rights, the people armed, and told him that if he did not give them the privileges of Englishmen, they would compel him by the point of the sword.... Would you not rather govern a country of spirited men, than cowards?

(cited in Fryer 1984: 219)

Along with four of his co-conspirators, Davidson was charged with high treason, hanged and then decapitated on 1 May 1820 (Wilkinson 1972; Fryer 1984; Edwards and Dabydeen 1991). Working class opposition to slavery continued, in part inspired by the contributions made by diasporic African outsiders such as Equiano, Wedderburn and Davidson. Between 1826 and 1832, more than 3,500 petitions were submitted to the House of Lords which eventually contributed to the abolition of slavery in the British West Indies in 1833.

This 'bottom-up' account of the abolition of slavery in Britain represents an important corrective to the kind of top-down, elite-led explanation advanced by Colley (1996). Although she concedes there were strong levels of opposition to slavery within the working class, she rejects any noble motivation for such action claiming instead that

[s]laves, unlike the Irish or the Roman Catholics, or the working class, existed overwhelmingly outside Britain's geographical and mental boundaries.... Slaves, in short, did not threaten, at least as far as the British at home were concerned.

(Colley 1996: 376)

However, neither element of her explanation stands up to critical scrutiny. First, Colley's argument regarding working class opposition to slavery seems to be underpinned by the assumption that slaves represented no threat to them at home. However, this fails to understand how it was precisely those segments of the working population that would have been most affected by the end of cotton production by slaves – such as the new working class of Manchester – who were most supportive of abolition. Second, if the elites had abolished slavery to reaffirm their libertarian heritage, one is forced to question why, immediately following abolition in 1833, they saw fit to institute in 1834 what Hugh Tinker (1974) refers to as the 'new form of slavery' in the form of 'coolie' labour? Under this new de facto slavery, labourers from parts of southern India and China were transported aboard packed vessels and shipped to various parts of the British Empire, including the Caribbean, the Pacific Islands and South America. Many would die on the way, of malnutrition, disease, or other mistreatment. Though such 'coolie' labour was typically classified as indentured servants with a five-year contract, the remnants of slavery remained, and there was often a considerable gap between the law and its application. Many investigators of the 'coolie' trade reported dire and inhumane conditions, with many workers never able to regain their freedom after serving five years for a planter, as was stated in their contract (Rodney 1981).

Class over nation and the significance of the racialized outsider

Inserting the Irish Catholic and African worker into the history of the making of the working class in England allows us to re-write traditional accounts of its making. Demonstrating the significant presence of minorities at the moment of its inception enables us to unmask and recover a historical tradition of co-operation and solidarity that often transcended racial and ethnic boundaries. It makes transparent how racialized workers were absorbed relatively easily into the working class of England, how some became influential leaders of the class struggles being waged during this period and, that sometimes, such solidarity could extend to plebeian and working class support for the causes of abolitionism and Irish emancipation. Significantly, such an account also raises important questions about Colley's thesis, particularly the scale to which English workers voluntarily attached their flag to the mast of British nationalism.

While Colley's account of the making of the British ruling class in these years remains compelling, it becomes more difficult to support her claim that the working class had embraced a national identification of Britishness, and that it had become interpellated into the British nation to the extent that she claims. The situation was more fluid, unstable and uneven. Her account remains partial because she underestimates the impact of the Industrial Revolution in transforming traditional artisan and working class life and, with it, working class consciousness. This brought in its wake 'a new economic relationship between men, a new system of production, a new rhythm of life, a new society, a new historical era' (Hobsbawm 1990: 65–66) that included a division of the industrial population into employers and workers who owned nothing; factory production combining specialized machines with specialized human labour, the 'tyranny of the clock' and regularity of work and the 'domination of the entire economy – indeed of all life – by the capitalists' pursuit and accumulation of profit'. The ferocity of the class struggles that it unleashed between wage labourer and employer was unprecedented, and so stark in places like Manchester that it is worth recalling the words of a clergyman who wrote:

> There is not a town in the world where the distance between the rich and the poor is so great or the barrier between them so difficult to be crossed.... There is far less personal communication between the master cotton spinner and his workmen, the calico printer and his blue-handed

boys, between the master tailor and his apprentices, than there is between the Duke of Wellington and the humblest labourer on his estate.

(Hobsbawm 1990: 87)

A situation of open class warfare prevailed for much of the late eighteenth century and the first half of the nineteenth century accompanied by the emergence of a strong sense of working class identification. Whilst this class consciousness may at times have looked back into history and articulated with a mythical English nation encapsulated in the theory of the Norman Yoke (Hill 1968) to ideologically justify its collective action, over time it also came to envisage a better future shaped by utopian socialism; but it rarely sought to justify such action on the terrain of British nationalism. The significance of this form of class consciousness lay in its oppositional nature, and its capacity to generate collective solidarities that could not easily be contained within the dominant boundaries of Britishness defined by the elites. It was the formation of such a powerful working class consciousness which helped inoculate it, partially, from any illusions it might have had about the British state and the ruling elites. Against this conflict-ridden backdrop, how could the elites construct a stable, meaningful narrative about a common national interest when large swathes of the working class understood that it was those same elites, and the British state, that were responsible for their repression and desperate conditions of existence? Such antagonistic and contradictory forms of class and national identification were enduringly difficult to marry.

It is Colley's failure to appreciate the nature of this class conflict which leads her to overemphasize the scale and scope of working class patriotism, at least, of the British kind within the English working class. While I have no wish to deny that in some places under some circumstances, parts of the working class did actively embrace and identify themselves as British and Protestant, my argument is that throughout much of this period, the working class as unenfranchised, and therefore inactive citizens of a Protestant Britain, remained the least receptive social class to such integrative nationalist projects. Even Colley concedes this, albeit reluctantly, when she observes how the so-called patriotic worker actually volunteered for war because of reasons to do with economic compulsion and elite intimidation – not because of any intuitive loyalty to king and country.

Equally significant is Colley's silence on Ireland in her account of the making of Britons. By failing to consider Ireland's position as a colony of Britain – not thousands of miles away but in its own backyard – she fails to grasp the political significance of Irish Catholic migration to Britain. This population carried within them not only collective memories of colonial oppression at the hands of the British state, but also an understanding that this oppression had been consolidated by a racism that had conceived them as the 'wild Irish' and 'natural savages' incapable of civilization (Allen 1994). Through the migratory movements engendered by the uneven development of capitalism, the racialized in the Irish colony became the racialized outsider within the British nation.

The term 'racialized outsider' is employed to denote how this group's prior experience of subjugation and racialization as a people at the hands of the British elite helped inform their relative lack of enthusiasm for, and commitment to, the dominant politics and representations of the British nation once in Britain. After all, 'their' nation was under the iron heel of the British state, they were castigated as Catholics and increasingly as members of an inferior Celtic race. And this detachment from the dominant ideology provided them with a unique perspective, an alternative lens through which to interpret the social and political developments of the day. It was this unique, politicized consciousness of the racialized outsider which lent itself to dissent, and with English workers already locked in a bitter class struggle with employers and the state, Irish Catholic workers conjoined with them. This chapter has demonstrated how, alongside such active participation in many of the key class struggles of the day, some Irish Catholic workers went on to become leaders of trade unions, as well as other kinds of working class collective action.

Racialized outsiders were also of African descent. Individuals like Equiano, Wedderburn and Davidson and countless unknown others who actively participated in the class struggles and political formations of the day had firsthand experience of the repressive and ideological state apparatus of the British state abroad. They were more than familiar with the deployment of racism by British elites to justify colonial conquest because they were the objects of such ideological repression themselves. In British colonial America, a vulnerable colonial elite, fearful of a united rebellion of African and European labourers against class oppression and servitude, had deployed their racializing ethnocentric world view to put in place a number of statutes that differentiated the status of Africans from Europeans, including European labourers. Incrementally, statute by statute, state by state, over the course of the late seventeenth and eighteenth centuries, the elite of colonial English America thus enshrined within the institutional arrangements of the new nation a set of discriminatory practices that divided humanity into two – those who were English, Christian and free and those who were African, Negro and enslaved. By encoding these categories within the law, it gave stability to much of the racializing nomenclature that was to prove one of the crucial foundation stones for the formation of scientific racism in the late eighteenth century – terms such as Negro, mulatto, black and white displaced the earlier forms of self-representation.

It hierarchically ordered these two groups in the social, political and legal sphere in such a way that prevented any transgression of these racialized boundaries for fear of punishment. Significantly, the impact of such measures on the European labourer abroad were disastrous because a 'screen of racial contempt' was constructed between dangerous black slaves and dangerous free whites (Allen 1994: 249), ensuring that black slaves and the white poor remained divided and which ultimately served to ensure the continuation of capitalist rule. The white poor were drawn into this web of deceit because according to Allen; following Du Bois, they derived a compensatory wage in the form of political and social rights alongside a sense of psychological belonging to the ruling race – the white race. Similar developments occurred in the British West Indies, although a racial classificatory system was extended beyond the black–white dualism of American society.

Significantly, however, the working class in England at this stage in history remained relatively free of contamination by the ideology of white supremacy. It held little allure as they found themselves locked in their own struggles against the British ruling elites. Further, through the diffusion of their writings, and active participation in the corresponding societies and other radical organizations that flourished during this period, individuals like Equiano, Wedderburn and Davidson were able to bring to the attention of this public both tales of horrific degradation and heroic resistance by the African slave. As we saw with Wedderburn, such individuals helped mesh the ongoing struggles against exploitation with those against racist oppression in the minds of the radical working class in England. These individuals became the linchpin around which the militant, yet particularist, struggles of the working class in England leaked beyond the conventional boundaries of working class self-defence and took on a more universalist character (Linebaugh and Rediker 2001).

The corresponding societies and other radical organizations of the day played a critical role in facilitating this kind of knowledge transfer. As nodes in the political struggles of the day, they brought together black abolitionists, Irish migrants demanding the liberation of Erin from the British yoke, and of course, their English allies. They helped facilitate a rich exchange of ideas about rights and freedoms amongst diverse groups of activists, and alongside this became an influential transmission belt of political radicalism into the working class inculcating a vision of a different society in which all men – although only occasionally women (Taylor 1991) – could play a role. It was this conglomeration of factors that proved key to winning significant elements of the working class to the causes of abolitionism and Irish national freedom.

What is striking about this 'heroic age of the proletariat' (Anderson 1964: 33) then is the scale and scope of solidarity amongst the English, African and Irish Catholic strata of the working class. Alongside the formation of a multi-ethnic proletariat on the high seas of the Atlantic so ably demonstrated by Linebaugh and Rediker (2001), here was a significant process of inter-ethnic working class solidarity within England itself. The potent cocktail of class war unleashed by the devastation to traditional rural labourers' lives combined with the circulation of new radical ideas associated with the French Revolution and universalized through the presence of the racialized outsider within Britain simply proved too much for the ruling elites who, momentarily at least, seemed incapable of defusing such social struggles within the power container of the nation-state (Giddens 1987). This was the significance of racialized outsiders like Irish Catholics and Africans, who, by virtue of their contradictory location in the nation-state, could universalize the particularist concerns of individual struggles to the advantage of all who were exploited and oppressed.

Chartism and the multi-ethnic proletariat

It is surely no coincidence that it is amidst a series of catastrophic defeats in both the political and industrial spheres during the early 1830s that we begin to discern the emergence of a growing antagonism between the English and minority worker. The first of these defeats occurred when working men failed to secure the vote in the 1832 Reform Act as middle class and manufacturing interests switched sides and aligned themselves to the aristocracy to save Old Corruption. At first, 'working-class alienation was extreme' (Colley 1996: 363), leading to another cycle of protest and rebellion. In the industrial sphere, the Grand National Consolidated Trades Union (GNCTU) was established, whose aims were to

> rationalise the structure of combinations, to achieve a general control of movements for an advance of wages, and to co-ordinate assistance for strikes, especially strikes against a reduction of wages.
>
> (Pelling 1987: 29)

The establishment of the GNCTU marked the climax of those attempts 'to use unionism as a vehicle for the transformation of society' (Pelling 1987: 29). Although it quickly accounted for 500,000 members (Pelling 1987: 29–30), the employers refused to retreat. When rural unrest amongst agricultural labourers began in the village of Tolpuddle in Dorset in 1834, Lord Melbourne, the then Home Secretary, chose to make an example of six labourers from the village by prosecuting them for taking unlawful oaths for seditious purposes. They were sentenced to seven-years imprisonment in Australia. Despite further opposition, the trade unions found themselves unable to resist employer and state repression. The outcome was the almost total collapse of trade unionism with only craft workers retaining some level of union organization (Hobsbawm 1990; Thompson 1991). This constituted the second catastrophic defeat for the English working class.

And it is in this moment of defeat, in both the political and industrial spheres, that anti-Irish sentiment appears to gain some traction within parts of the working class public. Accusations of such labour undercutting English workers, and, thereby putting a downward pressure on the wages of all workers emerged (McDermott 1979; Engels 1987). Thompson (1991: 480) describes how 'pitched battles with mortal casualties took place among railway navvies' of English and Irish descent. It was particular elements of the English working class, namely those that worked alongside Irish migrants in unskilled jobs in parts of the cotton industry (Miles 1982), the railways and the building trade (McDermott 1979: 4–5; Thompson 1991) that became especially antagonistic towards the Irish worker. The roots of such working class opposition to the Irishman lay in the weak bargaining position such unskilled English labour found themselves in, which exacerbated concern about their employment prospects, especially during a period where their only means of collective defence – trade unionism – had been prohibited.

Alongside this, the elites began to place a new emphasis on national integration and the manufacture of consent among a broader cross-section of the population, including elements of the middle and working class. Key here was the attempt to remake Britishness by developing

> a far more consciously and officially constructed patriotism which stressed attachment to the monarchy, the importance of empire, the value of military and naval achievement, and the desirability of strong, stable government by a virtuous, able and authentically British elite.
>
> (Colley 1996: 154)

The aim was to integrate the population horizontally along the axis of nation, and thus, re-imagine the nation as a singular entity regardless of vertical divisions like class that emphasized material inequality within nations. With opportunities for collective working class action in the political and industrial spheres severely curtailed, perhaps segments of the English working class began to see advantages in re-imagining themselves as British in opposition to the Irish Catholic. After all, elite conceptions of both English and British nationalism since the English Civil War had been constructed on the basis of a strong allegiance to a Protestant identity, in opposition to the Catholic other. By doing so, they perhaps thought they could lay claim to a greater entitlement to jobs at acceptable rates of pay than the Irishman who could not be considered British, and was therefore undeserving. This may also help to explain the relatively muted support amongst the working class for the Catholic Emancipation Act of 1829 compared with that for the abolition of slavery, although we should also acknowledge that the working class remained even then the least hostile segment to its enactment since they invested 'their hopes and energies in political not religious activism, in the struggle for parliamentary reform' (Colley 1996: 352).

Even then, the defeats combined with such attempts at integrating the working class into the British nation were not enough to quite bring down the curtain on the 'heroic age of the proletariat'. Such nationalism failed to generate the scale and scope of working class allegiance to British nationalism that the elites had hoped for. This was as much to do with elite policies as working class rejection with the former continuing to mistrust the working class as a collective entity, regarding them with 'fear and suspicion and certainly not people who could be trusted with the vote' (Hobsbawm 1990: 89). In this sense, the worker remained outside the elite-constructed image of the ideal British nation – a social group that simply could not be trusted to be active citizens. It was this continuing outsider status that would give rise to one final mass social movement of the working class and middle class radicals – Chartism.

Chartism was a political movement whose aim was to win support for constitutional change that would combat privilege and extend democracy (Webb and Webb 1919).

In the aftermath of the failure to extend the franchise to the working man in the 1832 Reform Act and the restrictions imposed upon legal trade unionism, a political and educational body called the London Working Men's Association was established in June 1836. The following year, they launched a people's charter, designed to win working class support for annual Parliaments; universal male suffrage; payment of MPs; equal electoral districts; abolition of the property qualifications for MPs; and voting by ballot (Morton 1994: 370). By the spring of 1838, these six demands had been drafted into a parliamentary bill which was

> endorsed at gigantic meetings all over the country. 200,000 assembled at Glasgow, 80,000 at Newcastle, 250,000 at Leeds and 300,000 at Manchester. At all these meetings the charter received empathetic approval.
> (Morton 1994: 370)

Many industrial workers saw in them 'the means to remove their intolerable economic grievances' while Engels believed that the six demands were revolutionary, 'sufficient to overthrow the whole English constitution, Queen and Lords included' (Morton 1994: 370). To secure the Charter's acceptance, a campaign of large demonstrations were organized alongside a mass petition to Parliament and a national convention. If the petition was rejected, a political general strike would be launched, or what the Chartist leadership referred to as a 'sacred month' (Morton 1994: 371). A series of huge processions, protests and strikes involving thousands followed ranging from the Newport rising of 1839 to the General Strike of 1842. The latter marked the high watermark of the Chartist movement with 500,000 workers participating in strike action. This was followed by the 'Great Delegate Conference' in Manchester in August 1842 where amidst an angry mood, some delegates spoke of a 'final reckoning' against the ruling elites. The British state, steeled by war against France and internal rebellion at home, was not going to buckle easily. Instead, they set about cutting off the head of the rebellion by arresting many of the Chartist leaders. State repression continued over the next few years with more than 1,500 Chartists brought to trial, and 200 being deported to Australia (Saville 1987).

Dorothy Thompson (1982: 123) usefully reminds us how 'there was a very considerable Irish presence in the Chartist movement' as well as a concern for Irish questions more broadly. There were individuals of Irish descent who played a central role in the Chartist movement, including occupying positions in the national leadership, such as James Bronterre O'Brien – commonly referred to as the 'Chartist Schoolmaster' and the main theoretician of the movement (Morton 1994: 372). There was also Thomas Devyr, an Irish migrant from Donegal who became Secretary to the Chartist Northern Political Union (Thompson 1991: 483), and Feargus O'Connor, the leader of the physical force Chartists. The latter, from the beginning 'had the support of the great majority of the industrial workers, the miners and the ruined and starving hand workers of the North' (Morton 1994: 371).

Perhaps less well known is the scale of rank and file Irish involvement in Chartism (Thompson 1982; Kirk 1985). Half the Chartists in Bradford were Irish, and Irishmen like George White and shoemaker John W. Smith played an influential part in transforming northern towns like Bradford into hotbeds of Chartist activity involving both English and Irish workers (Thompson 1982: 124). Thompson (1982: 125–126) challenges the commonly held belief that 'concern for Ireland and support for Repeal were grafted on to Chartism because of a personal foible of its leader' O'Connor. Instead, concern felt about Ireland was born from a recognition by parts of the working class in England that '[t]he way Ireland was ruled and the living conditions of her people affected the rest of Britain intimately and immediately' (Thompson 1982: 126). When attempts were made to impose the Coercion Act in Ireland alongside the Poor Law Amendment Act of 1834 in Britain, it was Irishmen like Bronterre O'Brien who made the English worker aware of what was going on in Ireland, particularly the possibly disastrous consequences of extending coercion in Ireland, and the low living standards comparable to the Irish worker that would await the English worker unless they mounted effective collective opposition to such proposals:

> I have lived in Ireland, was born and bred in Ireland... I have seen thousands of Irish who have never tasted animal food, or fish, or wheaten bread twice a year since they were born... I have seen them clothed in rags, their heads full of vermin their legs and hands covered with scabs, their bodies broken out in sores, and their feet cut and hacked with chilblains and stone bruises until they were unable to walk... but you ask 'are we, the wealth-producers of England, to be brought to this?' I answer YES, unless you bestir yourselves in time, there is no escaping the Irish level if the New Poor Law Act be fully carried out.
>
> (cited in Thompson 1982: 128–129)

This argument linking oppression abroad with exploitation at home was consistently made and sustained by Irish and English radicals and gave the Chartists an outlook and political complexion that regularly transcended the traditional boundaries of British nationalism. It should also not be forgotten that O'Connor, Devyr as well as 'many of the other Irish in the Chartist Movement' had their roots in 'the Republican wing of the nationalist movement' (Thompson 1982: 134) – that of 1798 and the United Irishmen. It was this constellation of historical experience and unique personnel that was decisive in determining Chartism's strong support for Irish independence. As McDermott (1979: 16) points out, 'O'Connor's newspaper the "Northern Star" – the name of the United Irishmen journal – regularly preached the revolutionary potential of a union between Irish nationalism and the English working classes'. This unity was practically built upon on several occasions such as when

> [a] large contingent of Irish Confederates marched with their green banners to Kennington Common alongside the Chartists on the 10th April 1848 to present the Petition to Parliament.
>
> (McDermott 1979: 17)

Alongside the Irish Catholics, the Chartists also counted amongst its core leadership individuals of African descent. William Cuffay, born in 1788 in Chatham – an English tailor of African origin – joined the organization in 1839 and became an influential figure in London. He was one of three London delegates sent to the Chartist national convention in April 1848 and assigned the responsibility of organizing the march from Kennington Common that was to accompany the Chartist petition to Parliament. Elite concern about the mobilization was widespread with the royal family being evacuated to the Isle of Wight. The armed forces had also been put on standby. Fearing a bloody confrontation with the repressive state apparatus, the Chartist leadership called off the march. This was interpreted as an indication of its relative weakness by the state, and Cuffay was arrested shortly thereafter on a trumped up charge of proposing to bomb strategically important buildings as a signal for the working class to revolt in response to the expected rejection of the petition by Parliament.

This fear of working class revolt, of a working class revolt that was multi-ethnic in character and united in opposition to the state was the context in which elite use of racism grew exponentially. During Cuffay's trial, prominent parts of the media, including *The Times* newspaper deprecated Chartism as the 'black man and his party'. The newspaper went on to refer to Cuffay as 'half a "nigger". Some of the others are Irishmen. We doubt if there are half-a-dozen Englishmen in the whole lot' (Fryer 1984: 242). A central element of this elite racism was its attempt to portray the insurgent Chartist movement as foreign and alien, and therefore not an authentic expression of the wishes of the English masses. There was a pseudo-valorization of the latter group as virtuous, a group that had somehow been misled by foreign Irish Catholics and Africans to engage in unrepresentative forms of collective action that were incompatible with English traditions.

At first, such crude attempts at racializing the Chartist movement failed to gain the level of traction within the English working class that the British elites had hoped for. While it remained in motion as a collective actor, such messages were critically decoded by the radical strata of the working class, and an alternative interpretation placed on such unsavoury attempts at generating conflict and division. As the 'Reynolds Political Instructor' – a radical paper with a circulation of 30,000, noted: Cuffay

> was loved by his own order, who knew him and appreciated his virtues, ridiculed and denounced by a press that knew him not, and had no sympathy with his class, and banished by a government that feared him...Whilst integrity in the midst of poverty, whilst honour in the midst of temptation are admired and venerated, so long will the name of William Cuffay, a scion of Africa's oppressed race, be preserved from oblivion.
>
> (Fryer 1984: 244)

Other prominent newspapers such as the *English Patriot and Irish Repealer* also protested against such crude racism describing it as 'The Old Original Dodge! Divide and Govern!' (Belchem 1985: 94). Nevertheless, this form of elite racism continued to gather momentum and began to embed itself in the wider political culture of British life. *The Times* newspaper claimed it was appalled by 'that extravagance of wild sedition which, for want of any other adjective, must be denominated "Irish"', and London was endangered by 'the Irish love of knife, dagger and poison bowl' (cited in Belchem 1985: 93). Meanwhile, *Punch* – the weekly satirical magazine – regularly referred to the Chartist conspirators of 1848 as 'MOONEY, ROONEY, HOOLAN, DOOLAN' (cited in Belchem 1985: 94). Charles Kingsley – later to be chaplain to Queen Victoria – warned the Chartists against any association with the United Irishmen: 'What brotherhood ought you to have with the "United Irishman" party, who pride themselves on their hatred to your nation' (Thompson 1982: 143).

While it would be that other side of the state namely coercion and repression that would ultimately bring about Chartism's downfall (Saville 1987), it was clear that any attempt to remake the solidarity between the English working class and racialized minorities from the mid-nineteenth century onwards would have to contend with and overcome the growing penetration of racist and nationalist sentiment in British public life, including within parts of the working class. It is why 'the mid-nineteenth century remains an important – and distressing – watershed in labour history' (Belchem 1985: 94).

3
Racism and the Contradictions of Socialist Nationalism

Participation in the domination of the world market was and is the basis of the political nullity of the English workers...One is indeed driven to despair by these English workers with their sense of imaginary national superiority, with their essentially bourgeois ideas and viewpoints, with their 'practical' narrow mindedness.

(Engels cited in Cowden 1963: 35, 49)

For us neither geographical boundaries, political history, race, nor creed makes rivals or enemies; for us there are no nations, but only varied masses of workers and friends, whose mutual sympathies are checked or perverted by groups of masters and fleecers whose interests it is to stir up rivalries and hatreds between dwellers in different lands.

(*The Manifesto of the Socialist League* by William Morris and E. Belfort Bax 1885, 2nd edition)

Introduction

While the secret of the English working class' political impotence in the post-Chartist period may well be traced to Britain's worldwide industrial monopoly, what must also be considered is the sheer scale of the defeats suffered by the working class, leading up to the final catastrophe of 1848, the feeling of helplessness that arose in the aftermath and the fragmented political response that it engendered thereafter.

This chapter considers how in the middle decades of the nineteenth century, for the first time in its incendiary history, parts of the working class adopted strategies that relied more on negotiation than on collective action to defend their living conditions and traces the impact of such strategies on their consciousness. At the same time, it touches on how the British ruling elite learnt to govern in a more consensual manner, the political and economic reforms they introduced, as well as how ideologically and politically parts of the British working class were incrementally incorporated into the expanding imagined community of the British nation. Incorporation, however, also meant cutting ties with fellow members of the working class, and this chapter focuses, in particular, on the part played by racism in creating such a chasm, between those of Irish Catholic descent and the English working class. Racism, deployed by the ruling elites against the Irish in Britain since the 1830s and 1840s, now came to be used strategically by parts of the English working class to legitimize the exclusion of the Irish from key jobs and occupations. In the process, the nation was re-imagined as an Anglo-Saxon Protestant nation.

The downtrodden and destitute – the large majority of the working class in the second half of the nineteenth century – shared little in the way of such rewards and benefits. And it was from within these strata that the wave of industrial rebellion that we term the new unionism arose in the final years of the nineteenth century. Through a brief coverage of the principal disputes, the chapter explores how the working class in England was remade. Attention is drawn to the instrumental role played by socialists, many of whom were of Irish Catholic descent, who led the strikes and used those ethnic ties to cement a level of class solidarity not seen since the first half of the nineteenth century. But little commented on in the social and labour history of this period is that much of this socialist leadership of the new unionism – both secular and religious – didn't break with British nationalism but rather worked within an expanded conception of the imagined national community. Their aim was nothing less than securing the formal inclusion of the unrespectable working class – the unskilled, the Irish, women – into the British nation.

But as Nairn (1982) reminds us nationalism is 'Janus-faced', and so it proved in this instance when the foil, the racialized other of such a political project became the newly arrived migrants of Jewish descent. Those socialist activists that had just recently re-imagined people of Irish Catholic descent as British to further the interests of the working class could not extend such generosity to the Jews. The chapter assesses the efforts, sometimes successful, made by that tiny minority of socialist internationalists led by William Morris in trying to overcome such racism by uniting Jewish workers with their Irish and English counterparts. It not only explores how such working class solidarity was built with socialist nationalists and their working class constituencies during the high point of the new unionism, but also considers the reasons why such unity floundered once the new unionism had been defeated.

Racism and the unmaking of the working class

Its collective morale already weakened by the defeat of Chartism, the majority of workers now found themselves reduced to a subsistence-standard of living (Hobsbawm 1990; Thompson 1991) while unemployment rose to catastrophic levels:

> In the hard-hit areas of Lancashire between 30 and 75 per cent of the total population might have been destitute . . . in the woollen areas of Yorkshire, between 25 per cent and 100 per cent; in the textile areas of Scotland, between 25 per cent and 75 per cent. In Salford, for instance, half the population was wholly or partly out of work, in Bolton about one third, in Burnley at least 40 per cent.
>
> (Hobsbawm cited in Robinson 1983: 40–41)

A 'profound caesura in English working-class history supervened' (Anderson 1964: 33). The class that had been forged by the currents of Jacobinism and Owenite Socialism now retreated into a state of 'prolonged catatonic withdrawal. The most insurgent working-class in Europe became the most numbed and docile' (Anderson 1964: 36). Accompanying the disappearance of its 'élan and combativity' was the almost total collapse of its radical political consciousness, leading one prominent Marxist historian to ruefully observe how the entire body of socialists 'might all have been comfortably got into one smallish hall' (Hobsbawm 1997: 134). The 'heroic age of the proletariat' had passed.

Against this traumatic backdrop, racist ideas that had formed part of the essential ideological circuitry of British capitalism in the colonies, as well as at home, now began to be picked up by parts of the working class in England with increasing regularity. That is, in the moment of its political defeat, groups of workers turned in on themselves thereby unmaking themselves as a class. In parts of north-west England and elsewhere, 'paddy-bashing' quickly established itself as a popular social pastime amongst the English working class (Kirk 1985; Panayi 1993, 1994; Swift 2002). From the Stockport riots of 1852 (Millward 1985) to the anti-Irish sentiment promulgated against the 'Fenian enemy within' (Curtis 1968, 1971), the English workers' attitude towards the Irish became 'much the same as that of the "poor whites" to the "niggers" in the former slave states of the USA' (Marx cited in Draper 1978: 67). Alongside the traditional hate-trope 'No Popery', such violence and resentment came increasingly to be expressed through a virulent scientific racism (Barkan 1993) which portrayed the Irish as an inferior race, not only by virtue of 'their language and/or accent, their culture and their often shabby appearance, but also by their (supposed) physical characteristics' (Miles 1982: 140).

In mid-Victorian England, the traditionally religious underpinnings of British nationalism were over-determined by a form of scientific racism that re-imagined Britain as an Anglo-Saxon Protestant nation in opposition to Catholics of the Celtic race on British soil. Previously excluded from the imagined British nation as a result of their Catholic faith, they now found themselves excluded twice over – for their faith, and, increasingly as members of an inferior racial type, the Celts. And alongside the different and hierarchical ordering of the physical characteristics of the two 'racial types', members of the Anglo-Saxon race were imputed as being masculine, superior, freedom-loving and capable of self-government, whereas members of the Celtic race were conceived of as feminine, childish, addicted to violence and authoritarian control and, of course, closer to the ape than the Anglo-Saxon (Curtis 1968). The arch-Conservative, Thomas Carlyle – who, along with Charles Kingsley, would go on to support Jamaican Governor Edward Eyre's suppression of the Morant Bay rebellion (see Hall 2002) – is an important example of the promulgation of this form of racism. In the course of one particularly savage attack on the immigrant Irish in Britain, Carlyle described how

> [c]rowds of miserable Irish darken our towns. The wild Milesian features, looking with false ingenuity, restlessness, unreason, misery and mockery, salute you on all highways and byways. The English coachmen, as he whirls past, lashes the Milesian with his whip, curses him with his tongue; the Milesian is holding out his hat to beg. He is the sorest evil this country has to strive with. In his rags and laughing savagery, he is there to undertake all work that can be done by mere strength of hand and back ... The Saxon man, if he cannot work on those terms, finds no work ... he has not sunk from decent manhood to squalid apehood ... the uncivilised Irishman drives out the Saxon native, takes possession of his room. There abides he, in his squalor and unreason, in his falsity and drunken violence, as the ready-made nucleus of degradation and disorder.
>
> (cited in Thompson 1982: 143–144)

Such racism was readily absorbed by the English working class through the popular press, magazines and other forms of written and visual paraphernalia. Curtis in his remarkable work *Apes and Angels: The Irishman in Victorian Caricature* (1971) documents how cartoonists, in particular, digested many of the key tenets of such scientific racism and then reflected them in the comic weeklies produced for a working class audience amongst others. Ideas about Irish peasants slowly descending the evolutionary ladder from the human to the gorilla rungs, or Irish militants as sub-human creatures became common-place. And such anti-Irish racism was further amplified by the popular press who formulated a persistent caricature which

> emphasise[d] the prognathous features of the Irish labouring class: a bulge in the lower part of the face, the chin prominent, the mouth big, the fore-head receding, a short nose, often upturned and with yawning nostrils: the simianising of the Irish.
>
> (Saville 1987: 38)

An understanding of 'racial' difference embedded itself in the cultural and political life of the working class in England. Many English workers came to regard the Irish as an alien presence, an inferior race that didn't belong in England. This was a form of working class politics that was narrower and more exclusive than in previous years, one that could no longer accommodate different ethnic groups within its understanding of class. On the other hand, it was an understanding of class that nested more comfortably within dominant conceptions of British nationalism and, indeed, was increasingly shaped by it. Being able to lay claim to membership of the ruling race of the nation proved a powerful means by which to justify Irish exclusion from 'good jobs', as well as others who could not be imagined as an organic element of this island race. It gave the English working class another strategy for improving its economic and political standing – one no longer dependent on the manufacture of a broad class-based solidarity, nor a frontal confrontation with the state – by simply asserting their legitimate rights as members of the British nation. This process of national identification came to constitute a form of symbolic capital that English workers could instrumentally deploy to exclude the Irish worker from key areas of employment or whenever they believed such workers threatened the economic security of the English worker (Kirk 1985).

This growing attachment to racialized conceptions of class and nation also explains the political chasm that emerges between the English and Irish worker from the 1860s over the growth of the Irish Home Rule Movement and its calls to repeal the Act of Union of 1800. While Irish-descended workers strongly supported Home Rule – ranging from limited reform, encompassing an Irish legislature with responsibility for its domestic affairs, to the Republican concept of total separation from Britain, as represented by the Fenians and the Irish Republican Brotherhood – the English workers' response ranged from one of indifference to resolute opposition. That political current of English working class support for Irish freedom which traced its lineage back from Chartism to the days of the United Englishmen found itself almost extinguished in the third quarter of the nineteenth century. Race had became the ideological cement that bound the nation together in opposition to Irish-descended Catholics, and parts of the English working class were active agents in this process of common national identification. Marx, observing the changing nature of working class politics at close hand, carefully identified how the lived reality of such divisions, particularly the English workers' growing identification with the nation, was the primary guarantor ensuring the maintenance of capitalist domination over both.

> Every industrial and commercial centre in England now possesses a working class divided into two hostile camps, English proletarians and Irish proletarians. The ordinary English worker hates the Irish worker as a competitor who lowers his standard of life. In relation to the Irish worker he feels himself a member of the ruling nation and so turns himself into a tool of the aristocrats and capitalists of his country against Ireland, thus strengthening

their domination over himself. He cherishes religious, social and national prejudices against the Irish worker.

(Marx cited in Draper 1978: 66–67)

It was Marx's own organization, the International Working Men's Association (IWMA), established in 1864, and more commonly referred to as the First International, that was instrumental in sustaining English working class support for Irish independence during this bleak period. When members of the Fenian Brotherhood were put on trial for killing a police officer in Manchester in 1867 and subsequently sentenced to execution, meetings and demonstrations were held to protest at the sentences. In November 1867,

> a meeting of some 20,000–25,000 working men at Clerkenwell Green, London sent a petition to the Queen. On the day of execution, magistrates banned meetings in many places and hussars and artillery stood by in Leeds.
>
> (McDermott 1979: 19)

Many Irish working men subsequently joined the IWMA, leading Jenny Marx to note optimistically that 'the Irish in London are entering the ranks of the International. Irish sections are being formed in various parts of the East End' (McDermott 1979: 19). Occasionally, there were other reminders of a multi-ethnic solidarity reminiscent of the days of Chartism. In 1872, members of the International organized a demonstration demanding a general amnesty for Irish political prisoners which

> [s]ome thirty thousand people attended, over half of them Irish. It was, as Engels noted, a significant exhibition of friendship between the Irish and the native British population.
>
> (McDermott 1979: 20)

Further, there sometimes emerged local forms of solidarity action: 'In periods of rising industrial militancy (in 1853, 1859–61 and 1869) Irish and English cotton operatives generally acted together against the forces of capital' (Kirk 1985: 330). But the general co-ordinates of English working class attitudes and behaviours had been set, and they pointed away from such solidaristic and internationalist inclinations.

Liberalism and the aristocracy of labour

The dissolving of old inter-ethnic class solidarities by the growing material force of racist ideology within the English working class was accompanied by other developments that further increased the pace of working class fragmentation and signalled a wholesale unravelling of the process of class formation that had been forged in the first half of the nineteenth century. While for most workers, union organization had become a thing of the past, for those 'favoured minorities' like craft workers, union organization actually strengthened during this period. However, this was a form of unionism that was unrecognizable from earlier in the century. The strength of these new model unions derived not from their capacity to generate and sustain collective action but their ability to improve the working conditions of their members through negotiation, by deploying the 'irresistible weapons of truth and reason' (Morton 1994: 378). While the success of this negotiating strategy was in one sense the outcome of the workers' own powerful bargaining position in a moment of tight labour markets (Hobsbawm 1990: 109; Thompson 1991: 8–10), it was also a reflection of the softening of attitudes of employers.

The mid-nineteenth century was the era of diplomatic-industrial imperialism where the enforcement of international free trade contributed to Britain's rise to prominence as the hegemon of the capitalist world economy (Anderson 1964; Hobsbawm 1997). Employers in the dominant state of the world-system understandably felt 'rich and confident enough to be able to afford such changes' (Hobsbawm 1990: 124). Further, the catastrophic defeat of Chartism and the resultant collapse in working class consciousness in the 1840s meant the elites no longer regarded

> the British working class as revolutionary ... they now saw it as divided into a politically moderate aristocracy of labour, ready to accept capitalism, and a politically ineffective, because unorganized and leaderless, proletarian plebs, which presented no major danger. For the great mass movements which mobilized all the labouring poor against the employing class, like Chartism, were dead. Socialism had disappeared from the country of its birth.
>
> (Hobsbawm 1990: 126)

The British elites had discovered another way of ruling at home, through consent not coercion, including the granting of wage increases to the minority of the male working class, or what some refer to as the 'aristocracy of labour' (Hobsbawm 1967, 1984b). The effects of such gains – secured through negotiation rather than collective class power – on the consciousness of such craft workers was profound. Rank and file craft workers attributed such relative economic security, and its successful maintenance for more than a generation, to the more conciliatory tactics adopted by the new model union leaders. This enhanced their authority and consolidated their position as a permanent and distinctive social layer of full-time officials (Pelling 1987; Hobsbawm 1990). Occupying a contradictory class position between labour and capital, their power as negotiators came to be rooted in the continued maintenance of a stable and orderly relationship between their membership and capital (Hyman 1972; Anderson 1977; Kelly 1988). On the one hand, these full-time union officials were seen as indispensable intermediaries facilitating the gains made by elements of the skilled male working class, while on the other hand, the price to be paid by the rank and file membership for the continued extraction of such gains was the development of this distinctive layer of officials with interests that were somewhat different to their own. The days of such leaders assuming the role of 'tribunes' of the whole working class as John Doherty of the General Union of Cotton Spinners and others had done just a few years previously had passed.

Trade union leaders of the new type, men like George Odjer, Henry Broadhurst and Robert Applegarth believed that the improved social position of the skilled English working class would be best consolidated by the granting of manhood suffrage. In organizations such as the *Universal League for the Material Elevation of the Industrious Classes* and the *Reform League*, these trade unionists conjoined with former Chartists and members of the Liberal Party to press for suffrage to be extended. While Lord Palmerston, Liberal Prime Minister had repeatedly stated his opposition to expanding the electorate, on his death in 1866, the incoming Prime Minister, Lord Earl Russell introduced a Reform Bill designed to enfranchise the 'respectable' working man, and by implication, exclude what they termed the 'residuum' or the less respectable stratum of that class.

Such representational distinctions and gradations within the working class were increasingly significant in the public sphere of mid-Victorian England. A conception of the labouring poor 'fused into a homogenous mass of the discontented and the oppressed' (Hobsbawm 1997: 263) was replaced by discourses which separated 'the workers' from 'the poor', and 'the respectable' from 'the unrespectable' sectors of the working class. Respectability denoted the penetration of middle class values and standards and attitudes such as sobriety, sacrifice and the postponement of gratification. Significantly, such discourses were used to separate 'people like "the intelligent artisan", to whom British middle-class radicals were anxious to give the vote, from the "dangerous and ragged masses" whom they were still determined to exclude' (Hobsbawm 1997: 263).

While the 1866 Bill was defeated due to the intransigence of the Liberal Adullamites led by Robert Lowe and the Conservatives under Disraeli, the following year, Disraeli – keen to outflank the Liberal opposition – changed his view and enacted the Reform Act. The passing of the 1867 Reform Act represented a tacit acceptance by the elite of an electoral system dependent on working class votes. The Act effectively doubled the voting public in Britain from one million to two million adult males, with all male householders now enfranchised. When the Liberals returned to power under William Gladstone in 1870, further reforms aimed at improving the lot of the skilled working man quickly followed, most notably the 1871 Trade Union Act which removed those legal obstacles which had made it so difficult for workers to found unions, and instigate strike action.

Subjectively, the extension of the franchise and other reforms encouraged the belief amongst skilled workers that they too held a stake in the British nation. Psychologically, their sense of national belonging was consolidated because it was now undergirded by an unprecedented degree of political entitlement and economic security. With their interests as craft workers increasingly compatible with active membership of the nation, class was becoming nationalized (see also Stedman Jones 1983). It was the subtle changes in political consciousness induced by such reforms, and mediated through the actions of the new trade union leaders, that explains why this newly enfranchised stratum of the respectable, industrious working class would reciprocate by voting en masse for their benefactors – the Liberal Party of Gladstone – ensuring the latter remained in power throughout much of this period of British domination of the world-system.

The new unionism or the revolt of the 'residuum'

This hegemony that held firm for more than a generation began to unravel from the mid-1870s. Britain's leadership of the capitalist world economy was threatened by the loss of its manufacturing advantage to the French, German and American economies. When a series of economic slumps followed in 1875, 1880 and 1884 (Pelling 1987: 83; Hobsbawm 1990: 127), the major powers abandoned free trade and resorted to protectionism to shore up those industries that were in decline. Significantly, the economic security guaranteed to the respectable sections of the English working class also came under threat. That is, an integral component of the material foundation of the cross-class settlement that had held firm over the past quarter century was brought into question as employers sought to maintain profit levels at the expense of the working class. As a consequence, the Long Depression was characterized by widespread unemployment, including amongst skilled workers in engineering, shipbuilding, metals, buildings and textiles. Employers grew ever more determined to undermine the privileges of craft workers by substituting machinery for skilled labour, and introducing piecework thereby making the conditions of such labour the most precarious and unstable they had been for more than a generation (Duffy 1961; Hobsbawm 1984b).

Trade union leaders came under growing pressure from activists keen to rebut the increasingly aggressive actions of the employers. However, they refused to buckle, instead urging caution and restraint. Although the rank and file craft worker recognized that their 'existence as a privileged stratum was at stake' (Hobsbawm 1984b: 368), they also understood that it was precisely the established trade union leadership with its long-standing links to the Liberal Party that were responsible for the gains secured over the past two decades and more. Locked into this chain of reciprocal and binding relationships, their continued compliance was secured. Frustrated at such inertia, many of the activists including figures such as Tom Mann and John Burns – both members of the Society for Engineers – and Keir Hardie, leader of the Ayrshire mineworkers union, came to reject what they termed a 'non-political trade unionism' committed to 'middle class views' (Hobsbawm 1967: 359), and turned instead towards socialism with its stress on autonomous working class collective action.

Socialism had planted modest roots in Britain over the past half century. From the utopian socialists inspired by Robert Owen to the Marx-Engels circle and the IWMA in mid-Victorian Britain, socialist men and women had participated in, and occasionally shaped the course of working class struggles. However, from the mid-1870s, these currents were replenished in diverse ways. First, there was the arrival in Britain of numerous exiles flee-ing the defeated Paris Commune and Bismarck's anti-socialist laws. Socialists like Johann Most and Andres Scheu helped spread the ideas of Marx and Proudhon to a broader constituency than hitherto. Second, there was the Labour Emancipation League (LEL), a political formation established in 1881 by Frank Kitz and Joseph Lane and advocating a form of libertarian social-ism to the impoverished working class in east London (Quail 1978; Bevir 2000). By 1884, the LEL had merged into a broader socialist party called the Social Democratic Federation recently established by the former Tory, Henry Hyndman. It was through participation in this body that many trade unionists such as Mann and Burns first encountered the new and sometimes contradic-tory life-world of organized British socialism, including its links to the poor in the east end of London. And it would be parts of this poor, particularly the unskilled and unenfranchised – not the established working class of unionized craft workers – that would trigger a wave of collective working class action not seen in Britain since the days of Chartism.

The harbingers of the new unionism were the large demonstrations of 1886 and 1887 organized by socialists and radical Liberals protesting against rising levels of unemployment, and professing their support for Irish Home Rule. Serious violence followed the first meeting held in 1886 at Trafalgar Square with large crowds looting shops in the west end. According to Engels, the demonstration held on Easter Sunday in 1887 was 'without exception the largest meeting we've ever had.' And in November 1887, when radical Lib-erals and socialists called a further demonstration in Trafalgar Square, again on the dual themes of home rule for the Irish, and tackling unemployment amongst London's poor, much violence ensued between the protestors and the police. A clerk, Alfred Linnell, was run down by a police horse, dying later in hospital. This proved to be a formative moment with many protestors understanding that political appeals to Parliament to improve the conditions of the unenfranchised working class would be insufficient. At Linnell's grave-side, William Morris's powerful lament declared how socialists must make it their 'business to try and make this earth a very beautiful and happy place' so that such things shall not happen again (cited in MacCarthy 2010: 572). What

Morris was alluding to here was a turn to industrial unionism, and it would not be long before it would be put to the test.

Discontent among the young women working at the Bryant and May match factory in Bow, east London was growing. Most of the women were under 15 years of age, and suffered terribly from poor working conditions including low rates of pay, long working hours, excessive fines and life-threatening health complications such as phossy jaw from working intensively with yellow phosphorous (Beaver 1985; Raw 2009). Annie Besant, a socialist activist who had come to prominence during the unemployed demonstrations, drew attention to their plight in her newspaper, *The Link* describing their working conditions as a form of 'white slavery'. When three of Besant's informants at the factory were sacked for refusing to retract their claims, 1,400 mainly teenage girls walked out in protest. The women formed the Union of Women Match Makers, and struck demanding better conditions of work. After two weeks, despite facing a hostile employer, and many attempts to discredit their claims in the press, including in *The Times*, the union successfully won all its demands (Raw 2009).

This victory, secured by women located at the very bottom of the British class structure inspired other groups of unorganized workers in the east end of London, catalyzing their attempts to organize (Raw 2009). In March 1889, the gasworkers became embroiled in a dispute over pay and working hours. Will Thorne – a worker at the Beckton Gasworks – enlisted the support of socialists Eleanor Marx, John Burns, Tom Mann and Ben Tillett to help organize the workers. A Gasworkers and General Labourers' Union (GLWU) was established which rapidly grew to 20,000 members (Pelling 1987; Morton 1994). Faced with the threat of industrial action from a discontented and newly organized group of workers, and with no recognizable reserve army of labour to draw on, the employer – the South Metropolitan Gas Company – was forced to accept the union's demands, quickly followed by the other gas companies (Morton 1994: 386).

Dockers in the east end of London had long faced meagre wages and casual employment. Taking their cue from the matchgirls and gasworkers, they too established a union called the 'Dock, Wharf, Riverside and General Labourers' Union' to redress their poor working conditions. Led by Ben Tillett, John Burns and other socialists, the organized workers launched their strike action demanding a 'tanner an hour' representing an increase in wages from four pence/hour to six pence/hour. They also insisted on eight pence/hour for overtime, the abolition of the process of sub-contracting and piecework, and, minimum employment of four hours (Pelling 1987: 88). After five weeks of the dispute, the employers accepted the dockers' demands, raising wages to six pence/hour or as Burns termed it 'the full round orb of the docker's tanner' (cited in Pelling 1987: 90). By November 1889, the dockers union had grown to over 30,000 members (Pelling 1987: 90). Buoyed by the success of groups of workers previously thought 'unorganizable' helped galvanize other unskilled workers to join trade unions such that within a year of the dockers' victory, more than 200,000 unskilled workers had been organized (Morton 1994: 386), transforming the nature of British trade unionism in the process. The allure of industrial unionism to the labouring poor was compelling:

> ...incapable of using the orthodox tactics of craft unionism. Possessing 'merely the general value of labour' he could not, like the 'skilled man' buttress a certain scarcity value by various restrictive methods, thus 'keeping up his price'. His only chance therefore was to recruit into one gigantic union all those who could possibly blackleg on him – in the last analysis every 'unskilled' man, woman or juvenile in the country; and thus to create a vast closed shop.
>
> (Hobsbawm 1949: 125)

In contrast to Hobsbawm's (1949, 1967, 1984a, 1984b) classic account which claims that it was the male gasworkers and dockers that marked the birth of the new unionism, this chapter suggests those disputes denoted 'the culmination of an agitation and temper in industry which had been expressing itself in a new form of Unionism as early as 1886' (Duffy 1961: 309). The catalyst was the demonstrations of the unemployed and women workers – the lowest of the low in the hierarchy of labour. A further weakness at the heart of Hobsbawm's account is his failure to identify how this revolt of the 'residuum' was sparked, and led, at all levels, by those of Irish Catholic descent – the racialized outsiders of nineteenth century Britain. This oversight stems from Hobsbawm's narrow understanding of racism as colour-coded prejudice and discrimination, a form of white on non-white exclusionary behaviour (see, for example, his attempt to understand racism in the context of imperialism abroad (Hobsbawm 1990, 1997)). While this certainly allows him to analytically capture the development of a colour-coded scientific racism that accompanied the new imperialism abroad, such a narrow conception of racism blinds him to the dominant modality of racism within the British interior – anti-Irish racism. Further, it prevented him from investigating the extent to which the lived experience of such exclusion and denigration might galvanize this social group to engage in collective resistance on all kinds of social and political questions.

The significance of the Irish Catholic contribution to the new unionism can be drawn out, albeit briefly. The large demonstrations of 1886 and 1887 are regularly described by labour and social historians as focusing on the question of unemployment in London. While undoubtedly correct, what is neglected in such accounts is that they were also about the question of Home Rule in Ireland. A notable characteristic of the working class in London was its multiethnic character, and those of Irish Catholic descent formed a large element of this stratum. Many of these Irish workers retained links with their ancestral homeland, and the multifarious ways in which its population had been made

subservient to the British state over the years. Louise Raw (2009) has docu-
mented in exhaustive detail how many of the matchgirls were Irish migrants
or first-generation English women of Irish descent. Many of the leaders had
strong ties to the local Irish community and lived in streets described deroga-
tively by social commentators of the time as 'a regular Irish den ... all the vices
of the Irish rampant', and 'inhabited by many Irish ... a rough lot, given to
drinking, racing and betting' (Booth cited in Raw 2009: 178). As many as 23
of the women came from Limehouse, east London referred to disparagingly
as the 'Fenian barracks' – an area that Booth in his monumental survey of east
London had noted was responsible for sending more police to hospital than
any other block in London (Lees 1979).

Will Thorne and Ben Tillett, leaders of the gasworkers and dockers respectively, were also of Irish Catholic descent. Ethnic ties were crucial in cementing
class solidarity. In the course of the dockers dispute, Ben Tillett received the
support of many activists of Irish descent including Tom McCarthy, general secretary of the stevedores – the group of workers who undertook the
more skilled tasks of loading vessels – and James Toomey who went on
to become president of the Dockers' Strike Committee (McDermott 1979:
10). The scale and scope of such solidarity undergirded by shared ethnic ties
was directly responsible for paralysing the Port of London from 20 August to
16 September when:

> Processions of them, led by bands, toured the docks to bring more men
> out on strike. Stevedores, lightermen, coal porters, and others came out
> in sympathy – some of them formulating their own demands upon the
> employers.
>
> (Pelling 1987: 88)

Such ties were also significant in spreading the new unionism throughout
the industrial regions of Britain. It was Irish activists – Edward McHugh and
Richard McGhee – who established the National Union of Dock Labourers – a
union which laid strong foundations in Glasgow and Liverpool. James Sexton,
son of Irish migrants, would go on to become its general secretary, while
James Larkin, a Liverpudlian born of Irish migrants was an influential member at the time. And there were numerous others (McDermott 1979; Pelling
1987).

The new unionism however was not solely a revolt of the Irish Catholics
and their descendants. Rather what is significant is how the influential role
played by this group at all levels of this wave of contentious action has been
glossed over in many classical accounts, and how this participation stemmed
not only from this group's structural position facing conditions of unimaginable poverty and degradation, but also its sophisticated political understanding
that it formed a racialized minority group in a state that was responsible for
maintaining oppression in its ancestral homeland. It is worth remembering

here how the British elite at this point continued to defend a conception of the British nation underpinned by a shared allegiance to an Anglo-Saxon Protestantism. In this sense, the Irish Catholics were not only a minority, but one that was perceived to be incompatible with such a vision. The coupling of this experience of racialization alongside the conditions of class exploitation gave this stratum the role of a catalytic agent in the class struggles of the new unionism. Significantly, because the demands of this collective action were expressed primarily through the language of socialism and class solidarity, it was also able to draw into collective action other components of the 'residuum', including English workers. This universalist approach forged from the particularist material of the Irish Catholic condition over the course of the new unionism was responsible for the transformation of trade unionism in England with 'hardly a single occupational group, from laundresses and waiters to post office sorters, which was not brought into the movement' (Pelling 1987: 91).

A key inference that can be drawn from the solidarity established between Irish and English workers in the new unionism is that it represented a rejection of the elite imaginary of British nationalism, one which could find no room for the Irish, women or other parts of what they disparagingly referred to as the 'residuum'. Socialist activists like the Scotsmen John Burns and Keir Hardie, the Anglican communist Tom Mann, and the Jewish Marxist Eleanor Marx conjoined with Irish Catholic socialists like Will Thorne, Annie Besant, Ben Tillett and others to advance the case for the unrepresented and unskilled of British society. Such solidarity didn't remain restricted to the industrial sphere. Ben Tillett and Will Thorne confidently married their commitment to socialist politics and challenging working class exploitation to their advancement of the cause of Home Rule in Ireland in a way that was reminiscent of the days of Chartism (McDermott 1979; Pelling 1987). Such solidarity was especially noteworthy given the backdrop of the four-decade consolidation of anti-Irish racism amongst parts of the English working class in the mid-Victorian era, and highlighted the capacity of political positions to alter in the course of large-scale and sustained collective action. The new unionism posed an alternative working class vision, one of solidarity and collective action whose success was dependent upon the suppression of such racist divisions within the working class.

The significance of these events has led some Marxist historians such as Engels (see for example Torr 1942) and Hobsbawm (1967: 359) to interpret the new unionism as representing a 'recrudescence of a revolutionary utopianism', while others have claimed that it 'challenge[d] the very foundations of the capitalist system' (Gray 1999: 4).

Such an interpretation must be rejected. While there were many competing currents that informed the class struggles of the period, including the radical Irish republicanism of the matchgirls' leaders, the revolutionary socialism of William Morris and Eleanor Marx, the large majority of activists who shaped and consolidated the political trajectory of the new unionism adhered to a form of socialist politics that was more limited.

The most prevalent currents were those which married their belief in socialism with an almost unthinking loyalty to the British nation. The majority of the socialist leadership of the new unionism didn't wish to break with British nationalism but instead hoped to expand the conception of the imagined national community so that it might encompass the majority of the working class who currently remained unenfranchised and disadvantaged. In this respect, they sought the establishment of a broader, more inclusive British democracy. Therefore, it would be more appropriate to describe much of the leadership of the new unionism as being shaped principally by a form of socialist nationalism, not socialist internationalism. What they desired most of all was economic and political justice and the formal inclusion of all the working class, including the poor, the unrespectable, and the Irish, within the confines of the expanded British nation-state.

In its secular form, this trend was represented by the dominant Hyndman-wing of the SDF, which despite their avowed allegiance to Marxism, actually understood their commitment to socialism as neatly bounded by their allegiance to this state. Hyndman and his closest collaborators saw the party as a vehicle for securing inclusion of the hitherto passive citizens of the working class into the English/British state as exemplified in his manifesto *England for All* (1884). Significantly, Hyndman evoked a conception of the nation which, although racialized, was broad enough to encompass the Irish-descended population as can be seen by how he evokes a radical republican tradition when justifying his call for a socialist republic:

> Tyler and Ball, and Cade and Kelt, Vane and Blake and Harrison, Priestley and Cartwright, Spence and Owen, Vincent, Ernest Jones and Bronterre O'Brien – a noble band indeed! . . . How do courtly fuglemen and ennobled sycophants look by the side of these? A great democratic English Republic has ever been the dream of the noblest of our race . . . to bring about such a Republic is the cause for which we Socialists agitate to-day.
>
> (Bevir 2000: 355)

This majority wing of the SDF undoubtedly held a more democratic conception of the nation than that currently advanced by the ruling elites, but their expanded socialist vision remained firmly located on the terrain of the nation, with Irish migrants and particularly their English-born children re-imagined as part of the English race.

In its religious form, such socialist nationalism manifested itself in the Independent Labour Party (ILP) established in 1893 by the four non-conformist Christian socialists – Keir Hardie, Ramsey MacDonald, Bruce Glasier and Phillip Snowden. All rejected Marx and criticized him for doing 'harm to Socialism by emphasising the necessity of class war' (Knox 1988: 626).

It wasn't *Capital* that inspired these socialists but the Bible with Hardie declaring how he first learnt his 'Socialism in the New Testament' and describing this as the source from which he continued to find his 'chief inspiration' (cited in Knox 1988: 609). This brand of ethical socialism saw the struggle as 'one of good versus evil, of fairness and decency against rapaciousness and exploitation. The object was to "bring down a little more heaven to earth" ' (Knox 1988: 626). This didn't require overthrowing the existing nation-state but taking charge of it to make it 'easy to do right and difficult to do wrong' (Reid cited in Knox 1988: 616). Significantly, this strand of ethical socialism displayed little animosity towards the Irish Catholic-descended working class. Indeed, as fellow followers of the Christian faith, and, as members of the excluded working class poor, the ILP leadership had no difficulty in re-imagining this population as an integral component of their expanded conception of the British national community, mobilizing them to seek redress and inclusion within the nation-state, as active citizens demanding freedom from the degradations inflicted by poverty and disease.

The religious inflections of the ILP's socialist nationalism are profoundly important in understanding one of the great quandaries of this period, namely why given the influential role played by the SDF – as a first home and political training ground for so many influential socialist activists – they did not benefit more from this wave of contentious collective action. No doubt part of the answer lay in the regular bouts of sectarian in-fighting which characterized the SDF, as well as its often paternalistic attitude towards the working class. However, perhaps most important of all was that the working class, including much of the unskilled that participated in the new unionism, remained wedded to a religious worldview, a view that they believed was more compatible with the Christian socialism of the ILP.

The undoubted strength of these related forms of socialist nationalism lay in their authority to speak on behalf of the voiceless of Britain. Their demands for greater democratization of British society laid down an important marker for the extension of citizenship and economic and political rights to much of the working class poor, including the Irish-descended population. Through the ILP, and eventually the Labour Party, this stratum was given a voice to challenge the more restrictive conception of the nation-state defended by the elites.

However, when drawing up a balance sheet of the new unionism and its socialist leadership, it is important to critically evaluate not only its strengths, but also its weaknesses. Nairn (1982) usefully reminds us that nationalism is Janus-faced. What contradictions emerged in a period where the dominant socialist project entwined itself with nationalism? In particular, were there clearly defined limits to the calls made by socialist nationalists to extend democracy and secure economic security for the unskilled in Britain? Were those boundaries defined by a racism directed against more recent migrant groups, such as the non-Christian Jews?

Anti-semitism and the limits of socialist nationalism

Much of the conventional labour and Marxist historiography of this period has failed to note how temporally the mass migration to Britain of Jews, escaping the racist pogroms in modern-day Poland, Russia and the Ukraine, coincided with the upturn in the class struggles associated with the new unionism. More significantly still, these Jewish migrants settled overwhelmingly in those localities that constituted the epicentre of this revolt – East London, but also Leeds and Manchester. Between 1881 and 1914, the Jewish population increased from 60,000 to approximately 300,000 (Bourke 1994: 195–196) with almost a third locating to East London (Holmes 1988; Panayi 1993; Bourke 1994; Panayi 1994).

Opposition to their arrival in Britain was immediate and widespread, transcending all social classes. A strain of Christian anti-semitism which could be traced back to the eleventh century was drawn upon to frame elite concerns about the scale and scope of Jewish migration to Britain (Panayi 1993, 1994). The TUC – at this point, still the representative of respectable working class opinion – followed suit noting in 1888 that 'it was the duty of the trades to keep the matter of Jewish migration under close consideration' (cited in Buckman 1980: 223). Facing exclusion from the wider labour market due to such anti-semitism and their lack of proficiency in English forced Jewish labourers to draw on 'family and hometown networks' (Gidley 2003: 2) to find work in small Jewish-owned enterprises in the tailoring and garment industries (Buckman 1980; Williams 1980). However, their employment in such trades at significantly lower rates of pay accentuated English worker hostility in comparable trades, leading them to complain 'that a major economic problem in this area, that of sweating, was related to the ' "swarms of foreign Jews" who had "invaded the East End" and turned it into a sweater's paradise' (Holmes 1988: 68). In this way, older anti-semitic representations of Jews as 'Christ-killers' and 'usurers' were over-determined by a set of new representations which came to associate the Jewish worker with the threatened economic and social degradation of the English working class.

There were some socialists who extended the hand of solidarity to the Jewish worker, most notably those aligned with the politics of the Socialist League. The League was made up of Marxists and anarchists, both deeply committed to the politics of internationalism. In large part, this commitment had been forged in opposition to the Social Democratic Federation (SDF). Most of the League's leadership, including William Morris, Eleanor Marx, Belfort Bax and Edward Aveling, had originally been members of the SDF, but had decided to quit over the incessant production of a racializing nationalist discourse by Henry Hyndman, the SDF leader, and Harry Quelch, the editor of the party newspaper, *Justice*. Such racism was integral to the politics of the SDF. As early as 1882, when it was still the Democratic Federation, it had passed a resolution – advanced by Hyndman – which committed it to opposing Chinese immigration to Britain on the grounds that the Chinese 'always remained a distinct race wherever they went. They could swamp us industrially and crowd us out of almost every occupation' (Hyndman cited in Crick 1994: 33). Eleanor Marx writing to Wilhelm Liebknecht in Germany in the aftermath of the split, and the subsequent formation of the Socialist League in December 1884, recounted how 'one of our chief points of conflict with Hyndman is that whereas we wish to make this a really international movement, Mr. Hyndman whenever he could do with impunity, has endeavoured to set English workmen against foreigners' (Crick 1994: 38).

Steeled by these earlier struggles against racism within the fledgling socialist movement, the League gave no quarter to racism or nationalism. Their conception of socialism refused to be limited by the narrow boundaries of the nation-state, instead it sought to transgress those boundaries by extending its hand of solidarity to a global working class that included 'Aborigines, Maoris, American Indians and black people everywhere' (Cohen 1984: 22). In its manifesto, first published in 1885, it boldly set out its position to the British working class:

> We come before you as a body advocating the principles of Revolutionary International Socialism; that is, we seek a change in the basis of Society – a change which would destroy the distinctions of classes and nationalities... The Socialist League therefore aims at the realisation of complete Revolutionary Socialism, and well knows that this can never happen in any one country without the help of the workers of all civilisations.
> (The Manifesto of the Socialist League by William Morris and E. Belfort Bax 1885, 2nd edition)

In the pages of their newspaper, *Commonweal*, they regularly confronted the racializing nationalist discourse of their fellow socialists in the SDF and accused them of squandering the opportunity to make common cause with Jewish workers: 'Are we then to allow the issues at stake in the struggle between the robbers and the robbed to be obscured by anti-foreigner agitation?' (cited in Cohen 1984: 22).

Confronted with the double threat of capitalist exploitation and working class racism, Jewish workers in the tailoring and garment-making trades had resorted to self-organization, forging Jewish unions to protect and improve their conditions of employment (Buckman 1980; Williams 1980). Although they achieved some measure of success with this strategy of racial formation (Omi and Winant 1994), it proved much harder to sustain such gains in the long run (Buckman 1980; Williams 1980). Alongside supporting those self-organized struggles of Jewish tailors and garment workers, in places like Leeds, members of the League also advocated the spread of industrial unionism such that all workers, including Jews, would be organized into one big union. In relation to Jewish employment in the tailoring trade, they determined that having the power to call out other groups of workers in support would strengthen the bargaining power of the Jewish tailors. In 1890, an amalgamation took place between the tailors' union and the gasworkers' union in Leeds whose leaders included important socialist activists such as Tom Maguire and William Cockayne. Drawing on this new-found organizational strength, they, along with Jewish activists, set about bringing the hours and pay of Jewish workers into line with English workers. In August 1890, when the employers rejected a union circular calling for a uniform working day for all types of workers, the tailors took strike action. Supported by the gasworkers, the tailors quickly won their demands such that '[w]ithin a few days, fifteen masters had conceded a uniform working day' which was quickly 'followed by a further twenty-six during the next week' (Buckman 1980: 234).

Five strikes in Manchester in the tobacco, tailoring, cabinet, boot and garment-making industries, involving English, Irish and Jewish workers, drew attention to the influential role played by Jewish and socialist activists in organizing this collective action (Williams 1980). Williams (1980: 290), summarizing the relationship between organized labour and Jewish workers in Manchester at this time, claims that there were

> no signs of hostility to Jewish workers amongst English trade unionists during 1889–90: on the contrary, it was in the interests of the English labour movement to support Jewish workers in a 'levelling-up' of conditions in the workshop trades. This strategy was...the outcome of the general state of trade union development in England.

The interventions of activists in the Socialist League during these years offered a brief glimpse into a different way of advancing class interests which rejected racism and was instead rooted in a commitment to forging a broad-based multi-ethnic class solidarity. The Socialist League's reach, however, was never extensive and remained restricted to particular occupations in cities such as Leeds, Manchester and parts of East London. Consequently, their anti-racist internationalist standpoint was an exception rather than the norm in the newly emergent socialist movement of Britain.

The majority of socialists remained wedded to a politics of socialist nationalism – either of a secular or of a religious kind. Their support for Jewish workers remained lukewarm at best and was shaped fundamentally by a pragmatic, instrumental collectivism which recognized the need to curtail expressions of anti-semitism because it risked fatally undermining the broader class solidarity forged in opposition to the employers over the course of the new unionism. Typical of this standpoint was Ben Tillett, the dockers' leader and himself the son of an Irish migrant. When referring to the Jewish workers engaged in collective action he declared: 'yes, you are our brothers and we will stand by you. But we wish you had not come' (cited in Meth 1972: 5). With Morris, Marx and other League members, working alongside Tillett, Burns and the socialist nationalists in many of the key disputes associated with the new unionism, an uncomfortable tension scarred relations between them over the 'Jewish question' throughout this period.

Often the socialist nationalists would resort to anti-semitism. In May and June 1891, Ben Tillett and Tom Mann, the Anglican communist, sent letters to the *London Evening News*, demanding the imposition of immigration controls against Jews. Tillett used this opportunity to formulate a proto-fascist discourse that not only called for the removal of Jewish workers from British soil, but blamed the current plight of the British worker on the failure of Britain's ruling class to stand up to the power of the Jewish bankers:

> Our leading statesmen do not care to offend the great banking houses or money kings... For heavens' sake, give us back our own countrymen and take from us your motley multitude.
>
> (cited in Cohen 1984: 28)

Similarly, in late 1891, in Keir Hardie's newspaper, *Labour Leader*, was to be found the astonishing claim that imperialist wars were being planned to suit the interests of Jewish finance:

> Wherever there is trouble in Europe, wherever rumours of war circulate and men's minds are distraught with fear and change and calamity, you may be sure that a hooked-nosed Rothschild is at his games somewhere near the region of these disturbances.
>
> (cited in Cohen 1984: 20)

In this period, Christian anti-semitism was increasingly over-determined by a discourse of scientific racism which constructed an especially pernicious set of physical and cultural representations of the 'Jew' (Miles 1993). However, it would be the defeat of the new unionism that would open up the political and cultural space for this virulent strand of racist anti-semitism to consolidate itself within the English working class.

Concerned at the success of the new unionism in organizing more than 350,000 unskilled workers, and doubling overall union membership from 750,000 in 1888 (6 per cent density) to 1,576,000 (13 per cent density) in 1892 (Hatton et al. 1994: 436, Table 1), the state and employers instigated a co-ordinated response to undermine trade union organization. Industry-wide employer federations were established and the legal position of trade unionism, including the right to picket was undermined (Pelling 1987: 113–114). By 1896, the employers had clawed back many of the gains from the new unionism and reduced unskilled labour unions to around 150,000 members (Hatton et al. 1994). By the mid-1890s, the cycle of protest (Tarrow 1998) initiated by the unemployed demonstrations and the matchgirls' strike had drawn to a close.

Demoralization and despair within the working class followed, and the Jews became one of the first casualties of the defeat of the new unionism. Those socialist nationalist leaders, who had largely suppressed their anti-semitism during the high-point of the new unionism now chose to deploy such racism opportunistically to provide English workers with a way of making sense of their present distressed condition. Certain deficiencies in the Jewish character, or simply their presence in Britain, comprised key elements of this resurgent socialist anti-semitism. G.D. Kelley, secretary of Manchester and Salford Trades Council, who was 'cheered as the champion of the sweated Jewish workers in the waterproof industry's strike of 1890 ... slip[ped] into anti-Semitic imagery with the failure of the Jewish tailors to maintain their union organisation' (Lunn 1985: 5). Against the objections of James Sexton – the then President of the TUC – a special TUC conference was organized to discuss immigration controls against Jews. In 1896, this was followed by the TUC sending an official delegation to the home secretary demanding the introduction of legislation (Cohen 1984: 21).

The Socialist League, always small, was no longer in a position to challenge the spread of such racism in working class communities. William Morris had resigned from the organization in 1890. Eleanor Marx had left even earlier in 1888 to form the short-lived Bloomsbury Socialist Society (Kapp 1976). Comprising anarchists and socialists, the League had been an unstable formation since its inception. Engels, long frustrated by the inability of the English to establish a socialist party with working class roots, had acerbically noted in a letter to Eduard Bernstein that he held out little hope for a party made up of anarchists and socialists and led by two poets (Morris and Aveling) and a philosopher (Bax): 'three as unpractical men ... as it is possible to find' (Engels 1894). His concerns were to prove well founded as those divisions, including over the place of violence in political struggles, came to a head during the peak years of the new unionism, causing the organization to eventually split.

As the working class suffered defeat upon defeat, socialist internationalists like Morris and Marx could do little to arrest the growing despair and despondency that gathered pace within it. Without a significant organizational base, they became increasingly marginal figures in the socialist movement, unable to mount any kind of effective opposition to such growing divisions. Meanwhile, many of its former industrial activists, including Burns, Thorne, Mann and others, had returned to the Social Democratic Federation, before finally de-camping to the newly established ILP in 1893.

The failure of the Socialist League to implant deeper roots in the working class during the formative years of the new unionism proved its undoing. It left few traces of its socialist internationalist outlook after its demise. Further, in the space of three years between 1895 and 1898, some of the most resolute figures of socialist internationalism in Britain – Engels, Morris, Marx and Aveling – were dead, the latter two having committed suicide. Eleanor Marx's death was especially poignant, effectively marking the end of the era of 'making socialists'. A more pragmatic working class politics born out of defeat and demoralization would become hegemonic, and accompanying it would be an all-pervasive racist anti-semitism.

Alongside the propagation of anti-semitism by the socialist nationalists, there was also its growing manipulation by the established political parties with a view to securing some electoral advantage. In parts of London, 'the Jew' increasingly became the scapegoat for Britain's economic woes, as well as the plight of the English and Irish working class. David Hope Kyd, a Conservative parliamentary candidate, warned in 1903 that prolonged association with Jews would lead to the 'extermination of the British working man in the East End of London' (cited in Holmes 1988: 69). In Bethnal Green in 1901, the Liberal and Radical Club passed a resolution that prevented Jews from becoming parliamentary candidates. Jews found themselves denied job opportunities with increasing regularity throughout Britain: in Leeds 'it was not unknown for immigrant Jews in search of employment to encounter the four-word stumbling block "No Jews need apply"' (Holmes 1988: 69–70). Racist violence also increased with Holmes (1988: 70–71), cataloguing incidents in Bethnal Green, in the Leyland area of Leeds, Salford and South Wales.

The first fascist organization, the British Brothers League (BBL), was founded in 1902 and constituted 'an alliance of east end workers and back-bench Tory MPs such as Sir Howard Vincent and Major William Eden Evans-Gordon' (Holmes 1988: 70). Its brand of racist anti-semitism warned English workers of the dangers of Whitechapel becoming the New Jerusalem (Holmes 1988: 69) and, in 1902, at a meeting held at the People's Palace in East London:

> [T]he hearty rendition of popular nationalist songs was followed by torrential speeches attacking Jewish immigrants by varying degrees of violence. Such hostility came from the mouths of Conservative MPs and spokesmen of various East End interests and resulted in shouts from the audience of 'Wipe them out'.
>
> (Holmes 1988: 296)

Such racism was exacerbated by the local press with the *East London Advertiser* opining that Jews were inherently different, incapable of adaptation and, therefore, alien to the British way of life:

> People of any other nation, after being in England for only a short time, assimilate themselves with the native race and by and by lose nearly all their foreign trace. But the Jews never do. A Jew is always a Jew.
>
> (cited in Holmes 1988: 68)

Amidst this worsening climate of racist hatred the demands for immigration controls gathered pace, leading to the establishment of a Royal Commission on Alien Immigration in 1903 to determine the impact of Jewish labour on employment and wages. In April 1904, Hyndman wrote to *The Jewish Chronicle* declaring that the SDF was against the 'free admittance of all aliens' and supported legislation that would restrict Jewish entry to Britain (Cohen 1984). The response of the ILP was equally problematic. Bruce Glasier, one of the four founders of the party, wrote in the *Labour Leader* that

> [n]either the principle of the brotherhood of man nor the principle of social equality implies that brother nations or brother men may crowd upon us in such numbers as to abuse our hospitality, overturn our institutions or violate our customs.
>
> (cited in Knox 1988: 626)

Keir Hardie was one of the few leading figures of the labour movement who opposed the introduction of an immigration act on the grounds that it would 'injure Britain's position as an asylum for political refugees and hurt our prestige' (cited in *New York Times*, 10 January 1909). However, his form of ethical socialist politics remained bound by a banal, almost unthinking, attachment to British nationalism. Such politics proved incapable of generating the vocabulary required to hold the line against the rising tide of an aggressive, racializing nationalism to be found throughout society, including much of the working class. The Jewish worker was effectively left defenceless against such racism, with disastrous consequences:

> [T]he notions of 'immigrant' and 'alien' became synonymous in everyday life with that of Jew. Moreover, Jewishness was increasingly interpreted as a quality determined by blood, and therefore as hereditary and ineradicable. References to the existence of a Jewish 'race' became common. This 'race' was signified as an alien presence that had the potential to destroy civilised society through the promotion of an international conspiracy: consequently, the Jews became the racialised 'enemy within'.
>
> (Miles 1993: 135–136)

Although the Royal Commission on Alien Immigration failed to come to a definite view about the impact of Jewish labour on wages and employment (Holmes 1988: 45), under such heightened political circumstances, the government chose to enact the legislation regardless, with the Aliens Act coming into force in 1905 (Miles 1993).

Many socialist nationalists were complicit in this surge in anti-semitism that led to the introduction of such racist legislation. Whether it was because the Jews were members of an 'alien race' or the bearers of a culture that they deemed was unassimilable, socialist nationalists' refusal to integrate the Jewish worker into the broader class struggles of the new unionism was a profound failing. While the conceptions of national belonging that underpinned the politics of socialist nationalism were undoubtedly broader than those forged by the elites, and highlights the significance of how even oppressive and exclusionary ideologies like nationalism can, under given concrete political and historical circumstances be appropriated and re-imagined to further the struggle for democratization by the oppressed, this expanded imaginary was never extended sufficiently to encompass the Jewish migrant. Indeed, one could argue that this expanded understanding of national belonging gained growing legitimacy amongst all sections of society, but especially the unskilled working class, precisely because it was able to portray elite conceptions of national belonging as unjust due to their exclusion of those like themselves who were British and therefore deserving of fair and equal treatment. In that sense, the Jew at home (as well as Asians and Africans abroad as we shall see in the following chapter) served as useful foils in making the case both to the elites, and themselves, about who was British and who was not. In that historic moment when socialist nationalists re-imagined the racialized Irish as an integral part of the working class of Britain, they excluded another – the Jews. The nation was being broadened and remade but only at the expense of consolidating another modality of racism – anti-semitism. That is the tragedy of this period.

4
Race, Empire and Its Discontents

By the end of the nineteenth century, Britain had seized the largest empire in history...which saturated and 'set' British society in a matrix that it has retained to this day...It is clear that the existence, maintenance and constant celebration of the empire affected all classes and institutions in Britain, it could not have done otherwise.

(Anderson 1964: 34)

It is certainly true that imperialism penetrated deeply into the labour movement and even into the socialist groups...[But] the suspicion with which...[it] was regarded...would reveal a very much more complex picture.

(Thompson 1965: 340)

Introduction

We saw in the previous chapter that one response of the British elites to the Long Depression was to unsettle the cross-class settlement that had been established in the mid-nineteenth century. This, in turn, generated a sustained wave of industrial class struggles known as the New Unionism that transformed the political landscape of British politics. A second response from the elites was to initiate a new imperialism, one that would provide Britain with export markets free of foreign competition. This chapter maps the impact of this new imperialist strategy within British society itself. In particular, it explores the growth in invented national traditions and social reforms that accompanied it, and which attempted to inculcate a sense of racialized national belonging and ownership of Empire amongst a much broader stratum of society than hitherto.

The chapter then moves on to consider how this process of working class integration into the Empire project was not only a 'top-down' elite construction, but one that relied heavily for its success on the fateful decisions taken by the Independent Labour Party (ILP). Successive defeats in the industrial and political sphere forced much of the ILP leadership to place less emphasis on the autonomous power of working class organization and the efficacy of socialist politics, and more on forging alliances with liberal trade union leaders and the Fabians. It was through this mediation that working class demands for greater democratization of the national polity and the provision of social welfare came to be redefined not as an end in itself but as a means to maintain and justify the defence of the British Empire. From the institutions of the ILP and the Labour Party, to music hall and the education system, even the unrespectable elements of the working class that had triggered the new unionism began to slowly but surely imbibe an increasingly virulent British nationalism underpinned by a shared allegiance to race and Empire. As the electoral threat of the Labour Party increased at home alongside resistance in the colonies abroad, so too did the recognition amongst the British ruling elites that the working class had to be brought into the orbit of the imagined national community.

The chapter also asks whether there were alternative voices and pathways available to the working class that might have enabled it to pursue its aims for a better and happier life without compromising on racism, nationalism and Empire. It focuses in particular on the struggle waged by a minority within the Social Democratic Federation for a socialist internationalism, as well as the political standpoint of the Socialist Labour Party in Scotland. By 1900, central to this current of socialist internationalism in Britain was a tiny community of socialist racialized minorities, figures like James Connolly, Zelda Kahan and Theodore Rothstein. Although history shows their efforts in advancing a politics of proletarian internationalism were largely in vain as much of the British working class voluntarily went to war, it would be from within this stratum that the nucleus of the future Communist Party of Great Britain would emerge.

'Half-devil and half-child': Elite racism and the new imperialism

If one elite response to the Long Depression which began in the mid-1870s was to tear up the settlement reached with parts of the working class during the mid-Victorian era of diplomatic-industrial imperialism, another was to launch the new imperialism in search of new markets. Key factions of the British elite, particularly prominent leaders like Joseph Chamberlain and Lord Rosebery, backed by powerful industrial lobbies, campaigned strongly for a new imperialism that would provide Britain with export markets free from foreign competition. Inaugurated by the acquisition of the Suez Canal in 1875, the new imperialism came to be symbolized by the scramble for Africa, and what some have termed 'empire for empire's sake'. The intense rivalry between the European powers meant the mission to colonize the world was ruthlessly pursued with no quarter given. From the 'Great Game' in central and south

Asia to the re-mapping of Africa, the colonial powers of Britain, Germany, France, the Netherlands and Portugal extended their reach across much of the world.

While the scale and scope of this wave of European colonialism was unprecedented, it was met by an exponential growth in rebellions of the colonized. In sub-Saharan Africa alone, there were revolts and wars in South Africa by the Bambatha in Natal, by the Asante and the Ndebele, Zulu resistance to the British, the first and Second Mandinka wars (Young 2001: 161–162). To the jaundiced eyes of the Western elite such rebellion was not only indicative of peoples who were incapable of adaptation to the ways of the West, but also suggested that the old ways of ideologically legitimizing their presence had failed. Kipling exhorted the Americans to join the British in taking up 'the white man's burden' of rule over 'new-caught sullen peoples, half-devil and half-child' (cited in Porter 1999: 24). Consequently, alongside the deployment of growing numbers of troops to suppress such rebellions there was a turn to scientific racism to justify Britain's imperialist practice. This form of racism was already well established in Britain having been deployed against the Irish and Africans in Britain. There is also evidence to suggest its increasing usage abroad in the aftermath of the Indian mutiny of 1857, and the suppression of the Morant Bay revolt by Governor Eyre in 1865 (Hall 2002). However, with the onset of the new imperialism, and particularly resistance to it, the status of such scientific racism changed from emergent to dominant as it was pressed into service on a universal scale.

This is hardly surprising since the number of such theories had increased exponentially over the course of the nineteenth century (Banton 1987) informed by, and giving rise to, new academic disciplines like phrenology, physiognomy and anthropology. What they shared in common was a fundamental belief that (i) humans could be sorted into a finite number of racial groups using a limited set of physical markers (for example skin colour, nose shape, hair type, skull shape and skull size); (ii) these groups were endowed with differing capacities for cultural and social development with Whites, especially Nordics/Anglo-Saxons/North Europeans at the top of this hierarchical order and sub-Saharan Africans at the bottom; and (iii) each group's capacity for civilization was fixed and immutable over time and space such that African and Asian societies were effectively imagined as lying in a state of arrested development akin to European societies at an earlier stage in their civilization (see Fanon 1961/2001; Said 1978). Fundamentally, this was an understanding of society where biology had become destiny. Further, such race-thinking was absorbed and integrated into the newly emerging Social Darwinian and eugenicist perspectives of the late nineteenth century, strengthening the allegedly scientific basis of racism and lending it a moral and intellectual legitimacy which was wholly undeserved (Hofstadter 1967).

While this type of thinking in its earliest stages informed the aggressive new imperialist drive to conquer the non-white world, the experience of conquest itself helped to consolidate, renew and sharpen the arguments of scientific racists. Scholars from the newly emerging disciplines of anthropology and phrenology provided questionnaires for missionaries, military officers and administrators to log and record every detail of the populations they encountered. Some made their own trips to the newly conquered territories, equipped with their latest head-measuring instruments to calculate the cephalic index of the 'natives'. These anthropologists as Mackenzie (1999: 286) observes 'worked within Imperial structures, utilizing the authority gleaned from power' – they were, as Levi-Strauss astutely noted, 'the handmaidens of colonialism'. Such so-called scientific findings proceeded to be integrated into the existing work on race-thinking and employed retrospectively to justify the imperial mission to 'civilize' the 'native' and 'save them from themselves' by training officials to rule. It was this reciprocal interaction of material and ideological processes which is fundamental in understanding how scientific racism both informed colonial conquest, and helped legitimate it.

The old thinking (and the policies that were constructed upon them) informed by a racializing ethnocentrism which presumed that the 'other' could be raised to a higher, Western/British plane of civilization didn't disappear entirely in this period. Cannadine (2002) usefully draws our attention to how other ways of representing the colonized, especially its elites, using the framing device of class existed alongside racializing conceptions. At the same time, he mistakenly construes class and racial categorizations as somehow competing and mutually exclusive identifications; by the 1880s, metropolitan elite class identities had been so thoroughly racialized that the colonized elite, and their class identification was nearly always racially inscribed within the boundary of the class position that they shared with the colonizing elite. That is, they were seen, and saw themselves, as distinctive racialized fractions within the elite class, reflecting the differing levels of status and esteem accorded to each in a world shaped increasingly by the idea of white supremacy.

What is unquestionable however is that the balance between this older type of thinking and the new, more aggressive scientific racism shifted decisively in favour of the latter, particularly in response to the collective resistance mounted by the colonized populations. A corollary of these developments was that British elite self-conceptions were also remade, coalescing increasingly around a sense of shared whiteness forged in opposition to the 'non-white' colonized other of Asia, Africa and the Caribbean. This understanding dovetailed neatly with the ongoing elite re-imagining of Britain at home as an Anglo-Saxon Protestant country in opposition to the Jews and Irish Catholics of the so-called Celtic race. That is, the idea of race had become the glue, the social cement which bound the nation together in opposition to Irish Catholics and Jews at home, and Africans and Asians abroad. A White, Anglo-Saxon Protestant Britain was emergent – a form of racist nationalism that became emblematic in the imperialist age of *fin-de-siècle* Britain.

Empire in the working class imaginary

What did the working class make of the British Empire in this era of the new imperialism and scientific racism? Did they recognize the Empire as *their* Empire? Or were they indifferent to it amidst their perennial and pressing search for material and psychological security? While a plethora of literature exists exploring social relations between what might be termed colonial states and the subaltern peoples exploited by colonial rule, including from a postcolonial perspective (see for example Said 1978), few systematic attempts have been made to disentangle working class reactions to Empire and imperialism from those of other classes. Even that influential body of literature produced about the impact of empire in Britain itself (see for example McClintock 1995; Hall 2002) has focused mainly on middle class communities. Amid this silence, there has sometimes been a tendency to infer working class attitudes and behaviours from a purely textual analysis of western elite artefacts, and assume as some prominent postcolonialists do (see for example Said 1978; Young 2001), that such arguments were uncritically absorbed by the working class thereby ensuring their seamless symbolic and political incorporation into the dominant discourse of a racializing nationalism committed to Empire-building. While working class embrace of empire in this period is undeniable (Mackenzie 1999; Attridge 2003), postcolonial accounts of the dominant ideology thesis kind must be rejected because they unnecessarily flatten British history, eliminating the bitter class conflicts that erupted and structured society in this period, and because they fail to give adequate consideration to the loss of legitimacy the elites suffered in the process. Instead, the working class acquired their understanding of race and Empire through a different, more mediated process that traversed the fields of education, culture and politics (MacDonald 1994; Attridge 2003; Driver and Gilbert 2003).

While their parents were heavily involved in the new unionism, participating in some of the largest class confrontations witnessed in Britain for more than a generation, the children of such workers were being educated about its Empire. The Elementary Education Act in England and Wales was introduced in 1870, and its effective enforcement from the mid-1880s set the framework for schooling of all children aged between 5 and 13. While the intention behind the act was to educate the children of the recently enfranchised working class, and meet the expectations of the industrialists for a more effective education system that would ensure Britain's dominance in the capitalist world economy, it also opened up another pathway for ideas about race and Empire to penetrate the lives and consciousness of the working class. The expansion of the education system meant that the school authorities became major purchasers of books, and the children, a large and captive audience (Heathorn 2000). The main books bought and used in the new elementary schools were 'readers' consisting of introductory history and geography books written by middle class educationalists. Their aim was not only to teach young boys and girls their 'letters' but also to provide a knowledge of their home country, and the British Empire. Alongside this learning, children were taught to be unyieldingly obedient to the dominant social order if they wanted to be recognized as active citizens, and members of the superior race. Effectively, they were being disciplined, and fashioned into a submissive class that would lend its weight to Britain's civilizing mission abroad through an internalization of its sense of national obligation (Heathorn 2000). By the end of the nineteenth century, two generations of working class children had been shaped by this education system, and the accompanying discourses of racism, patriotism and empire. The diffusion of such attitudes was consolidated by late Victorian publicists who packaged exciting imperial adventure stories that transmitted conservative values, including racism, to an eager teenage audience. With deliberate intent, a one-dimensional picture of the racialized and colonized other was manufactured that pointedly suggested it was the 'white man's burden' to bring civilization to the 'dark masses' thereby justifying Britain's imperial mission.

In late Victorian England, an imperial ethos was everywhere. If working class children came to internalize ideas about race and Britain's imperial mission through exciting adventure stories set in remote parts of Africa and Asia, their parents acquired this understanding through the medium of the music hall – the quintessential theatrical form for the working class audience in the late Victorian and Edwardian periods (Mackenzie 1986, 1999; see also Stedman Jones 1983: 229–230; Attridge 2003). The entertainment provided in these arenas invariably included '[p]atriotic song scenes, featuring uniformed performers, the showing of the flag, and even representations of Britannia and Queen Victoria' (Mackenzie 1999: 277). The tableau vivant was another form of cultural practice that appeared in church halls and theatres and which

> often featured well-known patriotic and Imperial events, re-created in frozen dumb-show. Sometimes they followed a well-known painting, thus providing an additional spark of visual recognition for the audience, or took up a key moment in the Indian mutiny, or Gordon's death.
>
> (Mackenzie 1999: 277)

Celebrated singers performed nationalist songs that appealed to the White Dominion to stand together against the African or Asian, while others featured 'heroic' working class figures fighting throughout the four corners of the Empire:

> And whether he's on India's coral strand,
> Or pouring out his blood in the Sudan,
> To keep our flag a flying, he's doing and a dying,
> Every inch of him a soldier and a man.
>
> (cited in Mackenzie 1999: 278)

It was precisely this type of cultural material that led John Hobson – the renowned anti-imperialist – to charge the music hall with being the fount of patriotism, a 'potent educator' of 'mob passion', 'appealing by coarse humour or exaggerated pathos to the animal lusts of an audience stimulated by alcohol into appreciative hilarity' (cited in Mackenzie 1999: 279).

Mackenzie (1999) also catalogues how imperial exhibitions were transformed in this period, from their earlier focus on the arts and industry to increasing displays of alleged British national and racial superiority. The most commented upon displays were those of the native villages – a form of ethnic 'peep-show' – which Mackenzie contends aimed to sharpen the sense of racialized difference by emphasizing the backwardness of the population compared to the British. This was accompanied by the display of human materials which were:

> ...increasingly used to illustrate concepts of social evolution according to stages of 'development', from hunting and gathering, through pastoral and agricultural modes, to commercial and industrial systems. Thus, other peoples were organized into categories which derived authority from their air of scientific objectivity but essentially reflected Europeans' views of themselves.
>
> (Mackenzie 1999: 285)

Other developments accentuated the consolidation of an ideological partition wall between the white Briton on the one hand, and the Asian and African on the other, including working class emigration to the colonies, and the development of a cheap postal service. The creation of a modern mass market accompanied by the associated paraphernalia of advertising, packaging and devices (such as tea and cigarette cards) designed to maintain brand loyalty also 'reflected patriotic pride, symbols of Empire and the excitement of Imperial events as well as racial ideas' (Mackenzie 1999: 288). Popular, as well as high culture became thoroughly suffused with an imperialist ethos undergirded by an unhealthy dose of racist nationalism.

One of the most influential mechanisms through which the working class acquired its understanding of Empire was through the political institutions it created in the immediate aftermath of the new unionism. The most important of these was the ILP established in 1893. A broad-based political formation committed to the politics of ethical or Christian Socialism, it confidently proclaimed its intention to secure, through majority working class representation in Parliament, 'the collective and communal ownership of the means of production, distribution and exchange' at its inaugural conference (Miliband 1987).

However, such early optimism was quickly checked by the ILP's poor electoral performance during the 1895 General Election when 29 candidates garnered a paltry 44,325 votes. Even Keir Hardie lost his seat, leading Beatrice

Webb to declare the ILP campaign as the 'most expensive funeral since Napoleon' (cited in Laybourn 1994: 154). In 1896, Hardie again failed to win a Parliamentary seat, this time at the Bradford by-election. Combined with the simultaneous defeat of the new unionism in the industrial sphere, this poor electoral showing forced the disappointed ILP leadership of Glasier, Snowden, MacDonald and Hardie to conclude that the prospects for socialism were more remote than they had imagined, or as the latter famously opined, socialism would be delayed until 1953 – denoting the 1,953 votes he had secured at the Bradford election (Laybourn 1994: 158).

Forced to change direction, the ILP set about forging alliances and electoral pacts with sympathizers of the 'working class cause' including Liberal-leaning trade union leaders and the mainly middle class members of the Fabian Society. In 1900, these different components came together in the Labour Representation Committee (LRC), and by 1906, the LRC had become the Labour Party, with the ILP providing much of its activist base (Miliband 1987). While the intention of the ILP leaders in manufacturing this arrangement had been to establish a party of labour (no longer socialist) that was electorally viable, could challenge the Liberals and Conservatives for state power, and thereby effect the inclusion of the previously unrespectable working class into the national polity as equal and active citizens, it also brought in its wake additional political commitments.

Attempts by the state to recruit troops from the industrial working class in the mid-1890s had exposed how many workers were medically unfit and unsuitable for military service. Elite anxiety about the physical decline of the British imperial race reached fever pitch during the Second Boer War between 1899 and 1902, when many expressed doubts about the long-term capacity of Britain to fulfil its imperial mission (McBriar 1963; Gupta 1975). Driven by such anxieties, the Fabians – Sidney and Beatrice Webb, George Bernard Shaw and others – who provided much of the intellectual stimulus in the newly founded Labour Party, reinterpreted the ILP objective of economic and social justice for the working class not as an end in itself, but rather as a means to maintain Britain's imperialist ambitions abroad (McBriar 1963; Gupta 1975).

A corollary of this welding of the cause of working class upliftment to the project of Empire were the attempts to make the previously uninterested working class (Rose 2002) more conscious of 'its' British Empire and the role it needed to play in its defence (McBriar 1963; Gupta 1975). In these years, Sidney Webb publicly commended Lord Roseberry for his imperial outlook (see Gupta 1975), while George Bernard Shaw, in *Fabianism and the Empire*, justified the British conquest of the Transvaal, and the opening up of China to European capitalism, on the grounds that 'states with a higher civilization had a right to take over backward states' (Gupta 1975: 11). What was significant about such expressions of support for Empire was that they emanated from a political organization and leadership that had emerged from the class struggles associated with the new unionism. In the eyes of the working class, this gave such statements a degree of authenticity, and, therefore authority which further consolidated the efforts made by the ruling elites to integrate them through relentless propaganda drives and invention of national traditions (Hobsbawm 1983). It also made it much harder to hold the line against these kinds of arguments as individual anti-imperialists like Hardie found to their cost (Gupta 1975: 9). The racializing logic of socialist imperialism had begun to permeate even those political structures the working class had manufactured in the course of the class struggles of the new unionism.

By the dawn of the twentieth century, the developments outlined in the fields of education, culture and politics had combined to increase the diffusion of racist representations of empire throughout most fields of working class life. Much of the English working class were now increasingly adept at displaying a more open enthusiasm for Empire than hitherto, drawn into a world of white superiority that had begun to exercise a magical hold over their imagination. Further, in Edwardian England, and despite the continuing antipathy between the social classes, there was little to distinguish between the mental conceptions of race, nation and Empire held by the working class, and those held by the elites. Working class demands for democratization of the British political system were increasingly expressed, and, indeed legitimated in opposition to the 'non-white' African and Asian outwith its borders, just as they were already being legitimated in opposition the Jewish enemy within. Through this racialized narrative of re-imagining, much of the British population came to know themselves afresh – as a white, Christian people.

Integration in the nation

Two obstacles stood in the way of the establishment of a new settlement between the classes that would replace the hegemony which had fallen into disrepute amidst the Long Depression and the class struggles of the new unionism – the continuing exclusion of the majority of the working class from the democratic political process, and the stark social inequalities that remained between the social classes. Even after the implementation of the 1884 Reform Act, 40 per cent of working class men and all women remained unenfranchised, while the defeat of the new unionism exacerbated the poverty suffered by the lower stratum of the working class. Consequently, despite the growing symmetry in attitudes towards race and Empire amongst all political parties, what distinguished the Labour Party from the Liberals and Conservatives was its commitment to redress these anomalies, and extend democracy and social justice to the entire British population through the conquest of state power.

Two developments were to break this political deadlock. First, Liberal imperialists like Edward Grey, Herbert Asquith and Lord Roseberry recognized that the state had to play an active role in ensuring the economic well-being of the working class. These pillars of the Liberal establishment had been horrified to discover that large numbers of working class men from urban areas had been classified as medically unfit and incapable of military service during the Boer War (Hay 1983). This concern about the physical decline of the imperial race, and the resultant doubts about Britain's long-term capacity to fulfil its imperial mission became particularly acute in the light of the unprecedented scale and scope of resistance that the British faced in parts of Africa and Asia. Set alongside the compelling social investigations documenting poverty in London and York conducted by Charles Booth and Seebohm Rowntree, and the Fabian advocacy of social imperialism, a consensus began to emerge across the Labour–Liberal divide that the state had an important role to play in uplifting all members of the British imperial race. The second factor responsible for breaking the political deadlock was the growing electoral threat posed by the Labour Party. While the majority of the working class remained disenfranchised, including much of the unskilled stratum that drove the new unionism forward, the Labour Party had still managed to secure 29 MPs at the 1906 general election. The skilled working class vote that had been the mainstay of the Liberal years in power was eroding, and the Liberals keen not to be outflanked from the Left, were forced into forging a new settlement.

The Liberal government of 1906 under Lloyd George introduced a series of social welfare reforms aimed at both preventing any further fragmentation of its skilled working class vote to the Labour Party, and uplifting the 'race' for its imperial mission. Some of the more important items of legislation introduced included compensation for injury at work, the provision of free school meals, and, medical inspections in schools. Pensions of between one and five shillings a week were also granted to those aged 70 and over. With the Labour Party increasing its Parliamentary representation to 40 at the 1910 General Election, it began to behave 'less like an opposition party than as a pressure group' (Miliband 1987: 22) pressing the Liberal Party to introduce further redistributive measures. From the delayed People's Budget of 1909, the Liberal-led coalition government responded by introducing the right to sick pay, free medical treatment and unemployment benefit in exchange for contributions to national insurance (Hay 1983).

The implementation of such measures represented real, tangible gains for the British working class that undoubtedly accelerated the on-going process of subjective integration of large parts of the working class into the nation. Set alongside the cultural and political developments that had taken place in the lives of the working class over the past three decades, such economic reforms represented the final pieces of the jigsaw through which much of the English working class voluntarily succumbed to the message that the British nation was 'their' nation, embedding this attachment deep in its collective consciousness such that it became part of its habitus. The granting of universal franchise in 1918 to all working men and women over the age of 28 simply confirmed the convergence of the working class and national interests that had taken place over the past three decades. The previously 'unrespectable' working class now joined its 'respectable' cousin and found itself relentlessly drawn into the ever more complex web of British civil society. A subliminal message was pumped out – 'that *you* belong, that *we* have a responsibility to educate, clothe and feed *you*', and 'that *you* are an integral member of the superior race that rules the world' that bound them, at least in their imagination, to their British masters. The English working class had travelled a long and difficult path since the Chartist demands for manhood suffrage. They were now active citizens of an imperial Britain with political representation in Parliament.

The effects of such integrative measures were to neutralize potentially powerful working class opposition at home, and, actively engage them in Britain's imperialist mission abroad. Ernest Renan, the noted French historian and philosopher, once remarked that nations are built on 'collective forgetting' – in this instance, the working class was invited to forget the contentious history of class war that had raged at regular intervals between themselves and their rulers since the 1780s, and, to re-imagine themselves afresh as integral members of an imperial nation united by race.

It was this set of profound transformations in the economic, political and cultural arrangements of British society in the three decades leading up to the First World War that allow us to better understand how it was that hundreds of thousands of British workers signed up for the Great War, voluntarily, and with pride. The 1914 military recruitment poster depicting Lord Kitchener, the British Secretary of State for War, above the words 'WANTS YOU' was merely the catalyst for enlistment; British workers, including some of the most militant workers from the new unionism, had been socially conditioned to answer the call of their country for more than two decades. The co-ordinates of British working class politics were now set and would follow a trajectory where the class struggle would be neatly contained, by the Labour Party and trade union leadership, within the accepted boundaries of the nation-state. The long-desired wish to democratize the British political system had been achieved, but at a cost, in that it bound the working class ever more closely to the politics of British nationalism, and a shared commitment to race and empire.

Internationalism in the age of imperialism I: James Connolly

Were there any currents of organized working class opinion that rejected such incorporation into the British imperial state in the years leading upto World War One? Were there political pathways available to the working class that might have enabled it to pursue its class objectives without succumbing to the allure of racism and Empire? And finally, were there any parts of the socialist left and the working class that might have prevented the head-long rush into world war?

There was the Social Democratic Federation, Britain's oldest socialist party. Ever since its formation in 1884, the SDF had been characterized by deep internal divisions, particularly between socialist internationalists and nationalists. Eleanor Marx and William Morris had left the organization almost immediately to form the Socialist League because of the SDF's consistent attempts to marry socialism to the politics of racism and nationalism, and its adamant refusal to support the industrial class struggles that were unfolding during the new unionism. However, while the internationalists of the Socialist League imploded during the peak years of the new unionism, the SDF – still led by Henry Hyndman and Harry Quelch, editor of the party newspaper, *Justice* – continued to maintain a presence in some working class communities with around 50 functioning branches and an active membership of around 1,000 in 1900 (Challinor 1977: 12).

At the dawn of the twentieth century, the most sustained challenge to Hyndman and Quelch's continuing attempt to marry socialism to racism and nationalism came mainly from racialized minorities within Britain, particularly those of Jewish descent in England, and a significant contingent of Scots of mainly Irish Catholic descent. The most notable amongst the latter was the Edinburgh-born James Connolly. When *Justice* boasted of 'dealing effectively with those malcontents who are bent upon following the lead of the German-Venezuelan Jew Leob, or "de Leon", to the pit of infamy and disgrace' (cited in O'Riordan 1988: 122), Connolly (1903) – in an article in *The Socialist* newspaper – condemned the Hyndman-Quelch wing of the SDF for 'appealing to racial antipathies and religious prejudices' to undermine the growing support for syndicalism amongst its left wing. He contended that attempts to blame 'the Jew' represented a missed opportunity to demonstrate to workers the real source of their oppression – the capitalist class:

> . . . instead of grasping at the opportunity to demonstrate the unscrupulous and bloodthirsty methods of the capitalist class [the SDF leadership] strove to divert the wrath of the advanced workers from the capitalists to the Jews.

Connolly mocked such 'racial antipathy' making transparent why it was incompatible with a socialist politics:

> . . . comrade de Leon is a Venezuelan, and the descendant of an old family, famous alike in the history of Spain and the New World, but if he were all that the *Justice* phrase has him, what of it? Suppose he were a German-Venezuelan-Jew, or a cockney-Irish-Scotsman, or even horror of horrors, an Anglo-Saxon, what is it to us or to Socialists generally?

Two inter-penetrating elements helped Connolly to navigate the treacherous waters of race, nation and empire and develop an innovative brand of politics informed by a commitment to anti-racism and proletarian internationalism.

First, the early formative years growing up in Edinburgh deeply marked Connolly for the rest of his life. Born in 1868 to Irish parents, Connolly grew up in an area of the city referred to as 'Little Ireland' centred on the Cowgate. Housing around 14,000 people from an Irish background, most of whom had arrived in Scotland in the aftermath of the Great Famine of 1845–1852, it was characterized by extreme poverty, poor housing and severe ill-health. In the local labour market, the Irish formed what the elites referred to as the 'unrespectable' elements of the working class, and Connolly was part of this stratum, working as a manure carter for Edinburgh Corporation (Ellis 1997; Armstrong 2013). Such economic and social hardships were overdetermined by a deep sense of exclusion from dominant constructions of the Scottish nation underpinned by a shared allegiance to Protestantism. Further, this exclusion was racially defined such that it was commonplace to refer to the Irish as a distinct race distinguishable from the British (Miles 1982). Just as in England then the Irish Catholics were the racialized outsiders of the Scottish nation, negatively evaluated by the official structures of Scottish society:

> This very high proportion of the Irish race in Scotland has undoubtedly produced deleterious results, lowered greatly the moral tone of the lower classes, and greatly increased the necessity for the enforcement of sanitary and police precautions wherever they are settled in numbers.
>
> (Census official cited in Miles 1982: 140)

Connolly's experience of this exclusion imbued in him a sense of racial and national consciousness such that he considered himself to be a member of a different race and nation to the British. Throughout his writings there are regular references to the 'Irish race' as distinct from the 'British race' (for example *The Fighting Race* (1898)). While for some, this might have helped stimulate and strengthen their attachment to the Catholic Church and its associated networks in Britain, in Connolly the lived experience of class-based poverty entwined with a sharp sense of racialized national exclusion combined to produce an interest in socialism, internationalism and Irish nationalist politics.

Second, when Connolly moved to Dublin in 1896, he further developed his understanding of socialism and nationalism in the era of imperialism. To those few remaining socialists who held fast to the abstract proletarian internationalism reminiscent of the days of the *Communist Manifesto*, he emphasized how 'our Irish nationality plays a large part in forming this conception of international [socialist] politics' (cited in Ellis 1997: 134–135) drawing to their attention the untapped potential of lived identities forged by the experience of racial and national oppression in producing resistance to the dominant order. At the same time, to those Irish nationalists who believed that the sole aim was to secure independence from the British state he declared:

If you remove the English army tomorrow and hoist the green flag over Dublin Castle, unless you set about the organisation of the Socialist Republic your efforts would be in vain. England would still rule you. She would rule you through her capitalists, through her landlords, through her financiers, through their whole array of commercial and individualist institutions...

Nationalism without socialism – without a reorganisation of society on the basis of a broader and more developed form of that common property which underlay the social structure of Ancient Erin – is only national recreancy (sic)...As a socialist I am prepared to do all one man can do to achieve for our motherland her rightful heritage – independence; but if you ask me to abate one jot...the claims of social justice, in order to conciliate the privileged classes, then I must decline.

(cited in Ellis 1997: 124)

For Connolly, the project of Irish independence from the colonial British state was indivisible from the struggle for socialism throughout that state. Anticipating Lenin's (1914/1983) more well-known work on the national question by several years, Connolly recognized earlier than most European Marxists how imperialism and mass nationalisms had greatly distorted relations between the workers of the world, and how this obliged socialists at the dawn of the twentieth century to combine their commitment to working class emancipation with active support for the struggles of racially and nationally oppressed peoples. That is, the desires and longing for national freedom and social justice amongst any subjugated population could, if harnessed to an internationalist socialist politics, lead both to national independence for all subjugated peoples, and the emancipation of the world working class from exploitation.

An example of his deep-felt commitment to the politics of anti-racism and socialist internationalism, and how it extended beyond his immediate concern for Irish independence, can be demonstrated not only by his consistent opposition to the anti-semitism of Britain's oldest socialist party – the SDF – but also in the manner that he embraced the migrant Jewish community in Ireland. In 1902, when Connolly stood as a candidate for the United Labourers' Union in the Wood Quay Ward of Dublin – an area with a significant population of Jewish migrants – he refused to indulge in the anti-semitism that characterized the campaign. Instead, recognizing that many of the Jews had been members of the Jewish Bund in eastern Europe, conscious efforts were made to reach out to them. He enlisted the support of Boris Kahan – secretary of the East London Jewish branch of the SDF – to produce a leaflet in Yiddish outlining that only James Connolly was a true 'Arbeter Fraint' (Worker's Friend) (O'Riordan 1988: 125). The election was bitterly fought with one of Connolly's opponents, the publican P.J. McCall denouncing him as a renegade from Catholicism by suggesting that socialism was incompatible with adherence to the Catholic faith. The scale of the effort taken to defeat Connolly is revealingly captured by his observation that

> ... the paid canvassers of the capitalist candidate – hired slanderers – gave a different account of Mr. Connolly to every section of the electors. How they said to the Catholics that he was an Orangeman, to the Protestants that he was a Fenian, to the Jews that he was an anti-Semite, to others that he was a Jew.
>
> (cited in O'Riordan 1988: 126)

I have focused on James Connolly not only because he constitutes a rare example of a socialist who forged an anti-racist and internationalist position in an era of ascendant imperialism, but also because in 1903 he co-founded, with George Yates and Neil Maclean, a political organization – the Socialist Labour Party – which was distinguished by its commitment to industrial unionism and proletarian internationalism. In the course of the 'great labour unrest' that unfolded throughout Britain from 1910, activists from the SLP played an influential role in shaping working class rejection of racism, especially on Clydeside – encompassing the city of Glasgow and the surrounding urban areas on the banks of the River Clyde such as Paisley, Clydebank and Greenock.

In March 1911, 12 female cabinet polishers went on strike at Singer's Kilbowie factory in Clydebank – the world's largest factory manufacturing sewing machines – against employer attempts to introduce scientific management techniques that would intensify their pace of work, and reduce wages. The 11,000 workforce was overwhelmingly female and ethnically diverse, comprising Protestants, Catholics and Jews. Given the long history of anti-Irish Catholic racism that had shaped patterns of working class formation in the west of Scotland since the mid-nineteenth century (Miles 1982), special efforts were made by activists like Arthur MacManus from the Socialist Labour Party, along with others like Tom Bell from the Industrial Workers of Great Britain, to challenge any attempts to divide the workers on the grounds of ethnicity. It was this emphasis on solidarity that was to ensure that within two days of the initial walkout, the vast majority of the 11,000 workforce would follow suit. One study concluded about the dispute:

> The confrontation ... was characterised by remarkable solidarity between the workforce – divisions based on occupation, skill, gender, religion and locality being subsumed during the strike. The philosophy of the industrial unionists played a part here ... they helped to raise levels of consciousness and were instrumental in organising and directing the escalating struggle. Their call for working class solidarity was encapsulated in their slogan, 'An injury to one is an injury to all'.
>
> (GLHW 1989)

This call for solidarity was in one sense an organic outgrowth of James Connolly's earlier forceful advocacy of industrial unionism and proletarian internationalism. It instilled in a generation of activists in the Socialist Labour Party the necessity of fashioning a political strategy that rejected divisions based on racism, gender and skill, and that relied instead on mobilizing the collective strength of the working class to effect radical social change. Within a decade, activists from the SLP including Arthur MacManus, Tom Bell, Willie Paul and many others would go on to establish the Communist Party of Great Britain (CPGB), and play influential roles within it.

Internationalism in the age of imperialism II: Jewish socialists

While a contingent of mainly Catholic socialists in the SLP were playing a critical role in sustaining a current of proletarian internationalism in Scotland, it was mainly Jewish socialists in the Social Democratic Party (formerly the SDF) who were the most consistent advocates of such a perspective in England. Already marginalized within an organization that was deeply infected with anti-semitism, Jewish socialists like Theodore Rothstein, Zelda Kahan, Boris Kahan, Peter Petroff and Joe Fineberg were now forced to contend with the pages of *Justice* resounding with attacks on 'the jack-boot bullying of Berlin' and offering advice to the British state to expand its Navy, and arm the citizenry in preparation for war with the Kaiser's Germany (Crick 1994: 231). A manifesto on *Social-Democracy and Foreign Policy* (1905) authored by Hyndman justified such a call for war by suggesting that 'we are all a bit Nationalist at bottom'. In reality, it simply reflected his own long-standing attachment to a politics of socialist nationalism that had remained unchanged since the publication of *England for All* in 1884. The other main socialist proponent of such warmongering was Quelch, who regularly used *Justice* to dismiss calls for proletarian internationalism on the grounds that it was 'about as practical as the beating of tom-toms to scare away an eclipse' (cited in Crick 1994: 231).

Nevertheless, the fact that Quelch considered it necessary to make a statement rejecting calls for a politics of socialist internationalism suggests there was at least some opposition from within the British socialist movement. Ernest Belfort Bax, the last surviving member of the original leadership of the Socialist League was certainly one opponent of this line of thinking. Although he had subsequently rejoined the SDP, Bax continued to challenge Hyndman and Quelch's calls for war condemning socialists who 'return to their patriotic "vomit" like the scriptural dog' (Crick 1994: 232). There were other socialist internationalists too in the SDP, including the socialist-feminist Dora Montefiore, along with a layer of younger activists such as E.C. Fairchild and Arthur Inkpin. However, it was Jewish activists such as Zelda Kahan, Theodore Rothstein and Boris Kahan along with the East London branches of the SDP in Central Hackney, Whitechapel and Bethnal Green that were the most consistent opponents of war, racism and nationalism (Kendall 1969: 49–54; Challinor 1977).

As émigrés from the pogroms launched by the Black Hundreds in Tsarist Russia these activists were highly sensitized to the destructive logics of racism and nationalism. Further, it was precisely because of such racist discrimination and their systematic exclusion from Russian society coupled with their continuing familiarity with the degraded conditions of existence faced by the Jewish community left behind that they came to embrace Marxist socialism as a route to emancipation. That is, from the particularity of their ethnic exclusion they had forged an attachment to the politics of proletarian internationalism with its promise of universal human emancipation. The regular calls for war with Germany from the SDP leadership combined with their vociferous anti-semitism naturally concerned such Jewish activists for it brought into question the universalist nature of the socialist project, and its promise of delivering the Jews from the curse of anti-semitism. This is why many Jewish socialists were at the forefront of anti-war activity.

When Hyndman renewed his calls for war with Germany, it was Zelda Kahan, supported by her brother Boris, her Irish partner WP Coates, and EC Fairchild who issued a statement urging the SDP to 'repudiate such bourgeois imperialist views' (Kendall 1969). Rothstein reinforced such opposition by accusing Hyndman of 'Teutonophobia' rejecting his calls for socialists to unite with their national ruling elites:

> We find you joining your voice in the war chorus of the Imperialists, and calling upon the people … to forget the class antagonisms … in a common effort to stave of the 'national peril'. If that is Social-Democracy I for one refuse to accept it.
>
> (cited in Crick 1994: 232)

.The outbreak of industrial unrest from 1910 must have filled the socialist internationalists within the SDP with hope that even at this late hour, the organized labour movement might yet embrace an internationalist outlook, and reject its attachment to a racializing nationalism, and thus avoid war. Nationally, the number of days lost to strike action increased from 4,576,000 days/year between 1900 and 1910 to 20,908,000 days/year between 1911 and 1913. Similarly, the number of workers involved in strike action increased from 240,000/year between 1900 and 1910 to 1,034,000/year between 1911 and 1913 (Hinton and Hyman 1975: 15, table 1). This industrial action was successful in arresting the decline in 'real wages and brought a flood of recruits into the unions such that membership rose from 2,369,067 to 3,918,809' in just four years (Morton 1994: 441).

An integral feature of this strike activity was the radicalization of previously acquiescent groups of workers with women and unskilled workers playing an instrumental role in the disputes over wages, conditions and demands for trade union recognition. Significantly, within the SDP itself – and from 1911 what became the British Socialist Party (BSP) – important victories were secured during this upswing in the cycle of protest. In 1912, Zelda Kahan's resolution demanding the BSP disassociate itself from any call demanding the strengthening of British national defence as a prelude to war with Germany was endorsed. However, it was to prove a hollow victory which served merely to unmask the embedded, proto-fascist beliefs of some of her socialist colleagues. Hyndmanites like F. Victor Fisher responded aggressively to the defeat contending that its anti-war sentiment had been 'largely inspired by comrades alien in blood and race' (cited in Crick 1994: 252). 'Hyndman wrote in similar vein in the *Socialist Record* and it was obvious that the old anti-semitic, nationalist tone of the SDF was reasserting itself' (Crick 1994: 252). A principled stand against war informed by the politics of socialist internationalism couldn't be secured in such an unprincipled party of British socialism as the BSP.

Equally, the Labour Party – the party of the majority of the working class – offered little opposition to the coming war. Although some of its founding members like MacDonald and Hardie would oppose World War One on pacifist grounds, the party formally committed itself to the defence of the national interest. It was a political machine that sought inclusion and social justice for the working class *within* the capitalist nation-state. Their world-view never extended beyond the nation, and it was this attachment to the nation-state, and the defence of the national interest which explained its compliance. When war was finally declared, the trade union and Labour Party leaderships immediately came out in support adopting a resolution which effectively called for the suspension of the class struggle until the war was over:

> That an immediate effort be made to terminate all existing trade disputes, whether strikes or lock-outs, and whenever new points of difficulty arise during the war period a serious attempt should be made by all concerned to reach an amicable settlement before resorting to a strike or a lock-out.
>
> (cited in Pelling 1987: 140)

This statement, along with many others like it passed by the socialist parties throughout the countries of Europe in the days leading up to, and just after 28 July 1914, ensured that the hopes and dreams of the Second International – established just a quarter of a century earlier – lay in tatters as workers from different nations turned their guns on each other in the killing fields of France and Belgium.

5

Class War, Racist Riots and Communism

White men appear determined to clear out the blacks who have been advised to stay indoors. Whenever a Negro was seen he was chased and if caught severely beaten.

> (*The Times*, 10 June 1919 cited in May and Cohen 1974: 114)

Communism is inextricably part of the history of British Labourism.... Communism has been present, since 1917, as the opposite pole to orthodox right-wing Labourism.

> (Thompson 1965: 347)

Introduction

The second decade of the twentieth century was not only characterized by world war but also an unprecedented wave of working class collective action. Central to the formation and subsequent development of the strike wave were socialists from the Independent Labour Party (ILP), the British Socialist Party and the Socialist Labour Party. State opposition to such industrial action served to further radicalize elements of the working class such that by 1919, Britain appeared gripped by a mood of working class insurgency. This chapter seeks to complicate this rather neat narrative of an undifferentiated working class moving collectively in one direction by focusing on a much neglected feature of this period; that alongside such collective working class action there took place a series of racist riots across many of the largest cities of Britain.

In particular, the relationship between such racism and the working class strike wave will be explored. It will demonstrate that such expressions were not necessarily artefacts of two different parts of the working class as Marxists might expect, but rather on occasion entwined, including Clydeside – the epicentre of the working class revolt. The part played by some of the leadership of the ILP in legitimizing such racism in Glasgow will be discussed briefly, particularly the dangers of ideologically locating the struggle for working class improvements on the terrain of the nation. The chapter also assesses the attempts by a minority of socialists who sought to challenge such racism, most particularly, those associated with the Socialist Labour Party. And it was from within this political current – inspired by the politics of James Connolly and syndicalism – along with that minority of internationalists in the British Socialist Party, that the bedrock of activists for the Communist Party of Great Britain would emerge. Thus, out of this wave of industrial and political class struggles there developed two, simultaneous but contradictory political processes. On the one hand, there took place a growing integration of the vast majority of the working class into the nation, mediated by the ILP, and through it, the Labour Party that finally forced the state to concede universal suffrage and the provision of a more comprehensive programme of social welfare than hitherto. And alongside this, there also emerged a small but significant oppositional current in the working class that rejected such attempts to nationalize the class struggle, rejected racism, and was instead informed by the politics of socialist internationalism.

The remainder of the chapter assesses the significance of the Russian Revolution and the subsequent establishment of the Third International in uniting these disparate internationalist forces in the CPGB, and in helping to draw out the importance of challenging the dominant racist and imperialist sentiment within the British working class. Concrete episodes discussing how activists from the CPGB challenged racism at home are briefly discussed, including in shipping, and at Cable Street in the East End of London. Alongside these actions, attempts to build a working class opposition to imperialism, and support for the right of the colonized nations to national self-determination are also explored. And through a focus on such episodes the influential role played by minority activists of Irish Catholic, Jewish and Indian descent is established. Finally, the significance of the growing nationalization of the Communist Party through Stalinism is discussed to understand how such CPGB participation in anti-racist and anti-imperialist activities marked not the seeds for the formation of a mass internationalist movement in Britain, but instead the remnants of a lost socialist internationalism extinguished in the midnight of the century.

War, proletarian rebellion and racism

By January 1915, more than a million British working class men had enlisted for war (Gregory 2007). While some were undoubtedly compelled to go to war because the Poor Law Guardians refused to pay support for military-aged men, the vast majority made that that fateful decision voluntarily. One striking detail about the early phase of recruitment in Britain was the formation of 'Pals Battalions' where groups of men from the same factory or football team would join and fight together. If confirmation were needed that proletarian internationalism had lost out to a deeply felt attachment to nationalism it was when the first British soldier picked up his rifle and fired at his comrade – the German worker.

Given the strength of nationalist feeling that manifested itself amongst all social classes at the onset of war, it is perhaps surprising how rapidly the harsh conditions of world war produced both disillusionment with the conflict, and a heightened sense of class consciousness paving the way for a wave of proletarian rebellion. In February 1915, steep rises in the cost of living caused by the pressing demand for war munitions led 10,000 engineering workers in Glasgow to take unofficial strike action in support of increased wages. This action along with the miners' strikes in South Wales greatly concerned the state because from its perspective, the struggle on the Western Front made it imperative that key workers 'abstain from demarcation disputes, substitute arbitration for strike action, and suspend union-imposed restrictions on output' (Wilson 2010). In March 1915, trade union leaders and employers, representing a range of war-related industries, were brought together at the Treasury Department where they established agreements that would curtail labour rights by making strikes illegal, and by allowing firms engaged on war contracts to relax or 'dilute' established trade practices and introduce less skilled labour to work in jobs that had previously been reserved for skilled labour (Hinton 1973; Pelling 1987).

In some areas of Britain, this agreement simply proved inoperable. On Clydeside, workers immediately reacted by establishing their own advocacy organization – the Clyde Workers Committee (CWC) – made up of 250–300 delegates elected directly from the workplace meeting every week. Among its leaders included Willie Gallacher of the British Socialist Party, Arthur MacManus from the Socialist Labour Party, and Manny Shinwell and David Kirkwood from the Independent Labour Party. The CWC quickly usurped the power of the local and national trade union officials, and its enhanced authority amongst the local workers was reflected in its uncompromising declaration: 'We will support the officials as long as they represent the workers, but we will act independently immediately they misrepresent them' (Hinton and Hyman 1975: 13). When the CWC instigated a strike against dilution, the state – already anxious about major social unrest in Clydeside impeding its war efforts – responded by invoking the Defence of the Realm Act, and ordered military authorities to arrest and deport (to Edinburgh) the shop stewards leading the disputes. While state repression effectively sidelined many of the key activists and suppressed working class opposition on Clydeside, struggles against workplace dilution now begun to spread elsewhere such that by 1917, 200,000 workers were on strike in London, Sheffield, Liverpool, Newcastle, Manchester and across more than 40 other towns (Hinton 1973).

This wave of strikes was now also joined by growing demands for peace. In June 1917, over 1,000 delegates attended a conference in Leeds to welcome the Russian Revolution of March 1917. The conference also recommended the establishment of 'Councils of Workmen and Soldiers' Delegates' in every town that would work for peace and ensure 'the complete political emancipation of international labour' (Hinton 1973; White 1974). However, when socialist activists attempted to set up local anti-war committees in at least eight areas, including London, Tyneside, Glasgow and Sheffield their meetings were disrupted by mobs of soldiers and 'public house loafers' incited by press headlines that declared, 'We shoot Huns at the front. Why are we more tender with the treacherous pro-Germans at home?' (Hinton 1973: 240). Despite such setbacks, it was clear that '[p]atriotic sentiment no longer absorbed, as in 1914, the social struggle' (Ferro 1973: 213).

In January 1919, this upturn in working class resistance climaxed on Clydeside as socialists concerned that rapidly dismantling munitions works and demobilizing large numbers of sailors and soldiers would lead to a sharp rise in unemployment launched the 40-hour movement to campaign for a drastic reduction in the working week (without any reduction in pay) to absorb the additional labourers returning from war. The Clyde Workers Committee (CWC) backed the demand by calling a general strike and within days, over 40,000 engineers and shipbuilders were on strike along with 36,000 miners and electricity supply workers (Gallacher 1936; Hinton 1973; Foster 1990).

However, the Liberal Government, long concerned about the industrial and political radicalism on Clydeside, feared the worst – major social disorder and possibly revolution – and began to take steps to avert it. At the Cabinet meeting, the Lord Privy Seal Andrew Bonar Law reported that 'he thought it vital for the War Cabinet to be satisfied that there was sufficient force in Glasgow to prevent disorder.... It was certain that, if the momentum in Glasgow grew, it would spread all over the country' (cited in Jenkinson 2009: 41). On 31 January, when over 60,000 demonstrators gathered in George Square in support of the strike, the police on horseback mounted a baton charge injuring 34 people. Nineteen police officers were also injured as demonstrators 'fought back, bringing the centre of Glasgow to a standstill as running battles spread out from George Square to surrounding streets' (Jenkinson 2009: 42). Many of the leaders of the CWC were arrested including Gallacher, Kirkwood and Shinwell. At the cabinet meeting held immediately prior to the riot, Secretary of State for Scotland, Liberal MP Robert Munro, had argued that 'it was a misnomer to call the situation in Glasgow a strike – it was a Bolshevist uprising' (cited in Jenkinson 2009: 42). After the riot, other Government ministers appeared to endorse Munro's assessment and refused to mobilize the battalion of Scottish soldiers stationed nearby at Maryhill barracks for fear they would be turned by the crowd. Instead, 12,000 English troops were deployed accompanied by over 100 lorries and six tanks (Jenkinson 2009: 42).

While the war years and those that followed immediately after marked an undoubted step-change in the political consciousness of influential sections of the working class, we must be careful to avoid the dangers of romanticizing this wave of proletarian rebellion, or interpreting it as marking some kind of undifferentiated large-scale shift to the political left as so much labour and socialist historiography is apt to do (see for example Hobsbawm 1964, 1984a; Hinton 1973; Hinton and Hyman 1975). Some have gone even further and claimed that in early 1919 Britain was on the 'brink of revolution' (Rosenberg 1987). What made it

> pregnant with revolutionary potential were the threats of the big battalions of the working class: the engineers on the Clyde...and at the very heart of the economy, the million-strong army of the miners, backed by the Triple Alliance, whose other members were the railway and transport unions.... If they all came out, as they threatened to do, the government could not have weathered the storm, as it would not have found enough reliable troops and police to suppress by violence a national upsurge of such dimensions.
>
> (Rosenberg 1987: 29)

There is no doubt that the numbers involved in strike action increased dramatically from an average of 632,000/year during the First World War to 2,108,000/year between 1919 and 1921. There was also a marked increase in the number of strike days lost to industrial action from 5,292,000 between 1914 and 1918 to 49,053,000 between 1919 and 1921 (cited in Hinton and Hyman 1975: 15, table 1). However, what such accounts have ignored is how this upturn in class struggle was accompanied by an intensification of racism and anti-semitism amongst all social classes.

When some parts of the Jewish population refused to enlist for war because it would have involved fighting alongside the Tsarist regime that instigated the pogroms that brought them to Britain in the first place (Holmes 1988: 103), it provoked great discontent amongst parts of the English working class in the east end of London. Most interpreted this act of refusal as unpatriotic, and accused such Jews of shirking their responsibilities to 'king and country' while simultaneously consolidating their economic and social position when 'British boys' were dying at the front (Holmes 1988: 104–105). Local institutions like Stepney Council's General Purposes, Staff and Education Committee demanded the calling up, internment or repatriation of all male 'aliens' of military age (Bourke 1994: 196). This representation of Jews as unpatriotic, and possibly even enemy combatants, continued unabated throughout the war years culminating in the introduction of the second Aliens Act of 1919 which

> required all Jewish 'aliens' to carry identity cards, to notify the authorities if they were to be absent from home for more than a fortnight, to eschew designated 'protected areas', and to sign special leave hotel registers.
>
> (Bourke 1994: 197)

The Act also introduced prison penalties for so-called aliens causing 'sedition or disaffection' amongst the military or civilian population; or attempting to 'promote industrial unrest in any industry in which he has not been bona fide engaged for at least two years'. It permitted immigration officers, the police, magistrates and the Home Secretary to detain and deport without right of appeal any 'alien' engaged in political or industrial subversion convicted of a crime, leading to hundreds of Jews being deported (Bourke 1994). It was in this increasingly feverish climate that coupled the Jew to the categories of 'alien' and 'subversive' that the *Protocols of the Elders of Zion* was first published in English in 1919.

And it was in 1919 – the year which supposedly marked the apotheosis of the strike wave and brought Britain to the 'brink of revolution' – that also witnessed an unprecedented series of racist riots throughout the port areas of most of Britain's largest cities including Liverpool, Glasgow, London, Cardiff, Manchester as well as Hull, Barry and Newport. While blacks and Asians were represented in a diverse range of occupations between the wars (Green 1990; Panayi 1994), their primary source of employment was as seamen. A significant factor in the riots was the large numbers of recently demobilized soldiers and sailors. With Lloyd George's promise to make Britain 'a land fit for heroes to live in' ringing in their ears, they returned home after four years of war to a civilian life characterized by unemployment and poverty (Leed 1981). Significantly, in the port areas of the main cities, this anger and disorientation entwined with racism as the soldiers and seaman found themselves competing for jobs against black and Asian people they refused to recognize as British. This sense of racial superiority generated by decades of social conditioning didn't dissolve amid the ongoing industrial unrest as some might predict but became activated and embroiled with it in a toxic cocktail.

Between January and August of 1919, many of these men rioted and attacked the minority seamen and their property leaving five dead, countless numbers seriously injured, and over 250 people arrested (May and Cohen 1974: 112; Jenkinson 2009: 1). In Limehouse, in the east end of London, several black men were attacked, leading to four days of rioting. In Cardiff, three people were killed, dozens hospitalized and over £3,000 worth of property damaged (Jenkinson 1996). Amid these racist riots, no section of British society saw fit to recall how the British state and employers had scoured the four corners of its Empire in search of labour to fill the gap left in the domestic labour market by several thousand British seamen volunteering for war (Gordon and Reilly 1986: 75). Instead, at the end of the war, white servicemen demanded their jobs back from the 'coloured' seamen, accusing them of 'crimping' or undercutting white seamen (Byrne 1977; Lunn 1985). The NUS – the main union for seamen – whose officials had for instrumental purposes muted their racism during the war when minority labour was essential, now began to deploy the prevailing racist imagery, including the dangers of 'miscegenation' to justify the replacement of minority labour with white labour:

> It is no use men trying to persuade us that the question of colour does not enter into national consideration, it does and very seriously. We have growing up in our midst a population, not of young Arabs, but of half-castes, which is undesirable in the extreme, and no prating of goodwill towards men of colour will alter this fact....We of this union killed the white crimp, and we are not going to stand idly by and see a coloured crimp take his place.
>
> (cited in Lunn 1985: 14)

The union also introduced proposals intended to restrict the employ-ment opportunities available to Black and Asian workers. Although the NUS claimed it was attempting to restrict the opportunities of migrant labour and not 'non-white' English labour, this subtle distinction was lost amid the racist sentiment that had been unleashed (Byrne 1977; Lunn 1985). Even long-established minority communities with no involvement in the shipping industry were adversely affected. In several large factories in Liverpool,

> the refusal of White workers to work alongside Blacks led to the dismissal of Black labourers. One local paper estimated that at the height of the riots 120 Black workers had been dismissed for this reason.
>
> (May and Cohen 1974: 118)

Faced with significant elements of the white working class mobilizing against blacks and Asians, alongside widespread industrial unrest throughout the country, the Government decided to act by establishing an inter-departmental committee to consider implementing a repatriation scheme to remove one of the so-called 'threats' to social disorder. Shortly afterwards, repatriation committees were set up in a number of cities with several hundred black and brown English, Welsh and Scots deported to their alleged countries of origin (Jenkinson 1996: 103–108). Parts of the British working class – long interpel-lated into racialized ways of thinking and acting – were complicit in this move, and in the process weakened the class solidarity that was necessary to ensure victory against the employers.

When viewed through the lens of race, the thesis – advanced by many labour and socialist historians – that this period marked some kind of univer-salist class awakening that brought Britain to the 'brink of revolution' requires considerable revision. A more nuanced explanation is required that can help us understand both the rising tide of working class industrial and political struggles, *and* working class deployment of racism, including violence and dis-crimination against Jewish migrants, as well as those from the British colonies.

In the 1910s, society was polarizing fast, not just along the faultline of class, but simultaneously along that of race and nation, within the working class.

Racists, Reds and the revolt on the Clyde

While the rise in workers' militancy was not accompanied by any diminution of racist sentiment some Marxists might contend that the co-existence of an upturn in class struggles and racism was an indication of the bifurcation of the working class. That is, racism emanated principally from the stratum of the working class that remained ideologically wedded to the elite project of national belonging underpinned by an allegiance to race and empire whereas those engaged in collective action in opposition to the state were part of a stratum that had broken from this project, and were moving in a political direction where the language of class and solidarity negated racism. However, such an argument is difficult to sustain when we consider events on Clydeside – arguably the epicentre of the working class revolt during this period – where racism was deployed by socialist activists to create a cohesive opposition to government and employer attacks.

On 23 January 1919, a racist riot occurred in the Glasgow harbour area when around 30 black sailors were chased out of the merchant marine hiring yard by white sailors, beaten in the street, attacked in their boarding houses and then targeted for mass arrest by police called in to halt the disorder. The mob was joined by white bystanders who bolstered the crowd to several hundred with many making use of 'guns, knives, batons, and makeshift weapons such as stones and bricks picked up from the street' (Jenkinson 2009: 73). Cornered in their boarding house, the black sailors offered no resistance when the police entered the premises. In contrast to the immediate arrest of the black sailors – all British colonial subjects from Sierra Leone – not one of the large crowd of white rioters was arrested (Jenkinson 2009: 74).

The riot wasn't a spontaneous eruption against the presence of black workers in Glasgow. Black people had lived and worked in the port area of the city for a number of years with many – along with Chinese labour – employed as seamen. Against a backdrop of rising unemployment, many white seamen branded the 'coloured' seamen as unfair economic competition. References to unfairness referred not only to the alleged tendency of such workers to accept lower wage rates than white workers, but also that minority labour was undeserving of such jobs because it was 'non-white', and, therefore not British. That is, what these white workers desired was that such labour make way for a more deserving category of worker that was white and British.

Jenkinson (2008, 2009) demonstrates how in the days leading up to the riot, socialist leaders on Clydeside actively expressed their support for such racist sentiment. Most notably, Manny Shinwell – leading member of the ILP,

President of the Glasgow trades and labour council, and leader of the Glasgow branch of the British Seafarers's Union – made a number of speeches expressing sympathy with the seamen. He encouraged them to participate in the strike action for the 40-hour week campaign which they could use as a platform 'to voice their concerns about workers from overseas undercutting their wages and threatening their job opportunities as part of the wider strike action' (cited in Jenkinson 2009: 43). A few hours before the racist riot broke out, Shinwell addressed a meeting of over 600 sailors at the mercantile marine yard where he attributed the existence of large numbers of unemployed seamen 'to the refusal of the Government to exclude Chinese labour from British ships' urging them that 'it was essential . . . that *action should be taken at once*' (cited in Jenkinson 2009: 43). When interviewed by a local newspaper in the immediate aftermath of the riot, Shinwell connected it to the hiring of overseas sailors stating that 'some of the best ships' out of Glasgow were employing black and Chinese labour while a number of recently demobilized (White British) Royal Naval reservists were unable to obtain employment (Jenkinson 2009: 43).

'In the days following the harbour riot, Shinwell continued to speak out at sailors' meetings against the threat to jobs due to the employment of "Asiatic" labour on British ships' (Jenkinson 2009: 43), and tried repeatedly to link this with the 40 hours campaign by calling for the removal of such labour from British ships thereby creating more job opportunities for white British workers. The day before the general strike descended into violence on Bloody Friday (31 January 1919), Shinwell presided over a third meeting of sailors in a week where he 'urged them to take effective steps to prevent the employment of Chinese labour on British ships' (cited in Jenkinson 2009: 44). Willie Gallacher – then chair of the CWC and leading member of the BSP – supported Shinwell and accompanied him to a meeting with seamen on 28 January 1919 to persuade them to take part in the strike action. As Jenkinson (2009: 44) notes:

> The tenor of this meeting was no different from the ones addressed only by Shinwell; again, the tactic was to import into the broad strike campaign the 'old demand' that black and Chinese crews should be expelled from British ships.

It was clear that 'the strike committee viewed support from white sailors as useful in widening the protest movement and were none too particular as to how such involvement was secured' (Jenkinson 2009: 44).

This episode draws attention to how even in those regions where working class militancy was most intense, the social and class struggles were sometimes animated and framed in racialized terms both by workers participating in such collective action, and many of the activists and organized social forces who led it. The ILP – of which Shinwell was a leading member – was a party that was deeply committed to securing economic and social justice for the working class. At the same time, it was also a party whose members often displayed a deep-rooted, almost unconscious attachment to nationalism. Shinwell himself claimed much later in life that the ILP's 'patriotism was of the subconscious variety . . . . Britain was the best country' (cited in Rose 2002: 337). This attachment to a form of banal nationalism (Billig 1995) defined the parameters within which they located the struggle for working class justice. They hoped the intensification of the class struggle would help pressure the elites into including the working class as partners within the confines of the existing capitalist nation-state. That is, leaders of the ILP aimed to use working class anger, the resulting strike action and the large-scale social unrest that ensued as political leverage to force the state to deliver a better economic and social deal to the working class of Britain, to force it to live up to its promise of building a 'land fit for heroes'.

However, there were clear dangers associated with grounding the struggle for working class justice on the ideological terrain of the nation because British nationalism had been thoroughly racialized since the mid-Victorian era. The ILP helped consolidate this discourse of racializing nationalism further within the working class by distinguishing those workers who allegedly belonged to the nation from those that didn't. When activists like Shinwell employed a discourse that equated the British worker with whiteness they effectively privileged the claims of this stratum for the limited jobs available in merchant shipping over those workers who were constructed as non-white. By creating an idealized image of the British worker as white, those workers who were represented as 'non-white' were deemed less deserving on the grounds that they weren't British, which in turn made them 'legitimate' targets for discrimination and violence, and eventually deportation.

At the same time, on Clydeside – unlike many other parts of Britain – there was a current of socialist opinion that vigorously opposed the manipulation of such racism. Leading activists like Arthur MacManus from the SLP and John Maclean from the BSP located the struggles of the British working class within a broader project of socialist internationalism. The twin pre-suppositions that informed this philosophical standpoint were an attachment to the cause of working class emancipation that transcended national boundaries, and the impossibility of achieving such social, economic and political equality within the confines of the existing capitalist social formation. Instead, for socialist internationalists, a radical social transformation was required that would inaugurate a post-capitalist socialist order. At the same time, it is important to emphasize that this wasn't simply an abstract commitment to proletarian internationalism but historically grounded in personal experience. Arthur MacManus was a Belfast-born Catholic who had witnessed the oppressive and exclusionary effects of the racializing nationalism generated by the machinery of the imperial British state in dividing Protestant and Catholic workers. It was this concrete assessment that led him, and many others to oppose such divisions from the standpoint of the international working class.

It was this political perspective – first inculcated by James Connolly – which enabled activists from the SLP in particular to directly intervene when attempts were made to racialize the class struggle on Clydeside. In an article entitled *Race Riots and Revolution* published in the SLP's monthly newspaper, *The Socialist*, the party mocked the seamens' union for deploying racism to remove black workers from certain occupations, and condemned them for deflecting working class anger away from the employers:

> The Trades Unions have prided themselves on having ousted coloured labourers from certain occupations....The very existence of capitalism depends upon driving all the elements of present day pugnacity, a trait always in prominence after a great war, into racial or national avenues. By forcing the workers to ease off their pugnacity over lines of colour, this blinds them to the class line which forms the focus of the struggle of the modern international proletariat.
>
> (cited in Jenkinson 2009: 16)

There was also opposition to such racism from Scottish women married to the black sailors. Letters submitted by these women to local newspapers tried to challenge the racist representations of their black husbands and 'mixed-race' children in the aftermath of the racist riots. One such person calling herself *Justice for the Coloured People* outlined how she had been married to a black merchant sailor for 25 years and reminded the readership of the many sacrifices that black sailors had made in defence of the nation. She went on to describe how her husband had been on ships that were torpedoed on four separate occasions. Three of the black sailors who had visited her house were drowned in these incidents while a further two burned to death 'at the hands of the German' (cited in Jenkinson 2008: 24) Such interventions by local working class women helped re-insert the contribution and sacrifices made by the black community (both British, and those from the colonies) into the national story of Britain. Informed by an emergent multicultural nationalism, they tried bravely in the face of great opposition to construct a counter narrative that would enable their husbands and mixed-race children to be treated like any white individual in British society.

Notwithstanding these important challenges, it was the ILP, and by proxy the Labour Party, that profited most from this wave of class struggles with many of the 'Red Clydesiders', including Shinwell and Kirkwood, eventually being elected to Parliament. The ILP's success lay in its ability to reflect faithfully the dominant cultural and political outlook of the working class at the time – both in terms of the ideas workers brought with them into this phase of class struggle, and the kind of actions they were willing to undertake in the course of such conflict. When confronted with an opportunity to challenge working class racism, the ILP instead chose to accommodate to it. Indeed, leaders like Shinwell went further by strategically deploying racism to cement solidarity between white workers at the expense of other non-white workers. In this sense, they reinforced and legitimized racist ideas existing within the working class and bound them ever more tightly to a racializing British nationalism. The task of those socialist internationalists in the SLP and the BSP was made doubly difficult; not only did they have to counter the racism and nationalism propagated by the elites, but also that emanating from political formations leading the working class unrest. Given the incremental incorporation of the working class since the mid-Victorian era accompanied by the growing penetration of racist and nationalist ideas, it is highly unlikely that the co-ordinates of the class struggle could have been re-set in the course of this phase of class conflict. There was too much ideological baggage to shed, and the SLP with its internationalist outlook was too small to affect it.

This more pessimistic account of the events leading up to 1919 lends weight to John Maclean's scepticism surrounding the legend of 'Red Clydeside' (see also Miliband 1987). Contrary to both the claims perpetuated by some government ministers – concerned about the prospect of revolution in Britain along the lines witnessed in Russia in November 1917 or Germany in late 1918 – and by later socialist writers, Britain, and more specifically Clydeside, was never on the verge of effecting radical social change. Certainly, the epicentre of this revolt on Clydeside produced many revolutionary socialists, most notably John Maclean, Arthur MacManus and Tom Bell, some of whom led influential campaigns for peace. They successfully mobilized workers in defence of transnational working class interests that prevented the delivery of armaments to Poland that were intended for use against the newly-established workers state in Russia (see Pelling 1987; Kelly 1988). Yet, the parties they were affiliated to such as the SLP and the BSP saw little growth in membership. The tendency of proletarian internationalism remained a marginal accretion on the culture and politics of the British working class – restricted in the main to racialized minorities like Irish Catholics and Jews along with other 'outsiders' such as those from the Highland Gaels or the South Wales mining communities.

A party of outsiders: The CPGB

Two waves of political and class struggles waged between 1885 and 1920 were instrumental in securing the formal political inclusion of the vast majority of the working class into the British nation-state. The first wave represented by the new unionism produced the ILP – a mainly Christian socialist formation that unified the Irish Catholic and English Protestant sections of the working class in a common quest for economic and social justice. Although unable to forge an independent political existence of its own, its alliance with the trade union leaders and the Fabians helped establish the Labour Party which went on to become the junior partner in the Liberal governments of the early twentieth century. The second wave, beginning in 1910 with the 'great labour unrest' and continuing beyond the war into 1919 proved decisive in breaking skilled workers away from the Liberal Party and into the arms of Labour. This development, combined with the decision in 1918 to enfranchise all men over 21 and women over 30 helped break Labour free from its dependency on the Liberals, and move into a position of political ascendency as the political party representing the working class interest. This was confirmed at the 1922 General Election where Labour displaced the Liberals and formed for the first time the principal opposition to the Conservative Party (Kelly 1988: 102).

It was the ILP's continued affiliation to the Labour Party throughout this period that ensured Labour benefitted politically from the sustained waves of industrial unrest, despite having played no substantive part in them. That is, its continued affiliation lent Labour a legitimacy, and served albeit unintentionally, as a kind of 'left cover' for the Labour Party, enhancing its socialist credentials amongst an ever broader and more class conscious working class constituency. It was amid this highpoint of workers struggle that the Labour Party adopted Clause 4 of its constitution which declared its intention:

> To secure for the producers by hand or by brain the full fruits of their industry and the most equitable distribution thereof that may be possible, upon the basis of the common ownership of the means of production and the best obtainable system of popular administration and control of each industry and service.
>
> (cited in Miliband 1987: 60–61)

Given the extraordinary economic, political and cultural pressures to conform and become an obedient member of an imperial nation-state, it is remarkable that small groups of socialist activists chose to remain outwith this settlement rejecting any attempt to narrowly locate the struggle for socialism and working class emancipation on the terrain of the nation. At the same time, this layer of political opposition to the hegemon of the Labour Party remained small, marginal, and deeply fragmented. Organizationally, it comprised the socialist internationalists of the BSP, the mainly Scottish worker militants of the SLP, the miners of the South Wales Socialist Society (SWSS) and the east end radicals of the Workers Socialist Federation (WSF) led by Sylvia Pankhurst. The relationship between these groups was often fractious, and they remained divided on whether or not to affiliate to the Labour Party.

Had it not been for the Russian Revolution of November 1917, and the establishment of a workers' state under the leadership of the Bolsheviks, it is quite possible that these socialist formations in Britain would have remained divided, and perhaps over the long run degenerated into inconsequential sects. The Bolshevik leadership led by Lenin were socialist internationalists who believed their conquest of state power in Russia represented an important step on the path to world socialist revolution. To further this aim, they placed great emphasis on encouraging the disparate forces of socialist internationalism to unify in a single united communist party in each nation-state. In Britain, it was this 'Russian Bolshevik initiative and influence' that was decisive in leading those 'diverse elements to unite into a Communist Party' (Pelling 1958: 41).

Unification was a complex, often torturous process conducted between the spring of 1918 and the summer of 1920. Eventually most of the BSP, the Communist Unity Group (consisting of the majority of the SLP) and the South Wales Communist Council (formerly the SWSS) agreed to establish a communist party. At the subsequent Unity Convention held in London on 31 July and 1 August 1920 and attended by 160 delegates, the CPGB formally came into existence. Fraternal messages were read from different parties and individuals around the world, including Lenin, who stated his agreement with plans to found the CPGB. He went on to criticize the WSF and Sylvia Pankhurst for not joining the CPGB, and declared that he was in favour of participation in Parliament, and, of 'adhesion to the Labour Party on condition of free and independent Communist activity' (cited in Klugman 1960). At the Second Congress of the Third International in August 1920, and again in his critique of the sectarianism of Sylvia Pankhurst in *Left-Wing Communism: An Infantile Disorder* (1920), Lenin reiterated his support for communist participation in parliamentary activities. Further attempts were made to draw the Workers Socialist Federation (now known as the Communist Party – British Section of the Third International) and the Communist Labour Party (comprising in the main of Scottish shop stewards), into the CPGB. By January 1921, agreement was reached and the CPGB was re-founded. The only major revolutionary figure in Britain who failed to join the CPGB was John Maclean – ironically the honorary vice-president of the Russian Congress of Soviets and the Bolshevik representative in Scotland – whose health and political intuition had been destroyed as a result of his many spells in prison.

At its inception in January 1921, the CPGB probably had no more than 2,500 members (Pelling 1958: 42; Thorpe 2000: 781, table 1) and they 'consisted to a remarkable degree, of persons of non-English origin' (Pelling 1958: 42). A Special Branch report similarly characterized one early CPGB audience as comprising in the main of 'Aliens, Jews and Sinn Feiners' (Morgan et al. 2007: 184). A year after its formation, over two-thirds of its members were to be found in South Wales, London and Scotland, with East London and Glasgow representing the main centres of strength – both of which were also key areas of Irish Catholic and Jewish residence (Thorpe 2000). In sum, the CPGB at its formation was made up of socialists drawn largely from the 'Celtic fringe' of Britain – Scotland and Wales – and racialized minorities including Irish Catholics, Jews as well as a sprinkling of Indians, Caribbeans and Africans. It is no coincidence that nearly all Stuart Macintyre's 'little Moscows' were located outside England, except for Chopwell in the north-east, and London's East End. The party was so marginal to English working class life in the 1920s that 'there were large parts of industrial England . . . [where] the party's activities simply did not reach' (Pelling 1958: 43).

Given that the dominant and exclusionary conception of British national belonging had been forged in opposition to those of Irish Catholic and Jewish descent at home alongside 'non-whites' in the colonies, it is understandable that some of these racialized outsiders would find their way to the CPGB – committed as it was to the radical social transformation of the British capitalist nation-state. Further, this memory and experience of exclusion from the British nation on the grounds of their race and/or religion imbued leading minority figures within the CPGB such as Arthur MacManus, Zelda Kahan, Rajani Palme-Dutt and his brother Clemens, with what Du Bois (1903/1994) refers to as double consciousness. Viewing British society through the lens of the 'alien eye' (Rajani Palme Dutt cited in Morgan et al. 2007: 185) enabled them to expose the moral illegitimacy of Britain's imperial mission abroad, as well as racism at home. At the same time, it is worth stressing that only a tiny fraction of the racialized minority population ever became Communist activists. Moreover, those that did believed that the victory of socialism would facilitate the transcendence from more parochial, particularistic attachments associated with race, ethnicity and nation. In that sense, we might wish to describe such minority communist activists as strategic universalists (Gilroy 2000). The phenomenon of the 'non-Jewish Jew' that Isaac Deutscher (1968) wrote so eloquently about was actually an important example of a much broader phenomenon encompassing diverse groups of racialized minorities, who by virtue of their outsider status helped expose the particularism through which contemporary capitalist society was constructed. Such an understanding was a prerequisite for plotting a more appropriate path toward a universalist future for all humankind.

The Russian Revolution was a defining event for many of these minority activists, helping to strengthen their resolve in revolutionary socialist politics when they were still small in number and influence in Britain. In particular, three factors bound them to the Bolshevik experiment. First, minority activists like Zelda Kahan and Theodore Rothstein – who had escaped the racist pogroms of Tsarist Russia only to come face to face with the racist anti-Semitism of British society, including from fellow BSP party members – were drawn to the Bolsheviks because of their resolute opposition to racism and nationalism, their opposition to world war, their commitment to socialist internationalism, and their perspective that the Russian revolution was a precursor to world socialist revolution. In their eyes, the Russian Revolution reinforced their belief in a better future for all humankind, one which offered redemption for the oppressed and exploited of the world. In this sense, the Russian revolution was interpreted as a revolution for hope. Further, Lenin in particular played an influential role in pressing the fledgling CPGB to become the organizing hub of anti-imperialist activity throughout the British empire and actively supported minorities within the party against those remaining individuals who retained any lingering attachments to racist sentiment. Tom Quelch – a London print worker and son of the notorious SDF racist and anti-Semite, Harry Quelch – drew rebukes from Lenin for warning against strikebreaking by 'jolly coons' during a Comintern meeting (Morgan et al. 2007: 213).

Second, Lenin's (1914/1983) sophisticated grasp of the national question, and his resulting support for the right of oppressed nations to self-determination within the former Tsarist Empire must have struck a chord with many socialist activists of Irish Catholic descent like Arthur MacManus and JT Murphy, and reminded them of James Connolly and his belief that the struggle for socialism and national liberation from colonial oppression were inextricably entwined in the age of imperialism. And thirdly, the composition of the Bolshevik membership itself reflected the successful forging of a multi-ethnic socialist formation with two-thirds of the Bolshevik leadership coming from minority groups within the Russian Empire, including Ukrainians, Latvians, Georgians and Jews (Riga 2008). These factors taken together lent themselves to an understanding of the Russian Revolution as an insurgency of the subaltern. Certainly, in the minds of racialized minorities in the CPGB, the struggle for working class emancipation in the west became firmly wedded to the struggle for liberation from colonial oppression of peoples in their ancestral countries of origin. The construction of a deracialized socialist society became indivisible from struggles against racism, for colonial liberation and working class emancipation.

The CPGB, anti-imperialism and anti-racism

Given the multi-ethnic composition of the CPGB, it comes as little surprise to find that over the next two decades it was at the centre of most organized campaigns against imperialism and racism. Through such campaigning and the production of literature, it tried to make the British worker more aware of the horrors and injustice of British imperial rule, and break them from their racist attachments. Shapurji Saklatvala – an Indian Parsi – played an instrumental role in these activities. Arriving in Britain in 1905, Saklatvala had first joined the ILP as a committed anti-colonialist, but inspired by the Russian Revolution and its support for national liberation struggles, had shifted his allegiance to the CPGB at the time of its founding.

Along with Arthur Field – an ILP activist – Saklatvala had already established the Workers Welfare League (WWL) in 1917 with the aim of forging unity between the Indian and British labour movements whose fortunes he believed were 'inextricably linked' (Squires 1990: 176). The organization was successful in securing the support of leading trade union activists like Arthur Pugh of the Iron and Steel Trades Federation and Duncan Carmichael – later secretary of the London Trades Council. Pugh and Saklatvala drafted a joint statement which outlined that the 'Indian labour problem is to be recognized as an English problem, seriously affecting the question of maintenance of standards of life among the workers working competitively in the same industries within the Empire' (cited in The Marxist 1996: 1–2). Further, they declared their aim was 'to bring together representatives of the working classes in Great Britain and India in order that they be of mutual aid to each other' (cited in the Marxist 1996: 2). Such calls for solidarity became more evident after the Bombay cotton strike of 1923 with Saklatvala making regular 'references to the jute industry of Bengal, and how necessary it was for the workers there and those employed in Dundee to make common cause' (cited in Squires 1990: 166).

There were also others in the CPGB who attempted to question aspects of Britain's relationship to its colonies. At the 1925 TUC annual congress, Harry Pollitt – the future leader of the CPGB – moved a resolution that drew the wider labour movement's attention to 'the domination of the non-British peoples by the British government' which served no interest other than that of 'capitalist exploitation' (cited in Callaghan 1995: 7). Alongside attempts to expose British imperialism, the CPGB attached great importance to challenging working class racism within Britain which they claimed was 'part of the imperialist rationale to stress the inherent backwardness of African peoples and . . . it was a mark of the political backwardness of British labour that it believed it' (Callaghan 1995: 17–18). In 1925, it passed a resolution at its annual congress that called on every party member to 'actively take up the fight against the imperialist prejudices still existing amongst large sections of the working class in Britain' (cited in The Marxist 1996: 2).

The establishment of the Comintern-backed League Against Imperialism (LAI) in February 1926 in Berlin marked an important step-change in anti-imperialist activity throughout Europe. Its primary aim was to 'mobilize a broad united front in western Europe' in support of the emerging movements of national liberation in the colonies (Hargreaves 1993). A major international congress was held in Brussels in February 1927 that was attended by 175 delegates, of whom 107 came from 37 countries under colonial rule. They included representatives from the National Revolutionary Army of China, the Chinese Trade Union Congress, the Kuomintang, the Indian National Congress, the Egyptian Nationalist Party, the South African Trade Union Congress, the nationalist movement of Indonesia, and the African Committee for the defence of the Negro race (The Marxist 1996). Alongside these organizations, several prominent individuals attended including Einstein, Nehru, Brockway, MacManus, with Reginald Bridgemann heading the British delegation. A British Committee of the LAI was constituted in April 1926 with regular conferences being held throughout the late 1920s. One such LAI conference held in Newcastle was attended by 136 delegates from 64 organizations, including various trade unions and the ILP (Hargreaves 1993: 256). Further, the WWL – now nesting within the CPGB – was beginning to make important inroads into the organized labour movement such that by 1927, it had gained the affiliation of 78 trade union branches (cited in Squires 1990: 169). And in 1928, a conference organized by them in Wales was attended by 148 delegates, including representatives from 33 miners lodges, 25 women's co-operative guilds and 20 local trades councils (cited in The Marxist 1996: 2). The ideological and political work patiently carried out by the CPGB since the early 1920s was beginning to resonate with parts of the organized working class.

Another feature of the CPGB's anti-imperialist activity was to provide support to the ongoing anti-imperialist struggles of peoples within the British Empire. The CPGB's head office on King Street was 'earmarked as the co-ordinating centre for anti-colonial activities, exploiting "[i]mperialis[t] means of exchange and communication...for the more speedy disruption of the Empire"' (Morgan et al. 2007: 213). The CPGB concentrated their extra-metropolitan efforts on India, with Phillip Spratt, Ben Bradley, and Lester Hutchinson helping to strengthen Communist support in the unions of Bombay and Madras despite facing strong opposition from the Raj authorities (Owen 1999: 201). In Britain itself, CPGB leaders in the 1930s were prominent in a series of Indian political conferences staged to promote the cause of independence with one author claiming that 'Communist influence among Indian students in Britain had never been stronger' (Callaghan 1995: 19).

While the CPGB drew into its anti-imperialist, anti-racist orbit some elements of the organized working class and others, the Labour Party as far as Empire was concerned remained dominated by two types of leaders – socialist nationalists who cared little about events or practices beyond the shores of Britain, and, social imperialists of the patrician kind such as Sidney Webb who continued to advocate some form of British imperial rule on behalf of trade union leaders and others so as to ensure there were places where (white) British workers could escape to if suffering from unemployment at home (Owen 1999: 194–196). The CPGB's internationalist outlook in those early years was an important, if somewhat uneven accretion within the British socialist movement that for so long had grounded its mission of working class advancement on the exclusionary terrain of nationalism.

However, from the late 1920s, the CPGB found itself engaged in such activity against ever increasing odds. The defeat of the General Strike in 1926 had a catastrophic impact on the organized labour movement, shifting the balance of class power decisively in favour of the employers and the state. The government acted swiftly by introducing the Trades Disputes Act in 1927 which made secondary strike action illegal. The following year, the Labour Party and many of the trade union leaders – committed to gradualism and the pursuit of the national interest – quietly acquiesced by endorsing the 'Mond-Turner' accord in 1928 and a 'compromise before conflict' model of trade unionism designed to promote harmonious industrial relations (Pelling 1987). The effect was to curtail rank and file trade unionists from taking industrial action to defend their rapidly worsening material situation.

This situation deteriorated further with the onset of the Great Depression in 1929. The effects on the industrial areas of Britain were immediate and devastating, as demand for British products collapsed. By the end of 1930, unemployment had more than doubled to 2.5 million and exports had fallen in value by 50 per cent (Hobsbawm 1990). Accompanying this was a dramatic decline in trade union membership from 35 per cent of the total labour force between 1920 and 1924 to 24 per cent between 1930 and 1934 (Grint 1991: 170, table 7). With trade union strength greatly weakened, the number of workers involved in strike action declined from 1,061,000 between 1920 and 1924 to 289,000 between 1930 and 1934, with the number of strike days lost declining from 30,277,000 to 3,980,000 over the same time period (Grint 1991: 170, table 7).

With the Labour Party now heading a minority government but unwilling to take the necessary steps to arrest the decline in material living conditions, many workers felt unrepresented, demoralized and angry. There is no doubt that the depression years of the late 1920s and 1930s greatly strengthened the influence of racist sentiment within the English working class, particularly in areas where migrant social groups and their English-born children had settled (Piratin 1978; Bourke 1994). In 1930, the Labour Secretary of State for India, William Wedgewood Benn (later Lord Stansgate), wrote how wherever he travelled in England, the working class seemed to be 'a mixture of ignorance ... and idealism, always with racial prejudice ready to be excited' (cited in Owen 1999: 199).

A key site of racist conflict remained the port areas where significant numbers of minorities were employed as seamen. In the 1920s, the National Union of Seamen successfully campaigned to restrict the employment of 'non-white' labour in the industry with the introduction of the Aliens Orders Act in 1920 followed by the Special Restriction (Coloured) Alien Seamens Order Act in 1925 (Byrne 1977: 264; Lunn 1985: 13). Two further aspects of NUS policy contributed to the aggravation of racist sentiment. First was the PC5, a union form commonly referred to as the 'slave ticket' (Gordon and Reilly 1986) which seamen had to be in possession of before they could be authorized to work on a ship in Britain. Such a requirement effectively gave the union leadership total power over its membership because the '£2 required to get a PC5 could be as much as three-quarters of the advance note (the percentage of wages a seaman received on signing on)' (Byrne 1977: 266). These

> subscription rules in the NUS meant that very few seamen on shore were actually financial members of the union and meetings were dominated by the full-time officials who used pensioners to carry the votes. The union was extraordinarily over-officiated. Officials were much better paid than working seamen and it is generally agreed that in the 1930s the NUS was effectively a company union for the British Shipping Federation.
>
> (Byrne 1977: 266)

Second, in 1930, the NUS and the British Shipping Federation (the ship-owners body) agreed a rota – a new system of registering seamen looking for work. This measure strengthened union power over the employment of black and Arab seamen because they now had to provide evidence of their British status; in effect 'the NUS acted as a second line of police in enforcing immigration control' (Gordon and Reilly 1986: 77).

Usually, the black and Arab seamen were forced to accept their second tier status. However in 1930, when Arab seamen in the South Shields area objected to the introduction of the PC5 and the rota and refused to comply they were supported by white workers active in the seamen's section of the Minority Movement. The Minority Movement was a rank and file work-ers' organization established by the CPGB in 1924 with Tom Mann as its chairman, and Harry Pollitt as secretary. Its primary aim was to encourage the working class – recruited mainly from the mining, engineering and trans-port industries – to mobilize against the deterioration in working class living conditions (Byrne 1977: 262). At its founding conference held in 1924, the delegates attending represented over 200,000 workers. Its influence spread rapidly over the next year such that by 1925, 683 delegates attended its sec-ond conference representing over 750,000 workers with affiliation peaking in 1926 at 957,000 members. After the bitter defeat of the General Strike, it came to represent those social forces opposed to the conciliatory politics of the Labour Party.

On South Shields, members of the Minority Movement organized a series of large meetings in support of the Arab seamen including one where 1,100 white seamen and 900 Arabs and Somalis declared their support for the boycott of the PC5. They were also influential in spreading the dispute beyond the South Shields area with sympathy strikes taking place in Liverpool, Barry and Stepney (Byrne 1977: 271). The dispute escalated into violence when the NUS and the local shipping federation attempted to replace Arab seamen with white labour (Byrne 1977: 272). Twenty Arabs and six white seamen of the Minority Movement were arrested and charged with incitement to riot: 'Virtually all charges were found proven at the trial at Durham Assizes in November and the vast majority of the Arabs were deported' (Lunn 1985: 15). Although the Arab seamen were defeated, the impact of such working class solidarity against racism was to resonate in the minds of working people throughout the South Shields area. It was because of the principled opposition from the Minority Movement seamen that 'attempts by the British Union of Fascists to exploit the situation later in the 1930s were prevented' (Byrne 1977: 274). By the 1930s, anti-racist action within the working class had become synonymous with workers and activists aligned to the CPGB and its affiliate organizations (Piratin 1978; Callaghan 1995; Watson 1996).

Elsewhere however, the British Union of Fascists (BUF) – established in 1932 and led by Oswald Mosley – was making inroads into the working class. Racist anti-semitism formed a crucial ingredient in the politics of the BUF.

In October 1934, at a meeting held at the Royal Albert Hall, Mosley attacked 'Jewish finance and Jewish Communism' (Thurlow 1987, 1998) as the twin evils responsible for Britain's precipitous decline from its position as the hegemon of the world-system. Further, the organization purposively linked questions of unemployment and poor housing to the presence of Jews. Their anti-semitism resonated in the economically depressed areas of the east end of London where there was a sizeable Jewish population resident in areas like Bethnal Green, Shoreditch and Stepney and where working people 'were living miserable, squalid lives. Their homes were slums, many were unemployed. Those at work were often in low-paid jobs' (Piratin 1978: 17). The area had a long history of anti-semitism, including socialist anti-semitism going back to the 1880s, and the BUF – following in the footsteps of the British Brothers League – exploited such pre-existing sentiments by opening its first branch in Bow, east London in 1934, quickly followed by branches in Bethnal Green, Shoreditch and Limehouse (Piratin 1978: 16; Bourke 1994: 199). By 1934, the BUF had grown to over 40,000 members (Skidelsky 1975: 331).

'Strife and tension characterised the atmosphere in east London in those years' (Piratin 1978: 17) as the BUF spread its anti-semitic message through the production of inflammatory literature, provocative street-corner meetings and demonstrations policed by the black-shirted Defence Force and supplemented by regular bouts of firebombing and Jew-bashing (Skidelsky 1975: 331). However, unlike the 1880s and 1890s when socialists failed to challenge working class anti-semitism, and even legitimated it, this time the CPGB and other socialists joined together with the Jewish community to challenge the BUF.

When the BUF announced plans to march through the East End on Sunday 4 October 1936 to build support for the forthcoming London County Council elections in 1937, the Jewish People's Council Against Fascism and Anti-Semitism organized a petition calling for the march to be banned (Piratin 1978: 19). Initially, the CPGB leadership – reflecting the growing influence of Popular Front politics – refused to countenance any direct confrontation with the BUF for fear of undermining their broader strategic objective of building alliances with so-called 'progressives', recommending instead that the main emphasis be placed on rallying support for the JPC petition. Further, it encouraged its members to '[a]void clashes...no excuse for Government to say we, like BUF, are hooligans' (Morgan et al. 2007: 195). However, the local branches of the CPGB in the East End contained many individuals, including Jews, who had joined the CPGB precisely because of its internationalist outlook, and refusal to compromise with racism and nationalism. As a result, the rank and file of the CPGB, along with activists on the CPGB's London District Committee, rejected the CPGB leadership's advice and accused them of becoming 'far too bloody respectable' (Morgan et al. 2007: 195). Joe Jacobs, CPGB secretary of the Stepney branch advocated direct confrontation with the fascists. The CPGB's national newspaper reflected this anger quoting one local resident as saying: 'We must give them such a reception that they will not march down here again' (cited in the *Daily Worker*, 1 October 1936).

When the JPC petition – signed by over 100,000 people – was rejected by the Home Office, the national CPGB leadership endorsed the strategy to mobilize for a counter demonstration alongside the Jewish Ex-Servicemen's movement (Piratin 1978: 22). They were quickly followed by local branches of the ILP – recently freed from the shackles of the Labour Party, and including within it a small layer of Trotskyists (Brockway 1942). The counter-demonstration was organized around the slogan 'The Fascists shall not pass', inspired by the resistance of Madriderios to fascism in Spain (Piratin 1978: 20).

The Labour Party on the other hand – both at a national and local leadership level – steadfastly refused to back the plans for a counter demonstration. George Lansbury, Labour MP for Poplar, even refused to endorse the petition calling for the BUF march to be banned, and encouraged members of the Labour Party to stay away from the demonstration in order that peace and order could be preserved (Piratin 1978: 20). This was an indication of how the Labour Party was increasingly compromised by racism. Unable to deliver the material security that working class people craved, parts of the Labour Party leadership, along with some trade union leaders, were actively pressing for the introduction of measures for the

> control of 'foreigners' on the grounds that Jews were detrimental to the welfare of the British worker. In the Trade Union and Labour journals *Clarion*, *Labour Leader* and *Justice*, Jews were identified as a threat to British self-preservation and a menace to the working class.
>
> (Bourke 1994: 200)

At the same time, many thousands of Labour Party members and activists refused to be bound by such calls and joined those mobilized by the Jewish groups and the CPGB in a demonstration against the BUF on 4 October 1936. On the day itself, tens of thousands of anti-fascist demonstrators gathered to oppose the BUF. Small scuffles ensued between the two groups throughout the day. The police tried to clear the streets with repeated baton charges but the anti-fascist demonstration was too large. Mosley, recognizing the futility of the situation, cancelled the march.

The CPGB emerged from this episode with enhanced prestige with membership increasing from 7,000 in February 1936 to 11,500 by December 1936 (Thorpe 2000: 781, table 1). Along with the Jewish community and local Labour Party members it had successfully mobilized a large and powerful multi-ethnic coalition against fascism. Yet, the events at Cable Street seem strangely out of kilter with the times, or at least mark an important crossroads in the history and evolution of the CPGB. On the one hand, they represented – along with rank and file CPGB participation in the International

Brigades during the Spanish Civil War – a formative moment in the history of large-scale collective action against racism and fascism inspired by a commitment to proletarian internationalism. On the other hand, the CPGB refrained from leading such large-scale collective action ever again indicating its increasing subservience to the shifting priorities and realpolitik of the Comintern, and in particular the Russian Communist Party under Stalin's leadership.

From the mid-1930s, it embraced the strategy of the Popular Front forcing it to nationalize its Communist message. The language of class war and proletarian internationalism was subsumed in an emergent discourse that spoke increasingly of the 'British nation' and the 'British people'. In *A Handbook of Freedom* (1939), writers like Jack Lindsay developed claims of a 'radical-patriotic lineage from Aelfric to Gallacher' (Morgan et al. 2007: 187) suggesting that the CPGB were the modern-day representatives of the Levellers and the Ranters (see for example Hill 1968; Morton 1994). As part of this attempt to make Communism authentically British, party members were forced to change political direction and develop opportunities to forge alliances with other so-called progressive forces such as Labour to secure for the British people – not the working class – what rightfully belonged to them. A corollary of this kind of political re-positioning was the pressure to develop more 'respectable' forms of protest against the growing threat of fascism at home (and abroad) than the previous focus on collective action so as not to frighten away those progressive forces to the right of the CPGB.

While many were drawn towards the CPGB precisely because of its changing orientation (Branson 1997), particularly its attempt to entwine the communist project with a radical British patriotism, the specific focus on anti-imperialism and anti-racism was increasingly sidelined. Long-term ethnic minority members like Clemens Dutt – brother of Rajani Palme Dutt, the party's chief theorist – was one of the first to raise objections, claiming that such activity was increasingly left to minority communists, and accused the party of 'white chauvinism' (Morgan et al. 2007: 216). Similarly, in 1934, Saklatvala complained about the 'adverse comments about Negroes and Asians' made by party members and how 'Many things happen among the coloured seamen in the East End of London . . . and members of the Party and of the unemployed workers' movement, living right in the locality know nothing about it' (cited in Morgan et al. 2007: 216–217). The Trinidadian George Padmore left the Stalinized Comintern in 1934 disillusioned that colonial liberation – which had been key to the goal of world socialist revolution in the time of Lenin – could now no longer be effectively pursued through nationally-oriented Communist parties dominated by the interests of the Soviet Union. Padmore, along with his boyhood friend CLR James, and Isaac Wallace Johnson – a Sierra Leonean worker's leader – would go on to establish the International African Service Bureau in London in 1937 – an anti-imperialist body formed 'to assist by all means in our power the uncoordinated struggle of Africans and people of

African descent against the oppression from which they suffer in every country' (cited in Adi 1998: 77).

What such political trends signalled above all was the extinguishing by Stalinism of the politics of socialist internationalism that had been ignited by the Russian Revolution, and unified under the auspices of the Communist International in the time of Lenin. Combined with the simultaneous and crushing defeat suffered by socialist and communist forces in Germany that heralded the brutal rule of the National Socialists and the bitter defeat of Republican forces in 1939 that concluded the Spanish Civil War and confirmed Franco as the victor, reaction was on the march. The current of socialist internationalism that had briefly flowered during the 1920s either fragmented or found itself devoured by the overwhelming pressure from the twin centrifugal forces of Stalinism and fascism, thus signalling working class defeat of world historical importance. Perhaps it was inevitable that at 'midnight in the century' (Serge 1939/1982), another world war loomed ominously on the horizon.

6

Racism: From the Welfare Settlement to Enoch Powell

It is true that the war effort of 1939–1945 produced much more social egalitarianism in England than any other event in her recent history.... Yet – paradoxically – it also contained the social upheaval more firmly than ever in a renewed "national" ideology of unity, a sense of patriotic purpose and regeneration.

(Nairn 1970: 16)

...the attitude of racial superiority on the part of white workers relegates their black comrades to the bottom of society. In the event, they come to constitute a class apart, an under-class: the sub-proletariat. And the common denominator of capitalist oppression is not sufficient to bind them together in a common purpose.

(Sivanandan 1977: 339)

Introduction

For the colour-blind scholar, the two decades immediately following the Second World War are almost uniformly heralded as one of unprecedented working class advancement with major gains being secured through a bipartisan commitment to the National Health Service, full employment and the guarantee of effective trade union rights. This was the era of welfare capitalism, which in the eyes of both Marxists and liberals represented a kind of golden age that to this day is favourably counterposed to the present conjuncture marked by the ascendency of neoliberalism. In contrast to this portrait, the race-conscious or anti-racist scholar would identify something more complex going on. Most significantly, we would see that such undoubted gains for one section of the working class were accompanied by systematic racism and discrimination against another section of the working class. The golden age of welfare capitalism and the social democratic settlement was also the golden age of white supremacy, of legal racist discrimination, and one in which 'nigger-hunting' and 'paki-bashing' became the unofficial sport of choice for many white workers.

The seeds of the bipartisan commitment to the welfare settlement that emerged in the aftermath of the Second World War were first sown during the time of war itself. It was then, as Tom Nairn astutely observes, that the ideology of national unity, so characteristic of the subsequent period of the welfare settlement, was more securely implanted than hitherto, as the Conservatives under Churchill and Labour under Attlee came together in a government of national unity representing all social classes, to thwart the threat of German expansionism under National Socialism. Arguably, the important reforms that were instituted by the first majority Labour Government in 1945 under Attlee represented the completion of the incremental but relentless process of working class inclusion into the nation instigated by the new model unions and the 1867 Reform Act. This chapter explores the extent to which the working class were active participants in the project of reconstructing a national identity built on the twin principles of a common citizenship and the welfare compromise.

Significantly, it was amid this unprecedented period of social peace and national unity that migration from the Indian sub-continent and the Caribbean began. The response of various institutions and social actors of British society, including the state, political parties and the organized labour movement, to such migration is traced. In particular, I demonstrate how British workers and their trade unions in this period enforced racist and discriminatory practices against such workers on the grounds that they were not white, and thus not British. The racialization of British nationalism was not new as previous chapters have demonstrated but what distinguished this period above all was the extent to which the state, employer and worker came to adhere to a common belief in British nationalism underpinned by a shared allegiance to whiteness.

The chapter then moves on to consider the scale and scope of opposition to such racism in the period, in particular from the CPGB. The CPGB had a history of principled opposition to racism and imperialism in the 1920s and 1930s, and by the 1940s and 1950s was a much larger political formation with two elected MPs. We find however a party that was a shadow of its former self, one that situated its political project on the terrain of British nationalism, and thereby politically disarmed itself when it came to challenging racism.

As demands for national self-determination in Britain's colonies grew, so too did the racism directed at migrants in Britain. This chapter traces how, during the late 1950s and 1960s, there was an exponential growth in street-level racism and violence directed against blacks and Asians accompanied by the introduction of racist immigration controls by the state. In effect, they came to represent in microcosm the populations of the newly-independent colonial nations as a whole; and projected on to them was the racist vitriol and bile that large parts of the British population felt at the loss of the British Empire. And it was from these dying embers of the British Empire that a new right emerged, and an essential underpinning to its programme of reconstructing Britain was racism. This was no more clearly demonstrated than in the founding figure of the new right, Enoch Powell. His 'rivers of blood' speech (Heffer 1998) is dissected and its political consequences mapped.

Against this backdrop of white racism from within all soci.   )se of Caribbean and Asian descent were forced to combat racism   own, relying on the cultural and material resources of their comm.   From the mid-1960s, a series of strikes by black and Asian workers ag.   acism and poor working conditions gave birth to a powerful anti-racist movement. This chapter traces briefly the roots of those individual disputes and how such action came to be informed by the ideology of political blackness where black and Asian activists appropriated the ascribed racial identity of black and infused it with new ideological meaning out of which were constructed black 'communities of resistance'. This chapter, by reading the 1950s and 1960s through the lens of race helps to unmask how deeply stratified Britain was by racism.

'You've never had it so good': Racism in the age of affluence and national unity

Although Britain lost its hegemonic position in the capitalist world economy to the USA at the end of WW2, the growth of light manufacturing indus- try and the production of white goods alongside the establishment of the National Health Service and other service industries helped initially to mask the long-term decline of British capitalism, and heavy manufacturing industry and textiles in particular. As British workers moved out of the latter, the labour shortage came to be filled by migrants. The Attlee administration granted the right of settlement to over 100,000 members of the Polish Armed Forces who had been in exile in Britain since the start of WW2. Between October 1946 and December 1949, a further 80,000 workers known as European Volunteer Workers (EVWs) were recruited from Displaced Persons Camps in Germany and Austria (Miles and Kay 1990: 1; Kay and Miles 1992). And this was sup- plemented by the arrival of between 70,000 and 100,000 people from the Republic of Ireland (Solomos 2003: 49) and around 125,000 West Indians and 55,000 Indians and Pakistanis (Renton 2006: 14). Alongside this more recent migration were the already established minority communities of long- standing, including most notably those of Irish Catholic and Jewish descent, as well as smaller communities of African and Asian descent (Fryer 1984; Ramdin 1987; Visram 2002).

The arrival of migrants in the early post-war period coincided with a historical conjuncture unique in British history, one where the scale and scope of horizontal integration into the imagined national community was unprecedented. Contrary to conventional socialist accounts (e.g. Benn 1982), the election of the first majority Labour government in a landslide victory in July 1945 didn't mark a radical departure from Britain's political past but represented instead the apex of an incremental but relentless process of working class integration into the nation that had first begun with the rise of the 'new model unions' and the enfranchisement of respectable working class men in mid-Victorian England. The seeds of this final phase of national integration were sown within a year of the outbreak of world war in 1940, when the Conservative government, led by Churchill, invited the Labour Party, under Clement Attlee's leadership to form a coalition government of national unity. As the Battle of Britain raged across the nation's skies, Winston Churchill and Ernest Bevin – the former leader of the militant dock workers, and now Minister for Labour – came to symbolize this cross-class alliance in the public imagination binding the population in a demonstration of unprecedented unity at a time of adversity and war.

Once in office in 1945, the Labour government introduced a series of reforms including most notably the establishment of the National Health Service that further strengthened working class attachment to the nation, reinforcing the impression that they too held a stake in the nation – a nation they had sacrificed much for, especially in wartime, and one that they now believed promised to deliver them a respectable level of material security. Confirmation of the existence of a bipartisan consensus was provided in 1951 when the incoming Conservative government, first under Churchill and then Anthony Eden, demonstrated their commitment to the main components of the welfare settlement. This included continued support for the National Health Service and the provision of other important social goods such as child benefit to mothers allowing Harold Macmillan to famously proclaim that the working class had 'never had it so good.'

While the majority of the working class secured important gains as part of this bipartisan settlement helping to cement their position as active citizens in the nation, another component – that of the newly arrived migrants – found themselves excluded from it (see also Rex and Tomlinson 1979). Solomos (2003: 52) shows how

> an increasingly racialised debate on immigration took place, focusing on the supposed social problems of having too many black immigrants and the question of how they could be stopped from entering, given their legal rights under the 1948 British Nationality Act.

Just two days after the *Empire Windrush* docked in Tilbury on 22 June 1948 – carrying 493 migrants from Jamaica – 11 Labour MPs sent a letter to the Prime Minister, Clement Attlee, calling for the restriction of black immigration on the grounds that:

> An influx of coloured people domiciled here is likely to impair the harmony, strength and cohesion of our public and social life and to cause discord and unhappiness among all concerned.
>
> (Carter et al. 1987: 2)

In January 1955, Churchill tried to convince the cabinet to adopt the slogan 'Keep England White' (Hennessy 2001: 205) at the forthcoming General Election adamant that restricting Caribbean migration was 'the most important subject facing this country' (cited in Gilmour 1977: 134). By the mid 1950s both Labour and Conservative governments had 'instituted a number of covert, and sometimes illegal, administrative measures designed to discourage Black immigration' (Carter et al. 1987: 3).

Significantly, many parts of the British working class were not uninterested bystanders in these elite debates, but helped inform them with their everyday racist practices and attitudes. Black and Asian migrants found themselves confronted with a workplace racism that represented them as an economic threat, a source of cheap 'foreign' labour deployed by unscrupulous employers with the intention of undermining the hard-won economic security of the white/British worker (Stephens 1956; Pinder 1961; Wright 1968). One branch secretary of a craft union reported:

> We are continually on the look-out for employers who seek to use coloured workers for cheap labour to the detriment of their countrymen; also employers who allow coloured workers to work unlimited overtime opposed to local and national agreements between federated firms and the union.
>
> (cited in Stephens 1956: 18)

Another union official opposed the recruitment of migrant labour claiming that 'many workers ... quite genuinely feel immigrants to be a danger' (Pinder 1961: 282). Major workplaces like Ford Dagenham, Vickers, Napiers and Tate and Lyle operated a 'colour-bar' jointly enforced by trade unions and employers (Watson 1996: 154). The use of discriminatory practices was particularly evident in the transport industry, and textiles and foundry work (Duffield 1988) where white trade unionists resisted the employment of black workers, or insisted on a quota system limiting them to around 5 per cent of available positions (Fryer 1984: 376). And when such racist practices came under threat of being breached, these workers took industrial action to defend them. In February 1955, in the West Midlands, workers employed by the West Bromwich Corporation Transport system began a series of Saturday strikes in protest against the employment of an Indian trainee conductor. In the same year, transport workers in Wolverhampton decided to ban all overtime in protest against the increasing employment of black labour, and the breaching of the 5 per cent quota agreed with employers (Ramdin 1987: 200; Wrench 1987). In these years, the principle of 'last in first out' was not applied in times of redundancy if it meant white workers would lose their jobs before black workers (Wrench 1987: 165) with one official of a general union confirming 'that in the event of redundancy occurring his members would insist on coloured workers going first' (Stephens 1956: 16).

A survey carried out in the mid-1950s of 61 trade union branches demonstrated that of the 22 branches with black or Asian members, only five had passed resolutions in favour of equal treatment (Stephens 1956: 18). Alongside such inaction, racist motions from white transport workers to the Transport and General Workers Union (TGWU) annual conference were passed demanding that black workers be banned from the buses while hospital branches of the Confederation of Health Service Employees (COHSE) passed resolutions objecting to the recruitment of Caribbean nurses (Wrench 1987).

One might have expected that an important source of opposition to such racism and division in the organized labour movement would have been the Trades Union Congress (TUC). However, in these years, the TUC and its executive body – the General Council – faithfully reproduced the dominant views of the major affiliated unions, singularly failing

> to acknowledge that there existed considerable hostility towards black workers amongst white trade unionists and increasingly came to adopt the position that the problems arose from the immigrant's refusal to 'integrate'.
> (Miles and Phizacklea 1977: 3)

Consequently, the response of the main institutional actors of British society – including the state, political parties and the organized labour movement – towards black and Asian migration in these years was uniformly dismal. Collectively, they enforced racist discriminatory practices against such migrants on the grounds that they were not white, and therefore not British. The racialization of British nationalism was certainly not new, as previous chapters have demonstrated, but what distinguished this early post-war period above all was the extent to which the British state, employers and workers came to share a common belief in British nationalism underpinned by a shared allegiance to whiteness. Colour-coded colonial racisms were being over-determined by an indigenous racism where

> the cruder, historically specific ideas of inferiority and lack of civilisation [were] replaced by feelings of cultural difference, of 'Britishness', of 'whiteness'....White colonial and cultural supremacy was being threatened 'on the streets' in Britain as well as in the former colonies. In response, the

black person was defined as 'alien', a threat to 'Britishness', a person with no right to be here.

(Joshi and Carter 1984: 66)

The CPGB and the British Road to Socialism

Did the CPGB – which had been the most consistent opponent of racism and imperialism in Britain during the 1920s and 1930s (see Callaghan 1995) – continue to play this role during the war, and the early post-war period? Certainly, the party had grown significantly in the aftermath of the events at Cable Street, and there was a further, more substantial growth from 1942 (Thorpe 2000) when many in the West came to believe that an alliance with the Soviet Union represented the most important bulwark against the increasingly ominous encroachments of Hitler's National Socialists in Europe and beyond. Benefitting from this construction of World War Two as an 'anti-fascist' conflict, the CPGB's membership grew to 45,435 by 1945 (Fishman 1995: 116). Significantly, along with its strong industrial presence it also developed a modest national profile with Willie Gallacher and Phil Piratin being elected as MPs at the 1945 General Election – the latter was a leading participant of the events at Cable Street providing a further reminder of the CPGB's anti-fascist association.

At the same time, its increasing insistence on locating its socialist project on the terrain of the nation created difficulties for the CPGB when it came to effectively challenging the racism directed at Asian and black workers. The Popular Front perspective which inspired this strategy of socialist nationalism was instigated in the mid-1930s, and was further consolidated when the Soviet Union entered the war in 1941 on the side of the allies. Typical of the activity that flowed from this perspective was CPGB participation in the Anglo-Soviet committees. One communist couple reflected approvingly of how they found themselves

> addressing large and influential audiences on the achievements of the Soviet Union. His Lordship the Mayor is in the chair, the leaders of local society are on the platform, where the grand piano, presently to accompany both 'God save the King' and the 'International' is prophetically draped with the Union Jack and the Red Flag, sociably intertwined.
>
> (Branson 1997: 5)

Such activity created the hope among many CPGB members that the quest for socialism could be aligned with the existing British nation-state. These trends were further consolidated in the post-war period when the CPGB openly proclaimed its capacity to 'manage' the British state more efficiently and effectively than the existing political establishment. The Party formally acknowledged the nature of these ongoing changes in strategy in its 1951 manifesto, *The British Road to Socialism* (1951: 10):

> The Communist Party declares that the leaders of the Tory, Liberal and Labour parties and their spokesmen in the press and on the BBC are betraying the interests of Britain to dollar imperialism. Our call is for the unity of all true patriots to defend British national interests and independence.

The manifesto went on to reassure those who still doubted the CPGB's loyalty to the British state by confirming its rejection of the Bolshevik model of Soviet power, and, reframed the CPGB's struggle for socialism as the latest chapter of the British peoples' long struggle for democracy inaugurated during the English Civil War:

> The enemies of Communism accuse the Communist Party of aiming to introduce Soviet power in Britain and abolish Parliament. This is a slanderous misrepresentation of our policy....British Communists declare that the people of Britain can transform capitalist democracy into a real people's democracy.
>
> (cited in Branson 1997: 236)

The CPGB aim was one of transforming Parliament, the product of Britain's historic struggle for democracy, into the democratic instrument of the will of the vast majority of her people. However, the danger with marrying their socialist project to British nationalism was that in the popular imagination the latter had been comprehensively racialized since the mid-Victorian period. Further, the CPGB's deepening attachment to this perspective coincided with the moment when many white British workers were excluding black and Asian workers from key areas of employment on the grounds that they were 'foreigners', not white, and therefore could not be classed as British. Consequently, when it came to challenging such racism, the CPGB found itself in a bind of its own making since it located its socialist project on the same ideological terrain of the nation and the 'British people' as the racists (see also Callaghan 2003). Challenging the presuppositions inherent in the racism directed against black and Asian workers would have involved exposing its articulation to British nationalism, but this in turn would have undermined the logic of the CPGB's own perspective of achieving socialism in Britain.

Unable to summon the repertoire of political education and collective action informed by the language of proletarian internationalism for fear it would conflict with its commitment to a more 'respectable' politics, of forging 'broad democratic alliances', the CPGB found itself incapable of effectively countering the mounting racism faced by black and Asian workers from parts of the white working class. Further, its elementary understanding of such racism as a form of historically-based prejudice rooted in colonial oppression and imperialism ignored the conditions for its contemporary reproduction in Britain and 'served to reinforce the "foreignness" of immigrant workers' (Smith 2008: 457–458) and confirm to many that they didn't properly belong in Britain. With the elimination of racism tied to a 'long-term programme of colonial freedom' (Smith 2008: 458) all the CPGB could offer in the interim were moral platitudes, grounding its objection to racism and 'colour bars' with reference to abstract arguments about the intrinsic unity of the human race.

Nevertheless, many black and Asian workers, as well as those from overseas, continued to join the CPGB during the 1950s, attracted by its continuing opposition to Western imperialism in Africa, Asia and Latin America, and seeking sanctuary from the racist hostility they faced from elsewhere in British society (Adi 1998). And some minority activists within the CPGB such as Ranji Chandisingh and Claudia Jones took a lead in drawing attention to the plight of racialized minorities in Britain. Jones was instrumental, along with others in the West Indian Workers and Students Association, in establishing the *West Indian Gazette* (WIG) in 1958 (Sherwood 1999: 126), and campaigned tirelessly for equality in education, employment and housing throughout the 1950s and early 1960s (Sherwood 1999: 89–124; Morgan et al. 2007: 202–204). Other minority groups were also drawn into the orbit of the CPGB through its increasingly federalist structure with significant autonomously-organized Cypriot and Indian sections (Morgan et al. 2007: 202–204).

However, apart from the influential contributions from minority individuals like Jones and others within the CPGB, and the undertaking of some educational work that highlighted the debilitating effects of racism on working class solidarity (see Pinder 1961), there is little evidence to suggest that the CPGB co-ordinated any sustained campaigns against racism. It was in this light that many activists like Trevor Carter and Frank Bailey eventually followed George Padmore in exiting the CPGB, with Bailey defiantly proclaiming that 'the British labour movement, neither Right nor Left had never done anything for the colonial liberation movement' (cited in Morgan et al. 2007: 203).

A further factor undoubtedly explaining the lack of CPGB activity in tackling racism, particularly in the workplace, was that despite its strong presence in key industries such as engineering, coalmining and shipyards (see Fishman 1995), its influence did not extend to those workplaces where Black and Asian workers were to be found. To its credit, in those few plants such as the Swift Scale aircraft parts factory in North London that were 'a stronghold of Communist Party industrial organisation', black workers were elected as convenors with no evidence of racist opposition (Watson 1996: 155).

Overall, however, these developments ensured that when black and Asian workers arrived in Britain during the 1940s and 1950s, there was no progressive, anti-racist political ideological framework which would have enabled the working class to 'make sense' of a black presence in Britain.

(Joshi and Carter 1984: 55)

Decolonization, 'nigger-hunting' and state racism

As the struggles for national self-determination intensified throughout the British Empire during the 1950s they added further fuel to the rising arc of racist reaction within Britain itself. The Conservatives, first under Churchill and then Eden, had come to power unwilling to relinquish Britain's colonies, regarding them as crucial to sustaining Britain's dominant position in the post-war world order. At the same time, the limitations of Britain's declining imperial reach were badly exposed by its seeming inability to repress movements for national independence in Kenya, Malaya and elsewhere. The nadir for the supporters of empire came in 1956 when the Egyptian radical nationalist, Gamal Abdel Nasser, unilaterally nationalized the Suez Canal. Having already lost India, the canal was seen as crucial to maintaining Britain's pre-eminent position in the Middle East and Asia. When Britain, along with France, colluded with Israel to engineer an attack on Egypt and retake the canal, the US government refused to back the invasion. UN intervention and US pressure forced Britain into a humiliating withdrawal of its forces, hastening Eden's resignation in 1957. This episode had a devastating effect on British national confidence, and it is probably the event that symbolically marked the beginning of the end of the British Empire, with many referring to it as 'Britain's Waterloo' (Brown 1998: 343).

Within Britain itself, the reaction to such imperial over-reach added new ingredients to an already toxic cocktail of racist sentiment and discrimination directed at Black and Asian migrants. Unable to prevent the loss of Empire to the 'dark hordes' of Africa and Asia, these 'empire loyalists' now projected their racism on to those non-white migrants already on British soil, who, in effect, became a kind of surrogate for the anger and violence they wished to inflict upon their alleged brethren abroad. According to the racist logic of this constituency, such migrant labour became the unwanted reminders of an empire lost, representatives of peoples abroad who wanted nothing to do with the British Empire. And, in the mind of the empire loyalists this invited the question, 'what are they doing here in Britain?' What late 1950s Britain was witnessing was the 'restaging of the colonial encounter', but this time at home with black and brown migrants in Britain in the crosshairs of an unprecedented wave of racist reaction (Schwarz 1996). The functional and political requirements of racism were altering, away from securing and legitimizing discrimination of blacks and Asians to one seeking to secure their expulsion.

In the summer of 1958, racist riots erupted in Nottingham in the East Midlands and Notting Hill, west London. On successive nights, thousands of white people gathered in the streets of St. Anns in Nottingham looking for black people to attack. In Notting Hill, mobs of white working class youth went 'nigger-hunting' armed with iron bars, butchers knives and weighted leather belts shouting 'Keep Britain White'. They attacked West Indian houses, breaking in and attacking any black people they found. The first night of racist violence left five black men lying unconscious on the pavements. Eyewitness accounts from policemen at the scene of such crimes recounted how they saw mobs of '300–400 white people in Bramley Road shouting "We will kill all black bastards. Why don't you send them home?" Another recounted how he was told to "Mind your own business, copper. Keep out of it. We will settle these niggers our way. We'll murder the bastards" ' (cited in Alan Travis, *The Guardian*, 24 August 2002, accessed 9 May 2009; see also Schwarz 1996). Schwarz (1996: 65) outlines how

> from the ruins of the colonial empires across the globe there emerged, among the white population themselves, a recharged, intensified self-consciousness of their existential presence as white. In the very moment of decolonisation and civil rights, amid all the rhetoric of families of nations, partnership and equality before the law, the white man once more gave birth to himself.

Such a white identity was not a benign term of self-description but one that had been fundamentally constructed in opposition to the political development that were forcing the governing class to take steps in relinquishing its empire, later to be formally acknowledged by Macmillan in his 1960 'wind of change' speech in South Africa (Schwarz 1996; Brown 1998). The aim of such a racist consciousness was to secure the future of Britain as a nation, for whites only. That is why this rising wave of racist reaction was fundamentally about 'how the end of empire impacted on English life' (Schwarz 1996: 65).

The consequences of such instrumental mobilization around a white identity were to prove catastrophic for racialized minorities as they marked the rebirth of domestic fascism. Crucial to the racist actions in Notting Hill and elsewhere had been fascists in the Union Movement and the White Defence League, who through active involvement in the racist rioting had begun to secure a small but vocal working class public for its white supremacist ideology. Alongside them was the growing presence of the League of Empire Loyalists – an organization established by AK Chesterton in 1954 and comprising 'retired military gentlemen, ex-colonial administrators, anti-communist and anti-semitic Roman Catholics, alienated sections of the conservative establishment and energetic upper-middle class ladies' (Thurlow cited in Hillman 2001: 9). A number of vociferous right-wing MPs with strong attachments to the racist colonial order also formed the Monday Club in response to Macmillan's speech on the 'wind of change' (Schwarz 1996: 72–73).

Within a decade of the mass migration from the Caribbean and the Indian sub-continent, and with no sign of organized opposition to the kind of orchestrated racism described above, the balance of political forces shifted decisively. There was a movement away from those elements of the British capitalist class whose industries had been given a new lease of competitive life through the deployment of a cheap and exploited migrant labour force and from those factions of the political elite wary of offending the newly-independent countries of the New Commonwealth towards those elements favouring the greater regulation and control of non-white migration to Britain. The Conservatives under Macmillan acted by introducing the Commonwealth Immigrants Act in 1962 claiming there was a need to halt black immigration because of the limited ability of the host country to assimilate 'coloured immigrants' (Solomos 2003: 57–58). Despite denials that the proposed statute was racist, William Deedes – minister without portfolio at the time – conceded many years later that the Bill's real purpose had been

> to restrict the influx of coloured immigrants. We were reluctant to say as much openly. So the restrictions were applied to coloured and white citizens in all Commonwealth countries – though everybody recognized that immigration from Canada, Australia and New Zealand formed no part of the problem.
>
> (cited in Solomos 2003: 56)

The Labour Party opposed the new legislation while in opposition on the grounds it would undermine Britain's privileged trading relationship with the Commonwealth, and its position as *primus inter pares* within it (Solomos 2003: 54). Representative of such opposition was Barbara Castle who argued passionately that:

> I do not care whether or not fighting this Commonwealth Immigration Bill will lose me my seat, for I am sure that this Bill will lose this country the Commonwealth.
>
> (cited in Foot 1965a: 11)

However, when it came to contesting the 1964 General Election, the Labour Party moved quickly to reassure the public of its intention to retain the 1962 Immigration Act. While the commitment to bipartisanship on racist immigration controls was confirmed, when the Labour Party did finally return to power in October 1964, it decided to make good on the promise contained in its election manifesto *The New Britain* (1964) to 'legislate against racial discrimination and incitement in public places' by introducing the first Race Relations Act in 1965. Left-wing MPs like Fenner Brockway played an influential role in pressuring the Labour government into introducing such legislation (see Sooben 1990) as did the boycott campaign led by the West Indian Development Council in 1963 against the Bristol Omnibus Company when it had refused to employ Black or Asian bus crews (Dresser 1986).

Arguably, it was in recognition of the need to protect Britain's national interests abroad, in particular its productive trading relationship with the Commonwealth countries, that was most important in forcing the Labour government's hand. The legislation effectively outlawed discrimination in public places like hotels and restaurants, and also established the Race Relations Board and the National Committee for Commonwealth Immigrants. This twin-track approach of support for racist immigration controls alongside a commitment to deliver racial equality for those blacks and Asians already legally resident in Britain was neatly encapsulated by Roy Hattersley (a former Home Office minister) in his pithy formulation 'Integration without control is impossible, but control without integration is indefensible' (cited in Solomos 1993: 84).

For the right-wing of the Conservative Party, and a large proportion of its activist and voting base, even such a relatively minor concession towards promoting racial equality as the 1965 Race Relations Act was considered beyond the pale. From their perspective, between the election of the Attlee government in 1945 and the Wilson government in October 1964, Britain had lost its empire with the number of people under British rule outwith the UK falling from 700 million to 5 million (of whom three million were in Hong Kong alone (Brown 1998: 330)). In the eyes of the political right – including the small but growing contingent of the extreme right – they had already been forced to concede the Empire that had helped to maintain Britain's role as the hegemon of the modern world-system; now it appeared to them they were being asked to accept that colonial migrants from Asia and the Caribbean be granted equal status in Britain both in law and in practice – effectively that they be recognized as black and brown Britons. For these influential elite strata of society such a scenario was unacceptable and they continued to question the legitimacy of those groups of black and Asian migrants who had arrived and settled legally in Britain between 1948 and 1962. For them and much of the British public, to be British one had to be white – this after all had been the cornerstone of British nationalism in the age of imperialism. Consequently, throughout the Wilson years, national political debate became further refracted through the prism of racism.

Early indications of the strength of support for the political right on the question of racism were provided during the 1964 General Election itself when the far right British National Party candidate John Bean secured 9.1 per cent of the vote in Southall – an area of significant Indian Sikh settlement – the highest vote for a minority party in the post-war era. During the same general election campaign, in Smethwick, a small industrial town near Birmingham, the Conservative Party candidate, Peter Griffiths had publicly endorsed one of the racist slogans circulating in the town at the time: 'If you want a nigger neighbour, vote Labour' (cited in Solomos and Back 1995: 54). And such racism worked as he successfully went on to oust the sitting Labour incumbent, Patrick Gordon-Walker.

It was against these increasingly adverse circumstances that the newly-established NCCI and the Race Relations Board commissioned a study from the liberal research institute, Political Economic Planning (PEP) – a forerunner of today's Policy Studies Institute (PSI) – to map the extent and nature of racist discrimination in Britain (Daniel 1968). In one of the first studies of its kind ever carried out in Europe, Daniel (1968) found that while the one-million strong migrant population of mainly Caribbeans, Indians and Pakistanis had occupied a diverse range of class positions in their countries of origin, they had undergone a profound process of proletarianization on their arrival to Britain. Seventy-one per cent of agricultural labourers and peasant farmers had been transformed into an industrial working class centred on manufacturing industry. While it was difficult to infer that this stratum of migrants had experienced any downward social mobility, such a conclusion could more easily be sustained for those who had worked as white collar employees prior to migration; 72 per cent of whom had found themselves forced into manufacturing industry (Daniel 1968: 60). Such a process of largely undifferentiated proletarianization of the migrant labour force, irrespective of their diverse class origins, was further demonstrated by the finding that:

> Half the people who formerly held clerical, administrative or professional positions are now employed as wholly unskilled manual workers, largely general labourers or cleaners in factories. Ninety per cent of them are employed in manual work of one kind or another. Only 7 per cent remain in white-collar jobs of any kind and there is no certainty that these are at the level of either their previous employment or their qualifications and abilities.
>
> (Daniel 1968: 61)

Daniel (1968) went on to establish the causes of such proletarianization by conducting research with employers and staff at various employment bureaux. He found 'a very substantial proportion of coloured people claim experience of discrimination... their claims are largely justified and... it is the most able ones [i.e. white-collar workers] that experience most discrimination' (Daniel 1968: 82). This pathbreaking study demonstrated conclusively that in 1960s Britain, racist discrimination ranged from the 'massive to the substantial' (Daniel 1968: 209) with an informal colour bar in operation which whilst 'more covert and insidious than that operated in some other societies with different legal status for people of different colours... [was] nonetheless effective, and perhaps even more distressing, for that' (Daniel 1968: 217).

In sum, the outcome of nearly two decades of sustained racist discriminatory behaviour was that Black and Asian migrant labour and their British-born children had come to occupy a distinctive position in class relations – as a racialized fraction of the working class (Phizacklea and Miles 1980; Miles 1982). In late 1960s Britain, there existed two working classes, one white, and the other black, politically and historically constituted in opposition to one another.

Faced with such compelling evidence outlining the depth and scale of racist discrimination in Britain, the Labour government was forced to concede that the remit of the Race Relations Board was too narrow and that a new, more comprehensive Race Relations Act would be introduced, making it illegal to refuse housing, employment or public services to individuals because of their 'racial' background. The Act also extended the powers of the Race Relations Board to deal with complaints of discrimination; and set up a new body, the Community Relations Commission, to promote 'harmonious community relations'.

The political right responded with outrage at the proposals and campaigned vociferously against them. When the Kenyan Asian affair broke in late 1967, they sensed a political opportunity. Kenyatta's plans to Africanize Kenyan society had effectively disenfranchised 200,000 Kenyan Asians – workers who had first been brought to the country to help build the railway line from Mombasa to the interior. Throughout the end of 1967 and early 1968, the right campaigned against the prospect of 200,000 Asians being allowed into Britain. Having already accepted the basic philosophical tenets underpinning racist immigration controls with its refusal to repeal the 1962 Commonwealth Immigrants Act, the Labour Party lacked any moral or theoretical armoury to resist such demands and caved in. Within three months James Callaghan, the then Home Secretary, introduced emergency legislation to end the freedom of entry of Asians – but not white settlers – from east Africa. *The Times* newspaper referred to the legislation as a 'colour bar' and 'probably the most shameful measure that the Labour members have ever been asked by their whip to support' (cited in Solomos 2003: 60).

However, to many in the wider population – the right wing of the Conservative Party, as well as those even further to their right – such concessions were never going to be enough. Indeed, their aim was nothing short of the recreation of an all-white Britain. It was in this politically-charged conjuncture of the supposed threat posed by continuing 'non-white' immigration coupled with attempts to promote racial equality on behalf of those black and brown Britons already resident in Britain that Enoch Powell – who in a previous incarnation as a Tory Minister of Health in the 1950s had warmly welcomed Caribbean nurses and Indian doctors to Britain (Kyriakides and Virdee 2003) – chose to make an incendiary speech that would not only reverberate through British politics for the next decade and beyond, but also effectively signalled the end of the era of bipartisanship built around the welfare settlement.

Enoch Powell, racist strikes and socialist inaction

On Saturday 20 April 1968, Enoch Powell, MP for Wolverhampton South West and shadow defence spokesman under Heath, delivered a speech to an audience of 85 Conservatives in a second floor meeting room of the Midland Hotel in Birmingham. He began by recounting a conversation with a middle-aged man from his constituency whom he claimed would not rest until he had seen his three children settled overseas because of his fears that 'In this country in 15 or 20 years' time, the black man will have the whip hand over the white man' (cited in Heffer 1998: 451). Employing this emotive anecdote to highlight the dangers of non-white migration to Britain, he claimed: 'I simply do not have the right to shrug my shoulders and think about something else' when some areas 'are already undergoing the total transformation to which there is no parallel in a thousand years of English history' (cited in Heffer 1998: 451).

> We must be mad, literally mad, as a nation to be permitting the annual inflow of some 50,000 dependents, who are for the most part the material of the future growth of the immigrant descended population. It is like watching a nation busily engaged in heaping up its own funeral pyre.
>
> (cited in Heffer 1998: 451)

According to Powell, this migration coupled with recent attempts by the Labour government to curb racism through the introduction of anti-discrimination legislation was effectively giving formal recognition to the existence of black and brown Britons or what he preferred to term the 'immigrant-descended population' and their right to expect equal treatment under British law. For Powell, the former arch-imperialist, this would effectively decouple the almost century-long association of whiteness with Britishness that had been so successful in cementing unity across social classes in pursuit of the state's imperialist ambitions abroad and the maintenance of hegemony at home.

So, precisely at the moment when the ideology of a racializing nationalism was losing some of its force among key elements of the political class, in particular the Labour Party and the one-nation Tories, as part of their realist accommodation to the forced relinquishment of Empire, Powell and what was later to become the new right (Hall 1983) sought to re-awaken it by instrumentally mobilizing those parts of the British population most enamoured of it. Hence, he claimed that it was not Blacks and Asians but whites that were the real victims: 'The discrimination and the deprivation, the sense of alarm and of resentment, lies not with the immigrant population but with those among whom they have come and are still coming'. He continued, it was white people who found themselves 'strangers in their own country...their wives unable to obtain hospital beds in childbirth, their children unable to obtain school places, their homes and neighbourhoods changed beyond recognition, their plans and prospects for the future defeated' (cited in Heffer 1998: 452).

The logic underpinning this racism however was now no longer designed to unify the nation with a view to recapturing its lost Empire. Powell was politically astute enough to realize that the Empire was lost forever. The intention behind this new racism was to expunge all memory of the Empire from Britain's national story, to redefine British 'national identity in terms appropriate to the times – and in particular, appropriate to the end of empire' (Nairn 1970: 5). Only then could Britain recover from the stupor into which it had fallen as a result of the wind of change that had brought forth decolonization. This was why he focused his racist ire on the migrant settler communities from South Asia and the Caribbean, together with their British-born children. They – both in his, and his public's mind – represented the living embodiment of the Empire now lost, a painful and daily remainder of their defeat on the world stage. England's rebirth was made dependent on their expulsion or rather what he termed their 're-emigration' to their ancestral lands of origin. Powell was offering a powerful re-imagining of the English nation after empire, reminding his audience it was a nation for whites only. In that historical moment the confident racism that had accompanied the high imperial moment mutated into a defensive racism, a racism of the vanquished who no longer wanted to dominate but to physically expel the racialized other from the shared space they occupied, and thereby erase them and the Empire from its collective memory.

This new racism was a postcolonial racism, summoned by former arch-imperialists who, seething at the loss of Empire, now decided to re-focus their energies on saving the nation as they imagined it. For Powell, there was

> this deep, this providential difference between our empire and others, that the nationhood of the mother country remained unaltered through it all, almost unconscious of the strange fantastic structure built around her.... England underwent no organic change as the mistress of the world empire. So the continuity of her existence was unbroken.... Thus, our generation is like one which comes home again from years of distant wandering. We discover affinities with earlier generations of English, who feel no country but this to be their own.... We find ourselves once more akin to the old English.... From brass and stone, from line and effigy their eyes look out at us, and we gaze into them, as if we would win some answer from their inscrutable silence.
>
> (cited in Nairn 1970: 5)

This was a powerful re-imagining of the nation whose aim was to revive what had previously been an unquestioning consensus over the association between British national belonging and whiteness in the face of contemporary non-white settlement. If the empire was lost, their nation was not, yet. At the same time, it laid the ground for an insular and defensive racism, born not out of self-confidence but anxiety and political retreat. It is no coincidence that Powell chose to make this speech just 16 days after the assassination of the US civil rights leader, Martin Luther King, and amidst the urban unrest that followed throughout most American cities. Contained within the speech is a warning to the British political class; that if they didn't take action and repatriate non-whites then they too would face the longer-term danger of American-style urban unrest, especially from those defined as the black and the brown English (Solomos 2003: 61). Quoting the Roman poet Virgil, he warned 'As I look ahead, I am filled with foreboding. Like the Roman, I seem to see "the River Tiber foaming with much blood"' (cited in Heffer 1998: 454).

The reaction to the speech was immediate. Powell was condemned by most of the political class, including much of his own party leadership. Four of his shadow cabinet colleagues – McLeod, Boyle, Hogg and Carr threatened to resign unless Powell was sacked. The Labour MP Edward Leadbitter reported he would refer the speech to the Director of Public Prosecutions. The Liberal Party leader Jeremy Thorpe spoke of a prima facie case against Powell for incitement whilst Baroness Gaitskell called the speech 'cowardly'. The PM, Edward Heath sacked him the next day, asserting the speech was 'inflammatory and liable to damage race relations' (cited in Heffer 1998: 461).

On the other hand, 'Working class support for Powell's speech was widespread' (Lindop 2001: 82):

> There were a considerable number of demonstrations and strikes in various parts of England, with the majority taking place in Powell's home base of the West Midlands. The first reported strikes – on Monday 22 April – were by fifty construction workers from a Wolverhampton firm who were working at Rugeley power station and fifty workers at the Metro-Cammell factory in Birmingham. In the following four days, there were some twenty or so strikes, involving perhaps 10–12,000 workers, with the largest ... involving some 400 workers at Motor Panels in Coventry, the Dunlop tyre factory near Gateshead, and Smithfield meat market in London. There were also a number of workplaces where workers, including shop stewards, circulated petitions supporting Powell's right to free speech and his opposition to further immigration.
>
> (Lindop 2001: 82)

The apotheosis of such racist strike action was reached between the 23 April and 26 April 1968 when London dockers struck in support of Powell. On Tuesday 23 April 1968, just three days after Powell's speech, 1,000 dockers from the West India Dock in Poplar came out on strike in protest against Powell's sacking. Some of them marched from the East End to Westminster carrying placards saying 'Don't knock Enoch' and 'Back Britain, not Black Britain' (Heffer 1998: 462). The following day, 600 dockers at St. Katherine's Docks in Wapping walked out in support of Powell while in nearby Deptford two wharves stopped work with a strike involving 150 men. On Thursday 25 April 500 men were absent from work at riverside wharves in the Upper and Lower Pools in Southwark and Bermondsey, and on Friday 26 April some 4,400 men stayed away from work in the largest sectors, the Royal Group of Docks in Newham (Lindop 2001: 82). Harry Pearman, leader of the strike at the Royal Docks, was quoted as saying:

> He wanted a total ban on immigration because there were enough immigrants here already.... Docklands felt the full weight of any influx of coloured people, he said. 'Docklands always feel it worst. You have every colour in God's earth down there. We've got as many Chinese as Mao and we're getting a bit browned off'.
>
> (cited in Lindop 2001: 84)

Overall, Lindop (2001: 82) estimates that 'about a third of the registered labour force – between 6,000 and 7,000 men – were involved in strike action in the week.' And amid these strikes by dockworkers, 600 meat-porters from Smithfield market struck and marched to Westminster handing Powell a 92-page petition supporting his stance. A Gallup poll carried out at the end of April 1968 showed that 74 per cent of the population agreed with Powell's speech with only 15 per cent disagreeing (Heffer 1998: 467). Through Powell, 'The English had begun to know themselves once more. In the obscene form of racism, English nationalism had been re-born' (Nairn 1970: 13).

There is little doubt that Powell had calculated correctly that summoning a racializing conception of English nationalism built around a white identity would strike a chord with important sections of the working class. However, where he miscalculated was in his reasoning that the resulting racist mobilizations by white workers would force the political class to place the repatriation of black and brown Britons on the immediate political agenda. While both Labour and Conservative governments had willingly introduced racist immigration controls to allay the fears of the wider population about the growing numbers of racialized minorities, their respective leaderships had tacitly accepted, however reluctantly, that one of the legacies of Empire would be the creation of a population of black and brown Britons. That was understood to be the opportunity cost of maintaining leadership of the Commonwealth – an important trading bloc as well as an institution through which to protect and maintain Britain's interests abroad. Powell's premeditated attempt to play the racism card had failed to have the desired effect on the political establishment.

Instead, the immediate beneficiaries of Powell's speech were the extreme right who began to acquire a public beyond disgruntled empire loyalists and reactionaries. The lead organizer of the dockers' strike was Harry Pearman. Pearman had headed a delegation that met with Powell in the House of Commons after which he is reported to have said:

> I have just met Enoch Powell and it made me feel proud to be an Englishman. He told me that he felt that if this matter was swept under the rug he would lift the rug and do the same again. We are representatives of the working man. We are not racialists.
>
> (Roth 1970: 361)

Secret intelligence reports from MI5 to Harold Wilson revealed that Pearman was also a member of the right-wing pressure group Moral Rearmament (see for example *The Guardian*, 1 January 1999). Pat Duhig, another leader of the dockers' strikes turned out to be a member of the Union Movement – the successor party of the pre-war British Union of Fascists – as did Dennis Harmston who led the strikes by meatporters in both 1968 and 1972 (Hillman 2001: 9–10).

Further, Powell's speech effectively legitimized the National Front (NF), a political party of around 2,500 members (Walker 1977) that had been founded the year before by the amalgamation of an assortment of small but increasingly active sects including AK Chesterton's League of Empire Loyalists, John Bean's British National Party and a faction of the Racial Preservation Society led by Robin Beauclair (Walker 1977; Taylor 1982). Their programme of opposition to all non-white migration and the repatriation of already settled migrant communities and their British-born children to their ancestral countries of origin mapped perfectly on to the contours of Powell's speech in Birmingham. In fact, it gave these former Conservative imperialists seething at the loss of Empire a new legitimacy in the minds of those on sections of the political right who saw them as more representative of conservative rank and file opinion than the one-nation Tories who had expelled Powell, and who currently dominated the leadership under Heath.

Thus, by the late 1960s, amid the end of the post-war economic boom, the hegemony constructed around a bipartisan commitment to the welfare settlement was disintegrating. Powellism was one early and important manifestation of a broader phenomenon that would later come to be referred to as the new right that sought to manage the coming crisis of British capitalism by manipulating a racializing nationalism to re-cohere the people around a new consensus, and thereby maintain its class rule. Although Powell's political career was to end in failure, the racializing nationalism he legitimized in his speech would, over the next two decades, come to form a constitutive element of the new right strategy to manufacture a new hegemony in the light of the demise of the welfare settlement (Solomos et al. 1982; Gilroy 1987). Crucial were the numerous overlapping social networks such as the Monday Club that acted as a bridgehead for the reciprocal transmission of ideas and persons between various parts of the Tory new right, including on occasion individual fascists, which would eventually result in the capture of the Tory party leadership by Mrs. Thatcher.

Within the labour movement, there was no organized opposition mounted to the racist strikes initiated in support of Powell other than some 'belated public statements exposing Powell's anti-union credentials' (Lindop 2001: 90). The CPGB at a national level, though formally opposed to racism, had, as we have already seen, lost its earlier commitment to a language of internationalism and class solidarity as a result of Stalinization. Party theoreticians of racism like Kay Beauchamp and Joan Bellamy offered crude economistic accounts of racism (Ben-Tovim 1978: 203) which reduced it to a capitalist conspiracy designed to 'make profit for a small handful of bosses, shareholders and bankers out of everybody's labour' and juxtaposed this to the British working class's 'traditions of tolerance' (see for example Bellamy 1968: 3, 8). In another document, Beauchamp claimed that the 'root and fruit of racialism is profit. For this reason racialism will never be eradicated under capitalism' (Beauchamp no date: 13). With few intellectual resources to understand and critique the material basis of working class racism other than to reduce it to a ruling class conspiracy, and constrained by its commitment to building broad popular alliances with Labour and trade union leaders, it was forced to draw on moral and abstract appeals to the unity of the human race to counter the materially-grounded expressions of working class racism.

Inevitably, such appeals fell on stony ground. Communist dockers like Jack Dash and Michael Fenn did distribute a leaflet at the West India Docks the morning after the strike 'attacking those who marched in violent language' (Lindop 2001: 91) but in the main 'most militants, including CP members, simply took the line of least resistance ... and kept their heads down' (Lindop 2001: 91). One concrete episode that encapsulated the ideological and political degeneration of the CPGB on the question of racism occurred at the Royal Docks on the morning of the strike on Friday 26 April when in an attempt to dissuade them from marching in support of Powell, a CPGB member of the liaison committee invited a Catholic priest and a Protestant minister to attend a dockgate meeting (Lindop 2001: 92). 'The irony of a communist appealing to the Roman Catholic Church for help was not lost on many dockers' (Lindop 2001: 92).

The libertarian socialist David Widgery (1976: 407) captured the feeling of disbelief and helplessness that gripped anti-racist socialists at the time:

> We were just completely shocked numb... You suddenly realized how little influence the left really had, how the roots of the political organisations like the Communist Party had been rotting in the soil. How pathetic the squabbling between groups all was. Just how urgent things had become... I seemed to spend the next few days leafleting solidly and I'll never forget the look on the faces of the Pakistani postmen when they

read the leaflets and found out they weren't fascist. For those few days after Powell, they were petrified. But so was I.

Widgery's (1976: 411) observation about how the CPGB (and the Labour Party) had failed to 'offer real, socialist alternatives to capitalism or to combat the racist upsurge' is prescient; the CPGB in particular had numerous working class militants whose response to racism was 'too little and too late.' Widgery himself was a member of the International Socialists which contained a number of intellectuals (e.g. Harris 1968; Foot 1965a, 1965b, 1969; Widgery 1976) who opposed racism by drawing on a language of class, solidarity and socialist internationalism that had once been associated with the CPGB. Further, Terry Barrett – the only IS member who worked in the docks in the east end of London at the time of Powell's speech – produced leaflets that attempted to challenge the racism of his work colleagues, and recalled Powell's persistent calls to make large-scale redundancies in the docks. However, it was to little avail; history shows such a message failed to resonate, in large part because the British left had hugely underestimated the depth of attachment considerable sections of the working class now had to a racializing British nationalism.

Black resistance

In the aftermath of Powell's speech, and the mobilizations in support by white workers, black and Asian communities responded by founding the Black People's Alliance (BPA). Led by Jagmohan Joshi – also leader of the Indian Workers Association (IWA-GB) in the West Midlands (Josephides 1990: 119) – it was a 'militant front for Black Consciousness and against racialism' (Sivanandan 1982: 25), and mobilized black and Asian workers against this latest escalation in racist sentiment. The BPA was emblematic of a growing trend within the minority communities of anti-racist organizing, independent of the official structures of the British labour movement. Long frustrated by its indifference to racism, black and Asian communities increasingly drew their political and ideational inspiration from the collective struggles against decolonization being waged across Asia, Africa and the Caribbean.

Equally significant was the struggle for civil rights being waged by African Americans and their allies in the US – the hegemon of the world-system. In late 1964 and early 1965 respectively, the leaders of the two wings of the American civil rights movement – Martin Luther King and Malcolm X – visited Britain. King stopped off in London en route to Stockholm where he was scheduled to receive the Nobel Peace Prize. Drawing inspiration from his visit, migrant groups representing the Caribbean, Pakistani and Indian communities came together with white anti-racists to establish the Campaign Against Racial Discrimination (CARD) in January 1965 to campaign for legislation to tackle racism and discrimination.

Malcolm X visited Britain in late 1964, and then again in February 1965 – just days before his assassination in Harlem, New York. In important talks delivered at the Oxford Union and the LSE he outlined his internationalist vision of a global struggle of subaltern peoples, of the 'exploited against the exploiter':

> ...the same pulse that beats in the Black man on the African continent today is beating in the heart of the Black man in North America, Central America, South America, and in the Caribbean.
>
> (Baldwin and Al-Hadid 2002: 348)

Significantly, he also visited Smethwick, the small town near Birmingham which had been witness to a vicious racist campaign less than a year earlier, where he encouraged black and Asian people to organize autonomously to combat such racism. The Racial Action Adjustment Society (RAAS) was established shortly afterwards exhorting 'Black men, unite...we have nothing to lose but our fears' (cited in Sivanandan 1982: 16).

In May 1965, when the mainly Asian and Caribbean workforce at Courtauld's Red Scar Mill in Preston, Lancashire – a large rayon mill producing industrial textiles – went on strike against the imposition of a 50 per cent increase in work for a 3 per cent increase in pay, it was members of RAAS that helped sustain the strike. On the other hand, the TGWU officials failed to support the collective action by refusing to make it official, and actively colluded with management to defeat the strikers. The vice-chair of the factory-wide shop stewards organization deployed racist imagery by claiming the dispute was 'tribal' in nature while another steward claimed that 'several hotheads' were stirring up trouble for their own selfish interests (Foot 1965b: 6). Despite this lack of solidarity from the official trade union movement, the black workers carried on their strike action for three weeks due in large part to the efforts of members of RAAS, and individual socialists like Raymond Challinor (Foot 1965b). The dispute marked an important 'progression in the organic unity of the (Afro)Asian, "coolie", and (Afro)Caribbean, "slave" ' with Asian strikers like Abdulla Patel subsequently joining RAAS (Sivanandan 1982: 16).

Another strike, this time by Indian workers, followed in 1967 which again drew attention to the widespread prevalence of racism, and trade union indifference to it. Management at Coneygre foundry in the West Midlands precipitated the strike by deploying racist redundancy procedures. Instead of operating the generally accepted trade union principle of 'last in first out', they identified 21 Indians (and no white workers) for redundancy. The Indian workers' trade union, the TGWU, refused to make the strike official while white workers organized in another trade union – the Associated Union of Foundry Workers (AUFW) – were actively encouraged by the local AUFW official to cross the Indian workers' picket line. On this occasion, it was the Indian Workers Association (IWA) that helped sustain the strikers until management was forced to take back the 21 Indian workers who were made redundant (Wrench 1987: 166; Duffield 1988: 86–89).

By 1968, and the formation of the BPA, it was increasingly evident that black and Asian activists had appropriated the ascribed identity of black previously used to disparage people of African descent, and infused it with a new ideological meaning out of which were fashioned powerful 'communities of resistance' (Sivanandan 1990). The Universal Coloured People's Association (UCPA) and the Black Unity and Freedom Party (BUFP) (Sivanandan 1982: 63) further consolidated this Caribbean-Asian unity – or anti-racist racial formation project (Omi and Winant 1994) – along with the Organization of Women of African and Asian Descent (OWAAD) which enabled women from these communities to develop a socialist-feminist strategy to challenge sexism, as well as racism (Parmar 1990; Shukra 1996: 28–29). Such black solidarity was also reflected in the plethora of local and national newspapers and journals such as *Race Today* that sprang up in this period. The intensity of the activity in this period is neatly captured by Shukra (1996: 30–31):

> The 'black' radical activist was usually an unpaid campaigner who operated intensively with a small group of like-minded people, went from meeting to meeting, distributed pamphlets, spoke at rallies, carried banners and organised demonstrations to convince what was termed 'West Indian', 'Indian' and 'Pakistani' people that their experience of inferior treatment at the hands of employers, schools, local authorities, government officials, politicians and the police was unacceptable. Crucially, they also argued that this situation could be changed through militant political activity, primarily against employers and the state ... the black activists used the term 'black' to build a movement to mobilize and cohere self-reliant communities of resistance to racism.

Importantly, the resolute insistence on black self-organization never implied any sort of permanent separation from white workers. Avtar Jouhl – General Secretary of the Indian Workers Association (GB) in the West Midlands – made transparent how:

> We feel unity will develop in struggle. This does not in any sense deny the need for black workers to have their own caucuses in every factory and place of work. But we do not advocate separate black unions; that would be to play the capitalists game of dividing the working class.
>
> (cited in Josephides 1990: 119)

By the close of the 1960s, Britain was two communites deeply stratified by racism: one black, the other white, historically, politically and economically constituted in opposition to one another by the events of the two decades since the docking of the *Empire Windrush* at Tilbury. Within the white community, there existed near unanimity about the need to limit the numbers of black and Asian migrants coming into Britain. At the same time, there was an important point of disagreement within the political elite about how to treat those racialized minorities who were already present in Britain. On the one hand, some in the Labour Party endorsed limited attempts to 'integrate' the British-born population of Asian and African descent. On the other hand, attempts to institute such measures had generated a further racist reaction on the political right which demanded the expulsion of all racialized minorities, irrespective of whether they had been born in Britain. The rise of Powell, the racist strikes in support of Powell, and the heroic but lonely struggle by black and Asian workers to combat the rising tide of racism that threatened to overwhelm them were all indicators that

> The political Establishment had begun to lose its old grip on the nation, and on the masses. It has – so to speak- started to shrink out of contact with the social realities over which, traditionally, it exerted an all-embracing and conservative control.
>
> (Nairn 1970: 24)

With the bipartisan consensus that had held steady since the Battle of Britain entering a moment of deep crisis, what would the 1970s bring?

7

Socialists, Anti-Racism and Working Class Bifurcation

A western European Left which does not seek to understand and then to tackle racism head-on is cutting its own throat. The loss of support from proletarian socialists who are sympathetic to racialist explanations...is better than endless equivocation, denial and ineffective compromise on this issue.

(Widgery 1986: 112)

In every town, in every factory, in every school, on every housing estate, wherever the Nazis attempt to organize they must be countered.

(ANL press release, November 1977)

Introduction

If 1968 marked the nadir of working class resentment towards racialized minorities in Britain, a historic moment where questions of class came to be refracted through the prism of race, the period between 1976 and 1979 represents the moment when collective action against racism and class exploitation in Britain partially entwined. How did such a dramatic turnaround come about? I begin by focusing on the economic, political and ideological factors that undermined the post-war hegemony constructed around the welfare settlement and the twin principles of active citizenship and full employment. As the state and employers attempted to make the working class pay for the profitability crisis of British capitalism of the late 1960s, key elements of the working class increasingly turned to collective action with Britain witnessing some of the most significant class struggles since the 1920s. Arising out of this process of industrial and political struggle was a broader conception of class consciousness that could not easily be accommodated within existing notions of the common national interest. Significantly, such collective action brought socialist activists to positions of authority throughout the trade union

123

movement particularly those aligned to the left within the Labour Party, the CPGB and the International Socialists.

These socialist activists played an influential mediating role in politically re-aligning the class struggles against exploitation to those on-going struggles against exploitation enveloped in racism by the black and Asian population. Through a focus on key events and episodes – such as the development of an anti-racist standpoint within the trade union movement, the formation of Rock Against Racism (RAR), the solidarity extended to Asian women workers involved in the Grunwick strike between 1976 and 1978, and the emergence of the Anti-Nazi League (ANL) – it will be demonstrated how the working class bifurcated on the question of racism in the late 1970s. Key to manu-facturing this bifurcation were those 'white' socialists who re-discovered their own histories of racial oppression over the course of the events in the 1970s. Those of Irish Catholic and Jewish descent played a bridging role helping to inculcate and transmit anti-racist ideas and actions into the trade union move-ment and the working class more generally – ideas that until then had been narrowly located within the black and Asian communities challenging racism and fascism. The resultant formation of an anti-racist, anti-fascist social move-ment in Britain was unprecedented in scale and scope that remains unseen anywhere on the European mainland to this day.

Class conflict, socialist activism and anti-racism

At first, it appeared that events in the 1970s would proceed along the tracks laid down in the preceding decade with the newly elected Conservative gov-ernment introducing a further Immigration Act in 1971 on the grounds that it would avert, once and for all, the 'legitimate fears' of 'our people' by assur-ing them that there would be 'no further large-scale immigration' (Miles and Phizacklea 1984: 80). The Act was even more restrictive than those intro-duced during the 1960s and effectively took away the right of black and Asian Commonwealth migrants to settle by declaring that all 'aliens' and Common-wealth citizens who were not patrials needed permission to enter Britain. Such state racism was vigorously challenged by the black community as 'Indian, Pakistani and West Indian organizations from all over Britain marched through London...A dozen organizations including the Supreme Council of Sikhs, the Indian Workers Association and the West Indian Standing Conference took part' (Renton 2006: 15). However, as in the 1950s and 1960s, the stand-point of the official representatives of the organized labour movement, the TUC, was noticeable only by its meekness: 'Insofar as the institutionalisation of racism by the state was concerned, the TUC had nothing to say' (Miles and Phizacklea 1984: 75).

If an increasingly virulent strand of working class and state racism was one signifier of the breakdown of the welfare settlement, another was the growing rift between organized workers on the one hand, and employers and the state on the other. This crack had first emerged during the late 1960s when the state and employers identified informal trade union activity as the primary cause of the poor productivity of British industry (McIlroy 1995), especially the increasing ability of shop stewards to carry out bargaining in an informal manner at plant level. According to the then Labour government this encouraged disorder, particularly wildcat strikes, which they were intent on suppressing. As a result, the 'shop steward came to be constructed as a symbol of trade union irresponsibility, and workplace conflict came to be seen as *the* major problem underlying poor productivity performance and Britain's economic problems' (Eldridge et al. 1991: 25). Although the Royal Commission on Trade Unions – the Donovan Report (1968) – found that shop stewards were not the problem but poor management, the Labour government continued to seek a legal resolution to the 'problem' of wildcat strikes, and the following year published a white paper called *In Place of Strife* which outlined its proposals for curbing such activity.

While the Labour bill was defeated due to the pressure brought to bear on the government by the trade union movement (Moran 1980; McIlroy 1995), the incoming Conservative government of 1970 was determined to succeed where Labour had failed, and quickly introduced an Industrial Relations Bill that proposed replacing the collectivist laissez-faire system of industrial relations with a comprehensive legal framework intended to restrict conflict (Moran 1980; Sheldrake 1991). These increasing interventions by the state in employer-labour relations induced a dramatic re-configuration of the class struggle. Recognizing that their living conditions could no longer be sustained solely through the operation of free collective bargaining and the use of exclusionary practices, workers increasingly resorted to strike action leading to some of the biggest class confrontations in nearly half a century (Grint 1991). The number of strike days lost increased from an average of less than 4 million days a year during the 1950s and 1960s to 24 million days in 1972 alone (Grint 1991: 172, table 7; see also Sheldrake 1991: 74). A significant proportion of these strikes were qualitatively different from those of the 1950s and 1960s because 'a wide range of traditionally moderate and peaceful workers, many of them women, embarked on strike action, many for the first time in their lives' (Kelly 1988: 107). Attempts to curb unofficial strike activity also saw the return of the political strike for the first time since the 1920s (Grint 1991). A series of one-day stoppages against the 1971 Industrial Relations Bill culminated in the TUC instructing its members to refuse to register as trade unions when the Bill became law. Such collective action was reinforced by over 500 occupations and sit-ins that took place during this period (Kelly 1988: 108–109; McIlroy 1995: 239).

There was no necessary, unmediated association between this upturn in class struggle and the formation of an anti-racist consciousness in the working class. We have already seen how in those early years of intensifying class conflict between 1968 and 1972, the organized white working class and its institutions remained resolutely indifferent to the struggles being waged by black workers against discriminatory practices in Britain as evidenced by their failure to confront everyday racism, state racism, Powellism and the resultant racist strikes by dockers and Smithfield porters. The rank and file participants of this early phase of class struggles against exploitation rarely interpreted their campaigns as intersecting with the on-going struggles of black workers against exploitation enveloped in oppression.

Nevertheless, a current of working class anti-racism did emerge from the early 1970s, and crucial to its formation were many of the socialist activists and stewards who found themselves elected to positions of influence throughout all levels of the trade union movement as the class conflict intensified. Over the course of those bitter struggles waged between 1968 and 1972, the idea that employers and workers shared some common national interest was undermined in the minds of many workers when they witnessed those same employers forcing them to pay for the crisis of British capitalism. As the old hegemony disintegrated, for the first time since the 1920s, many workers found themselves increasingly drawn to the socialist left and their principled advocacy of collective action to combat such attacks on living standards. These activists didn't attempt to put a brake on such workers' collective action, but encouraged it, and attempted to find ways of further strengthening it. As strikes and other actions increased exponentially throughout 1972 (Darlington 1994), it signalled above all that workers were increasingly looking beyond the conventional tactics employed to defend working class conditions achieved during the high point of welfare capitalism.

This growing synchronicity in ideological frame between the rank and file worker and socialist activists in a conjuncture of heightening class consciousness helped start the process of transforming the leadership of the trade union movement at all levels. It forced some traditional national trade union leaders to adopt a more combative class perspective, whilst others who refused to adapt to the changing relations of force were swept away in the maelstrom and replaced by left-wing leaders. Significant leftward swings in the leadership of several major trade unions took place during this period including the Amalgamated Engineering Union (AEU), the Transport and General Workers Union (TGWU) and the General, Municipal and Boilermakers' Union (GMB) (Kelly 1988: 109). At the district, regional and shop steward level, it brought to positions of influence a diverse layer of socialist activists including left-wingers in the Labour Party, members of the CPGB, as well as to a lesser extent, representatives of an unorthodox form of Trotskyism, the International Socialists (IS). By the mid-1970s, it was estimated that 10 per cent of all trade union officials were Communists (Verberckmoes 1996: 227; see also Kelly 1988). This wave of industrial struggle arrested the CPGB's long-term decline in membership (Smith 2008) while various Trotskyist parties saw significant increases in their membership (McIlroy 1995: 104), with the most significant of them – the International Socialists (IS) – growing from around 1,000 members across 47 branches to around 3,500 members with some implantation in the organized working class (Birchall 1981).

Amid this rising arc of contentious class protests, a new generation of social-ist, New Left and sometimes Marxist activists, who had been gestating in the womb of British society for a decade or more found themselves in positions of authority where they could shape and influence the direction of organized working class politics, not just in the workplace, but also beyond. Significantly, some of these socialist activists that came to prominence in the early 1970s were more alive to the dangers of racism undermining working class solidarity, and more willing to challenge it than socialists in previous waves of working class insurgency in British history.

This was because this New Left – the class of 68 – encompassing principally the socialist left in the Labour Party, the IS, and those that would go on to become the Eurocommunist–wing of the CPGB – were shaped by a conjunc-ture marked by a wholly different set of relations of force – a world of imperial retreat and decolonization where national liberation struggles waged by black and brown peoples was challenging the domination of the non-white world by the white, and bringing into question the powerful ideologies that sustained such rule, including racism. Alongside this were the struggles against white supremacy being waged by African Americans within the heart of the global hegemon, which when entwined with iconic figures of the age like Muhammad Ali, Angela Davis and Malcolm X and set to the soundtrack of Motown and Stax had ignited much of the world in righteous indignation. And perhaps most important of all were the domestic struggles against working class and elite racism that had been waged by Asian and Caribbean workers without any show of solidarity from the organized labour movement and its institutions since the mid-1960s.

Moral opposition to racism, which had been growing in the early 1970s, combined with an instrumentalist understanding that the working class could ill-afford such racist divisions amid employer and state attacks drove social-ist activists on to diffuse anti-racist ideas throughout the organized labour movement. The number of motions tabled at regional and national union conferences calling on the labour movement to take steps to combat racism increased (Virdee 2000). And at the 1973 TUC annual conference, social-ists were successful in moving a motion which called upon the next Labour government to repeal the racist 1971 Immigration Act, thereby reversing the decision taken at the 1971 TUC annual conference (Miles and Phizacklea 1984: 103). The first, modest indications that socialist pressure was finally beginning to shift the mainstream organized labour movement away from a position of indifference or of blaming migrants and their British-born children for their troubles to one where they recognised the scourge of racism, and the need to combat it – within society as well as its own ranks – were now clearly evident.

At the same time, the country was polarizing, rapidly. The growing inter-section of contradictions over Northern Ireland, black resistance, and an increasingly class-conscious proletariat on the one hand, and the rise of the National Front on the other provoked a powerful response from the state. A decisive shift in strategic direction was instigated towards a 'law and order society' effected through the construction and amplification of moral pan-ics and accompanying folk-devils (Hall et al. 1978). Amid this heightened atmosphere of social tension and crisis in 1970s Britain, the twin concerns associated with the black presence in Britain recurred over and over again: uncontrolled immigration and the problems arising from it (Hall et al. 1978: 299). Against this backdrop, the National Front saw its share of the vote rise from scarcely 12,000 votes at the 1970 general election to 77,000 votes in the February 1974 general election, before almost doubling again to 114,000 votes in the October 1974 election (Taylor 1979: 134). Significantly, as the events at Imperial Typewriters in Leicester in 1974 and elsewhere proved, the National Front was now increasingly drawing its support from the less well-organized sections of the manual white working class, residing in ethnically mixed areas of residential settlement.

For socialist activists, there was no turning back; as far as they were con-cerned such racism had to be challenged, or the working class would be defeated. According to their perspective, the rise of the National Front had only confirmed the lessons they had been forced to learn from a decade of autonomous struggles by black workers coupled with the horror of supposedly militant groups of workers like the dockers marching in support of Powell – that racism hindered the process of working class formation that was so crit-ical to defending the collective interests of the working class in the face of growing state and employer intervention. Socialist opinion by the early 1970s was forced over and over again to concede that it had greatly underestimated the depth of racist sentiment within the British working class, and that steps had to be taken to combat it (see CPGB no date; Foot no date; International Socialists 1974; Nicholson 1974; CPGB 1975). A pamphlet released by a rank and file docker in the TGWU, and formally endorsed with a foreword by Jack Jones – the leader of the TGWU – declared that

> [t]he harsh reality is that the working class is divided by racialism to a damaging degree. An urgent responsibility falls upon trade union activists to seek those remedies which can unify our class and meet head-on the racialism embedded in so much of our society.
>
> (Nicholson 1974: 7)

The collective pressure initiated by socialist activists, principally from the Labour Party, the CPGB, the IS and other smaller socialist formations, drove the TUC to introduce measures that set out to challenge racism in the trade unions and beyond (Miles and Phizacklea 1978). At the 1974 TUC Annual Conference, the General Council announced that it had submitted oral evidence and a memorandum to the Select Committee on Race Relations and Immigration where it acknowledged for the first time in its history that black workers were subject to racism and discriminatory practices. Moreover, this evidence went on to state that 'trade unions should actively oppose racialism within their own ranks' as well as the organized far right (Miles and Phizacklea 1978: 199). At the 1975 TUC Annual Conference delegates from several affiliated unions made speeches denouncing the racism and activities of the National Front and called upon trade unionists to warn their members of the dangers of racism to working class solidarity. Local committees and trades councils also became increasingly concerned about racism and began to develop ways of challenging it. Immediately after the 1975 TUC Annual Conference, the General Council established a new sub-committee of the General Council, the Equal Rights Committee, whose main responsibility would be to develop policies to promote equal opportunity. In the same year, the TUC General Council also established the Race Relations Advisory Committee to work with the Equal Rights Committee on issues relating to 'race relations' (Miles and Phizacklea 1978: 198). And in July 1976, the General Council issued a press release which called for the trade union movement to actively tackle racial discrimination:

> Much needs to be done to eliminate the discrimination and disadvantage facing ethnic minorities and for their part the General Council are advising affiliated unions about steps they should take to strengthen the organisation among immigrant and black workers and unity between work people.
>
> (Miles and Phizacklea 1978: 199)

Against this backdrop marked by a noticeable shift in position by the leadership of the organized labour movement, the Labour government also decided to make good on its manifesto promise of challenging racism by introducing several important pieces of legislation to curb discrimination, including most significantly the 1976 Race Relations Act (Marsh 1992). The Race Relations Act not only made acts of direct discrimination illegal, but also acts of indirect discrimination entailing treatment which may be described equal in a formal sense between different 'racial' groups but discriminatory in its effect on one particular 'racial' group (Home Office 1977: 4–5). Despite subsequent problems regarding its effective implementation (see McCrudden et al. 1991), this legislation stands today as testimony to the remarkable changes brought to bear on formal institutional politics in British society by the combined forces of black self-organization, and socialist activism in the organized labour movement.

Rock Against Racism (RAR)

1976 marked a step-change in the content and form of racist and anti-racist contentious politics in Britain. When Enoch Powell made a speech in April of that year warning how Britain was 'still being eroded and hollowed out from within' by 'alien wedges', the National Front again proved to be the beneficiary. In the 1976 district elections that followed immediately after, 80 National Front candidates garnered more than 10 per cent of the poll (Messina 1989: 114). In Leicester alone, they procured 44,000 votes while at the London County Council elections in 1977, the party secured 119,000 votes and nearly 250,000 votes around the country (Renton 2005: 1). Increasingly concerned about continuing 'non-white' immigration and unsure about the Conservative Party's ability to either arrest it, or prevent the continuing drift to the left taking place under a Labour government, growing numbers of working class Tories switched their allegiance to the National Front. Although its membership had peaked in 1973 at between 14,000 and 20,000 members in the aftermath of the Ugandan Asian affair, it gained a further 5,000 members following the decision of the Labour government to admit the Malawian Asians in 1976 (Messina 1989: 112).

Buoyed by its electoral success and its ability to draw in growing numbers of young white men from the unorganized manual working class (Taylor 1979), the political repertoire of the National Front diversified during the mid-1970s to encompass not only electoral contests but also attempts to mark out and reclaim territory that they believed had been conceded to racialized minorities by strategically deploying graffiti, random violence and increasingly, marches in ethnically diverse areas. Such action was driven by the national socialist element within the National Front which was by the mid-1970s ascendant within the leadership. Modelling themselves on the German National Socialists, they believed, according to Gerry Gable – veteran anti-fascist activist and co-founder of Searchlight – 'in Dr. Goebbels' maxim: who controls the streets will win the final victory' (cited in Renton 2005: 21). The aim was clear, as it had been in 1920s Weimar Germany: to intimidate the minority communities, and their anti-racist supporters among the socialist left.

In the summer of 1976, just months after the Front's latest electoral successes, and amid the continuing fall-out over the Malawi Asian affair, Dinesh Choudhri, aged 19, and Riphi Alhadidi, aged 22, were stabbed to death by white youths as the two students walked to a Chinese restaurant in south Woodford, Essex. In July 1976, Gurdip Singh Chaggar, aged 18, was also stabbed to death by a gang of white youths outside a cinema in Southall, leading John Kingsley Read – leader of a small far-right organization called the National Party – to allegedly claim 'One down, one million to go.' And in September 1976, a 60 year old woman, Mohan Dev Gautam, was murdered when a racist gang dragged her from her home in Leamington Spa and set her alight (Sivanandan 1982).

No part of British cultural or social life appeared immune from this rising arc of racist hate. Important cultural icons like David Bowie displayed an open affection for Nazism at the time (Buckley 2005: 250–255). Then, at a concert held in Birmingham in August 1976 – just a month after Gurdip Singh Chaggar's murder – a heavily drunk Eric Clapton, renowned musician of blues, rock and jazz, made an explosive outburst declaring his support for Powell before calling on the audience to 'keep Britain white' (Denselow 1989: 138–139; see also 'Blood and Glory' by Ed Vulliamy in *The Observer*, 4 March 2007).

Such racism didn't go unchallenged. In September 1976, the photographer Red Saunders and designer Roger Huddle along with four others published an angry letter in key music weeklies including *Sounds, NME* and *Melody Maker* that declared:

> When we read about Eric Clapton's Birmingham concert when he urged support for Enoch Powell we nearly puked. Come on Eric ... you've been taking too much of that *Daily Express* stuff and you know you can't handle it. Own up. Half your music is black. You're rock music's biggest colonist ... We want to organize a rank and file movement against the racist poison in music ... P.S. Who shot the sheriff Eric? It sure as hell wasn't you!
>
> (cited in Widgery 1986: 40)

Six hundred people wrote in to express their support, and a social movement called Rock Against Racism was born (Renton 2006: 34). Red Saunders described the mid-1970s as

> an emergency. People were being attacked and murdered ... We were music fans looking for a way for ordinary kids who loved black music to have a voice. Out of that came a youth campaign that wasn't about boring old-fashioned politics, but harnessed the energy of new sounds like punk and reggae.
>
> (cited in Sawyer 2007)

The intention was to change the political values of British youth, to use music as a means to transmit an anti-racist message to a young audience that wouldn't be inspired to take anti-racist action listening to socialist speeches. RAR's intentions were crystallized in the first issue of its fanzine, *Temporary Hoarding* in which it declared:

> We want Rebel music, street music. Music that breaks down people's fear of one another. Crisis music. Now music. Music that knows who the real enemy is. Rock Against Racism. Love Music Hate Racism.
>
> (Renton 2005: 33)

Within three months of its formation this aim was given concrete expression with the first RAR event held at the Royal College of Art on 10 December 1976 with Carol Grimes headlining (Widgery 1986: 56). This was quickly followed by further musical events involving Aswad, Steel Pulse and Matumbi. RAR's growth was dramatic moving rapidly in three years 'from a letter in the music press to a national organisation able to organise major outdoor festivals' (Widgery 1989: 119–120).

Paul Gilroy (1987), in one of the few scholarly accounts of RAR, links its success to the simultaneous 'growth of punk'. The borrowing of key themes and insights from reggae enabled punks to supply an oppositional language through which RAR could speak a truly populist politics:

> The dread notion of 'Babylon System' allowed disparate and apparently contradictory expressions of the national crisis to be seen as a complex, interrelated whole, a coherent structure of which racism was a primary characteristic, exemplifying and symbolizing the unacceptable nature of the entire authoritarian capitalist edifice.
>
> (Gilroy 1987: 159)

By 1976, the first breaches in the wall-to-wall racism faced by racialized minorities since the 1950s were clearly evident. The national leadership of the trade union movement – driven by rank and file socialist pressure – had formally committed itself to taking steps to challenge racism and fascism, and with RAR, there emerged the first indications that parts of white youth were also receptive to such a message. What it signalled above all was the beginning of a new-found confidence and desire among a small but growing element of the white community to join with those from minority communities in actively challenging racism.

The Grunwick strike

In August 1976 – just weeks before the establishment of RAR – a handful of mainly Asian women led by Jayaben Desai had walked out on strike in response to the 'arbitrary and oppressive management in a photographic print facility' in North London (Pearson et al. 2010: 409). Employing around 440 people, of mainly Indian descent, Grunwick was well-known for the harsh conditions under which workers were expected to labour. In part, these were a consequence of Grunwick's business which 'hinged on processing customers photos at low cost and with a short turnover.' However, instead of investing in automating different parts of the production process, the company chose to maximise productivity 'through constant threats of dismissal if workers did not respond to efforts to increase output' (Pearson et al. 2010: 414). Compulsory overtime was instituted without warning and racist harassment was commonplace. Further, management often subjected the staff to degrading treatment when it came to securing permission to go to ante-natal clinics, and restrictions were even imposed on when staff could take toilet breaks. Overseeing this intolerable intensification of work was a manager called Malcolm Auden, housed in a glass walled office from where he could watch over the female Asian workforce. The pressure was so overwhelming that 27 of the 102 workers employed in the mail order department had left in the six weeks running up to the strike (Pearson et al. 2010: 415).

The dispute itself was triggered when Jayaben Desai and her son Sunil refused to work overtime and resigned, along with Devshi Bhudia, Chandrakant Patel, Bharet Patel, and Suresh Ruparelia. Desai subsequently recalled how:

> I did not think – I just walked out with my self-respect intact. I did not want to work in such a place … So I left for my self-respect and because I had confidence in myself.
>
> (cited in Pearson et al. 2010: 418)

Shortly thereafter, 137 mainly Asian women followed Desai's example and walked out of the plant and joined the picket line she had initiated. The strike had begun. The strikers decided to establish a union, and after advice from the local Brent Trades Council and Tom Durkin in particular, joined the Association of Professional, Executive and Computer Staff (APEX). Once they had become members, APEX immediately made the strike official, and offered strike pay to those involved in the dispute. Grunwick's management led by joint owner George Ward responded by dismissing all the strikers. However, the strikers refused to buckle, stating defiantly to their employer that: 'If you refuse to talk to us, we will turn off all the taps, one by one, until you have to' (Phizacklea and Miles 1978: 270). To achieve this, they required support from other groups of workers, and, on this occasion, 'Support for the strike from sections of the British labour movement was quick and widespread' (Ramdin 1987: 289).

At the 1976 TUC Annual Conference, Roy Grantham, General Secretary of APEX called on trade unionists to lend their support to the strikers. He explicitly raised the issue of racism, arguing it was central to the exploitation that South Asian workers suffered. Similarly, Tom Jackson of the Union of Post Office Workers (UPW) pledged support, and agreed to stop the delivery of mail coming in or out of Grunwick thereby effectively preventing the business from operating. Solidarity action flowed not only from national trade union leaders but also large numbers of rank and file workers. Donations came in from local workers at the 'Milliner Park Ward, Rolls Royce Works Committee, Express Dairies, Associated Automation (GEC), TGWU, and the UPW Cricklewood Office Branch' (Ramdin 1987: 292). Significantly, on 1 November 1976, the post office workers in the UPW stopped delivering

Grunwick's mail. Despite such solidarity, management refusal to concede to the strikers' demands combined with the overly bureaucratic management of the dispute by APEX forced the local strike committee to call for a mass picket of the firm for one week in June 1977.

Ten months on from the start of the dispute, mass picketing began in the week of 13 June 1977 with between 1,000 and 2,000 pickets present. By the end of that week, those numbers had swelled to 3,000, including miners from the coalfields of South Wales and Yorkshire – the latter led by Arthur Scargill (Rogaly 1977: 178). On the 23 June, two coachloads of miners from Barnsley drove through the night to join the picket line, along with Scottish miners led by Mick McGahey. This solidarity action combined with the post office staff who continued to prevent the delivery of mail in or out of Grunwick, and the contracted TGWU drivers who refused to drive the police onto the firm's premises highlighted the importance of this dispute to the labour movement (Rogaly 1977: 173; Ramdin 1987). The largest picket occurred on 11 July 1977 when an estimated 18,000 people – among them workers, feminists and anti-racists – joined Desai and the strikers in an unprecedented show of solidarity (Rogaly 1977: 182). Particularly significant was the solidarity action from the London dockers who, in 1968, had marched to the Houses of Parliament in support of Enoch Powell's racist 'rivers of blood' speech shouting 'Back Britain, not Black Britain' and demanding an end to black immigration. Now less than a decade later at Grunwick, amid a rising tide of industrial and political radicalisation, some of those same dockers carried the Royal Docks Shop Stewards' banner at the head of a mass picket in support of the predominately Asian workforce at Grunwick (Virdee 2000).

The mass picketing continued into November 1977 when 8,000 pickets attended. Huge clashes with the police ensued resulting in 243 pickets being treated for injury, along with 113 arrests being made. However, thereafter support for the dispute began to ebb. The problems associated with the contradictory role played by the TUC as intermediaries responsible for arbitrating and managing the relationship between capital and labour increasingly came to the fore (Anderson 1977; Kelly 1988). Finding itself under pressure from the Labour government to enforce the Social Contract, and manage industrial relations more effectively, the TUC insisted that control of the dispute must be placed in the hands of the APEX executive. At the same time, postal workers who had boycotted Grunwick were laid off by the post office management. In November 1977, as part of one final effort, some of the Grunwick strikers went on hunger strike outside the TUC headquarters demanding more effective support. Desai perceptively observed how 'Support from the TUC is like honey on your elbow: you can see it, you can smell it but you can't taste it!' (cited in Pearson et al. 2010: 409). APEX responded by suspending the hunger strikers and took away their strike pay. Unable to effect change, the strike was eventually abandoned after 670 days on 14 July 1978 without any of the strikers' demands having been met.

Despite the disappointment of defeat, the dispute at Grunwick helped crys-
talize how – in the space of less than a decade – parts of the organized working
class had undergone a dramatic, organic transformation in their political consciousness. From being attached to a narrow understanding of class that nested
neatly within dominant conceptions of race and nation, key groups of workers
had moved towards a more inclusive language of class that could now also
encompass racialized minority workers. Key to facilitating this political transformation were socialist activists. A process of Asian, black and white working
class formation was taking place – uneven, contradictory, but most definitely
present amid the organic crisis of British capitalism in the 1970s.

'We are black, we are white, together we are dynamite': The Anti-Nazi League

As Hot Chocolate's 'So you win again' and Donna Summer's 'I feel love'
topped the UK pop charts in successive weeks in July 1977, the epicentre
of anti-racist activity shifted to Lewisham in South-East London – an area
of significant Caribbean settlement. Twenty one black youths had recently
been arrested and charged with conspiracy to steal purses. However, suspi-
cions about the validity of the charges and the heavy-handed treatment of
the suspects when arrested, combined with revelations that the police operation had been referred to by parts of the local force as Operation PNH – an
acronym for police nigger hunt (Renton 2006: 53–54), led the families of the
accused to form a defence campaign.

With tensions already high, the National Front announced its intention to
march through Lewisham wishing to draw attention to its alleged 'mugging
problem.' However, by the summer of 1977, a plethora of local and national
anti-racist organizations had sprung up alongside the well-established black
and Asian political formations, with many declaring their intention to oppose
the National Front with a counter-demonstration. There was the All Lewisham
Campaign Against Racism and Fascism (ALCARAF) chaired by CPGB member, Mike Power. ALCARAF was one of many local anti-racist committees
that were established throughout London in the aftermath of clashes with
the National Front at Wood Green in April 1977. Most were affiliated to the
All London Anti-Racist Anti-Fascist Co-ordinating Committee (ARAFCC).
ARAFCC and its local affiliates were essentially broad-based umbrella groups
bringing together anyone – ranging from Liberals to members of the CPGB –
who wished to collectively oppose racism and fascism.

In the days leading up to the proposed march on 13 August 1977, divisions arose between ALCARAF and those like the International Socialists
(IS) – recently re-badged as the Socialist Workers Party (SWP) – about what
tactics to employ to oppose the National Front. Specifically, the ALCARAF
committee was keen to publicly demonstrate its opposition to the National

Front, but at the same time avoid any confrontation with their opponents, whereas the SWP wanted to prevent the National Front from marching. Some in ARAFCC, including its feminist affiliate Women Against Racism and Fascism (WARF), chose to participate in both demonstrations (Bourne 2007).

On the morning of 13 August 1977, the ALCARAF march led by local dignitaries passed off peacefully. However, in the afternoon, as 800 members of the National Front assembled for their march along New Cross Road they found themselves confronted with 5,000 opponents made up of the local community, feminist activists, trade unionists, as well as members of the SWP, and other socialist formations. With the police unable to open a way, the NF marchers found 'a hail of bottles, bricks, wood blocks, beer cans, smashed paving stones and smoke bombs' raining down on them while at the same time their banners were 'seized and burnt' (Widgery 1986: 48). Although a third of the entire Metropolitan Police were on duty that day, with riot shields being used for the first time on the British mainland (Renton 2006: 67), they were unable to facilitate the NF's march through Lewisham.

Although those opposing the NF had come from a range of diverse political backgrounds, it was the SWP who took the initiative, and established a national organization that drew in those growing numbers of socialist activists in the Labour Party, trade unionists as well as unaffiliated Asian, black and white youth who wished to challenge racism and fascism. The Anti-Nazi League (ANL) was established in November 1977. The diversity of the social forces represented by the ANL was reflected in its organizational structure. The three executive positions were occupied by Peter Hain (press officer), a leading opponent of apartheid and racism; Ernie Roberts (treasurer), a left-wing Labour MP and deputy general secretary of the AEUW and Paul Holborow (organizer), a member of the SWP. Other members of the Steering Committee included a further four Labour MP's – Martin Flannery, Dennis Skinner, Audrey Wise and Neil Kinnock; a former Young Liberal Simon Hebditch; Maurice Ludmer of the anti-fascist organization Searchlight; Miriam Karlin, an actress of British Jewish descent; and finally, two members of the SWP – Nigel Harris and Jerry Fitzpatrick. The League also received endorsements from a further 40 Labour MPs, including Tony Benn and Gwyneth Dunwoody, as well as Arthur Scargill of the NUM, and Tariq Ali of the IMG. This overwhelmingly socialist-led anti-fascist coalition was supplemented by a diverse range of sponsors – high profile personalities who lent their support to the anti-fascist politics of the ANL. Among the more prominent were football managers Terry Venables and Brian Clough, writers Arnold Wesker and Keith Waterhouse, and actors Julie Christie and Warren Mitchell – the latter renowned for playing the racist character Alf Garnett in the television sitcom *Till Death Us Do Part* (Renton 2006).

The ANL was officially launched at the House of Commons with its opening press release declaring:

For the first time since Mosley in the thirties there is the worrying prospect of a Nazi party gaining significant support in Britain ... The leaders, philosophy, and origins of the National Front and similar organisations followed directly from the Nazis in Germany ... They must not go unopposed. Ordinary voters must be made aware of the threat that lies behind the National Front.

(cited in Renton 2006: 81)

It quickly built up a large network of members who helped arrange a series of activities aimed at exposing the National Front as fascist racists, associating their politics with those of the National Socialists in Nazi Germany and pointing out the consequences of remaining indifferent to them – the genocide of alleged 'racial inferiors', and the destruction of the organized labour movement. Alongside this, racist arguments about black criminality, unemployment and repatriation were actively challenged in a range of ephemeral literature.

The ANL also attempted to counterpose its own embryonic vision of the alternative society – one based on love not hate, multi-ethnic solidarity and not racial division. This was most clearly visible at the major carnivals it organized alongside RAR throughout 1978 and 1979. The first, held at Victoria Park on 30 April 1978, was a genuinely national gathering with amongst others more than 40 coaches arriving from Glasgow, a whole train from Manchester, and a further 15 coaches from Sheffield (Widgery 1986: 84). The march to the carnival site at Victoria Park in East London was led by giant papier mâché models of Martin Webster and Adolf Hitler, built by Peter Fluck and Roger Law – the makers of *Spitting Image*. At the carnival itself, the Clash, X-Ray Spex, Tom Robinson and Steel Pulse played to 80,000 people. Peter Hain, Vishnu Sharma – of the Indian Workers Association (IWA) – Miriam Karlin and Ray Buckton made speeches against racism and fascism. Raphael Samuel – a key member of the CPGB historians group – described the march to the carnival as one of 'the most working-class demonstration I have been on, and one of the very few of my adult lifetime to have sensibly changed the climate of public opinion' (Renton 2006: 121). The Victoria Park event was followed by carnivals in Manchester, Cardiff, Edinburgh, Harwich and Southampton, culminating eventually in the second carnival in London held at Brockwell Park on 24 September 1978. More than 100,000 watched Sham 69 perform alongside Crisis, Inganda, RAS, the Ruts and others (Renton 2006: 132).

These large events brought together thousands of disparate individuals in an open celebration of a multi-ethnic Britain, providing them with added confidence to challenge the racism they witnessed in their everyday lives. A plethora of local groups were established in the wake of ANL's formation, including Students Against the Nazis, Teachers Against the Nazis, School Kids Against the Nazis, Skateboarders Against the Nazis, Football Fans Against the Nazis – all with the aim of rejecting racist and fascist ideas in these diverse sites. Trade unionists – radicalised by the class struggles of the early 1970s, and eventually won to anti-racist ideas by socialist activists – also participated in ANL-led events. In February 1979, 200 people attended a Miners Against the Nazis conference held in Barnsley. Speakers included Arthur Scargill, television presenter Jonathan Dimbleby, Paul Holborow, and Alex Biswas. The Port of London shop stewards committee affiliated to the ANL – an important achievement given they had struck in support of Powell in 1968.

Racist attacks didn't suddenly stop with the formation of the ANL. Altab Ali – a Bangladeshi clothing machinist from Wapping – was murdered just days after the first ANL festival at Victoria Park. There were others too. As a result, running parallel to the Carnivals and other such events were the marches and demonstrations against the NF. Between November 1977 and April 1979, the NF and the ANL along with the black and Asian communities found themselves locked in a perpetual struggle with each side adapting their repertoire of actions to accommodate, negotiate and circumvent the other's activities. In one such demonstration held in Southall, West London on 23 April 1979, amid sustained fighting between the police and members of the ANL, IWA, Peoples' Unite and the Southall Youth Movement, Blair Peach – a New Zealand schoolteacher and ANL activist – was killed. Peach had come to demonstrate his opposition to the NF and their attempts to march provocatively though an area of significant Indian Sikh settlement. It was perhaps the NF's growing association with social disorder that was to dash their hopes of electoral success (Messina 1989). One month after Southall, and despite standing in over 300 seats, the NF managed to save only a handful of deposits at the General Election of May 1979 with their national vote reduced to 1.3 per cent.

The Anti-Nazi League: An assessment

Did the ANL contribute to the decline of the National Front? There is no simple answer to this question. The replacement of Edward Heath in 1975 – the arch enemy of the racist right in the Tory Party – by Margaret Thatcher – a leading representative of the new right – marked an important shift in Conservative politics, including their position on race, that was little appreciated at the time. In January 1978, Mrs Thatcher on Granada TV had claimed:

> I think people are really rather afraid that this country might be rather swamped by people with a different culture and, you know, the British character has done so much for democracy and law, and has done so much throughout the world, that if there is any fear that it might be swamped, people are going to be really rather hostile to those coming in.
>
> (Widgery 1986: 14)

Such a statement amounted to a political dogwhistle inviting those disaffected Tories that had joined the National Front in disgust at Heath's censure of

Powell, to come home to their natural party of affiliation because the house had been put back in order.

While this undoubtedly constituted the primary 'pull' factor in drawing disaffected Conservatives back into the fold, it was the activities of the ANL that constituted the 'push' factor which made many of those Empire-loving Conservatives – currently aligned with the National Front – realize that their concerns would be better served in the party of Margaret Thatcher. In 1982, when Peter Hain brought a libel case against Martin Webster – one of the leaders of the National Front – he recalled Webster claiming how

> ... prior to 1977, the NF were unstoppable and he was well on the way to becoming Prime Minister. Then suddenly the Anti-Nazi League was everywhere and knocked hell out of them. It obviously still hurt. He said that the sheer presence of the ANL had made it impossible to get NF members on the streets, had dashed recruitment and cut away at their vote.
>
> (Hain cited in Widgery 1986: 111)

It was precisely this capacity of the ANL to fashion, and then mobilize a community of anti-racists, of committed 'white' anti-racists in particular, that undermined the National Front, and forced many of the racist middle classes and deferential working class Tories to retreat back into the Conservative Party. Further, it is highly unlikely that such a community of mainly working class anti-racists would have emerged in the mid-1970s had it not been for the political radicalization that took place among important sectors of the working class (including working class youth). And key to bringing that working class revolt into some kind of alignment with the struggle against racism were the mediating forces of the socialist left.

Interestingly, the definitive scholarly assessment of the ANL – Britain's first and only mass anti-fascist social movement – provided by Paul Gilroy (1987) is extremely critical of the ANL. In contrast to his favourable interpretation of RAR, Gilroy levels two criticisms at the ANL. First, he contends that its formation reduced an emergent struggle against racism and capitalism to one of challenging fascism. That is, unlike RAR who operated with a broad conception of racism that linked 'the activity of the neo-fascists directly to the actions of state agencies, particularly the courts, police and immigration authorities' (Gilroy 1987: 157), the ANL sought to:

> ... impose the elimination of Nazism as a priority on the diverse and complex political consciousness crystallised by RAR ... The narrow definition of the problem of 'race' – as a product of fascism ... imposed a shorter life and more limited aims on the movement. The goals of anti-racism were being re-defined. The Rasta-inspired pursuit of 'Equal Rights and Justice' was being forsaken ... replaced by the more modest aim of isolating and eliminating the fascist parties at the polls.
>
> (Gilroy 1987: 172)

A key difficulty with Gilroy's line of reasoning however is how he sharply juxtaposes RAR to ANL leaving the reader with the impression that the ANL in some way replaced or subsumed RAR to its narrower form of political action. Instead, the two organizations were deeply complementary throughout their largely over-lapping existence. While RAR was established in September 1976 – 15 months before the ANL – it only arranged its first music event in December 1976 while the first issue of its magazine – *Temporary Hoarding* – was produced as late as May 1977, that is, just six months before the formation of the ANL (Widgery 1986; Renton 2006). RAR's existence not only largely coincided with that of the ANL's, but it markedly increased its activities after the ANL's establishment when its broader anti-racist, anti-capitalist message reached a far larger audience as a result of the exponential growth in musical events that took place from early 1978. RAR was never simply the 'ents. division of the ANL' (Widgery 1986). Its original founders had hoped for just such a complementarity when they had called for a 'rank and file movement against the racist poison in rock music' and for 'black and white to unite and fight along the fundamental lines of class' (Goodyer 2009).

Relatedly, Gilroy caricatures the ANL as operating within some kind of hermetically sealed box that prevented ideas about racism and capitalism 'leaking' into its work. Not only were there significant overlapping networks of personnel in RAR and ANL (see Goodyer 2009) but he ignores the extent to which the ANL itself was a broad, mainly socialist coalition of anti-racist and anti-fascist individuals and groups. There were those like the SWP and IMG who were socialist internationalists and others – in the CPGB and the Labour Party – who were mainly socialist nationalists. Alongside coming together to combat the NF, they also engaged in a healthy debate about fascism and its relationship to racism and capitalism. One indication of this broader discussion was the debate and then subsequent adoption of a policy of opposition to all immigration controls at the first ANL national conference held in 1978. Further, the SWP – the main political party behind the ANL's formation – regularly published material about state racism and produced placards for demonstrations that explicitly stated 'Stop the Nazis; No Immigration Controls', thus making clear to all who attended the links between state racism and fascism (Davidson 2006). Those who participated in ANL-related activities also carried on with their anti-racist consciousness-raising and other related work through their individual trade unions, in their communities, as well as in their own political formations. It is curious for example, that Gilroy has nothing to say about the emergent anti-racism in the trade union movement nor the Grunwick dispute in particular. The monochromatic picture of the ANL that Gilroy paints bears little resemblance to the complex, fluid, social movement of diverse political currents that the League actually was. And no hermetically sealed boundary between anti-fascism and a broader anti-racist consciousness could be sustained for very long in such circumstances.

The second criticism Gilroy levels at the ANL is that they effected a shift from anti-racism to anti-fascism by summoning a form of British nationalism and patriotism:

> The idea that the British Nazis were merely sham patriots who soiled the British flag by their use of it was a strong feature of ANL leaflets. This inauthentic patriotism was exposed and contrasted with the genuine nationalist spirit which had been created in Britain's finest hour – the 'anti-fascist' 1939–45 war.
>
> (Gilroy 1987: 171)

According to Gilroy (1987: 173), this shift in political direction was driven by the ANL leadership's desire to make a 'concerted appeal to older voters, and involved a direct appeal to their memories of anti-fascism in the 1930s and 1940s' (Gilroy 1987: 173). Further, he contends that while emphasising

> ...the Nazi character of neo-fascist and racist politics to the exclusion of every other consideration... may have lead to the electoral defeat of the NF, British Movement and their allies... this was achieved ironically by reviving the very elements of nationalism and xenophobia which had seen Britannia through the darkest hours of the Second World War.
>
> (Gilroy 1987: 174–175)

Again, it is difficult to sustain these claims, particularly in the light of the publication of Renton's (2006) history of the ANL. This book-length analysis of the ANL has the virtue of drawing on extensive archival research of original campaigning literature including newspapers, newsletters, fanzines, and other political ephemera and combining it with more than 80 interviews with leading activists. What emerges clearly from his account is that the images of war, of concentration camps, and of National Front members dressed in Nazi uniform were intended to draw the public's attention to the dangers of fascists acquiring state power. It aimed at constructing an association – both visually and in writing – of the NF being the modern-day exponents of Nazi racism. As Roger Huddle, founding member of RAR, and a leading ANL activist explains:

> The argument wasn't about the war; it was about what fascism was. We had to show that the NF stood for the camps, the swastika, the death camps for the Jews and the Roma.
>
> (cited in Renton 2006: 126)

After an exhaustive study of the archival material, Renton (2006: 127) concludes that

> such language is almost entirely absent from any of the ANL's publications. The references in League material to the heroes of the Second World War,

the positive descriptions of 'Britannia', are simply not there...these anti-fascists never claimed that the best alternative to the National Front was a return to Britain's wartime spirit.

Gilroy's insistence on reading the activities of the ANL by employing a colour-coded understanding of racism homogenizes the 'white' experience in Britain, and renders invisible the often related histories of racist oppression of social groups perceived as white. Applying a multi-modal understanding of racism helps to uncover how many of those activists leading and partici-pating in the ANL were themselves of minority descent. Alongside a strand of Caribbean and Indian activists including figures like Tony Bogues, Kim Gordon, Balwinder Rana, Avtar Jouhl and Vishnu Sharma there was also significant Irish Catholic and Jewish involvement. Some of the individuals of Jewish descent who played an instrumental role in the ANL included Miriam Karlin, Maurice Ludmer, Steve Jefferys, Dave Landau, Neil Rogall, Sherrl Yanowitz, David Rosenberg, Tony Cliff, Chanie Rosenberg and John Rose. Equally significant were the activists of Irish Catholic descent includ-ing Jerry Fitzpatrick, Mickey Fenn, Ted Parker, Eddie Prevost and Eamonn McCann.

These individuals were the most unlikely group of 'white people' to sum-mon a traditional conception of British nationalism to fashion an anti-fascist social movement as one could possibly find in 1970s Britain. Instead, they were instrumental in the ANL's formation because concern about the racism directed at Asians and blacks had activated their own histories of racist and religious oppression. Further, both those of Jewish and Irish Catholic descent continued to experience some degree of anti-Semitism and anti-Irish racism in 1970s Britain. While the National Front continued to reproduce its anti-Semitic racism by representing 'the Jew' as the 'enemy within', a mediating virus drawing 'coloured aliens' to British shores in ever increasing numbers, those of Irish Catholic descent were reminded of their own problematic status in Britain when, in 1969, the RUC moved into the Bogside in Belfast using CS gas against Catholics marching for civil rights (Hall et al. 1978: 259).

The troubles in Northern Ireland helped maintain a steady flow of Irish Catholic men and women into the socialist movement throughout the 1970s, not only from Northern Ireland itself, but also from within the mainly work-ing class Irish Catholic diaspora on the British mainland. Ted Parker and Jerry Fitzpatrick – organizers of the anti-fascist demonstration at Lewisham in August 1977 were both of Irish Catholic descent with Fitzpatrick an activist in the Free Derry campaign. 'I came from an Irish background. I had been at Derry in 1969. I had seen the resistance on the Bogside – that was a factor. We wanted to organize in the same way' (cited in Renton 2006: 51). These activists utilised ethnic networks of the Irish diaspora to help build the anti-NF protests at Lewisham:

There were lots of Irish people who provided us with logistics and support...There was an Irish hall next to our centre. We were allowed into there, and into the Irish pubs and dances, to raise money, to speak about the NF as the latest incarnation of British imperialism, and to appeal for support.

(cited in Renton 2006: 58)

This mobilization of the Irish Catholic diaspora continued with the formation of the ANL. Mike Barton – an activist in the ANL office – recalls the large numbers of Irish people 'involved in the Anti-Nazi League, second generation, whose families had been victims of discrimination in the past.' He recounted a particular incident involving Jimmy Fenn – a lightweight boxer – who found himself subject to taunts of 'race traitor' by NF members while attending an anti-fascist demonstration. Barton recounts how he responded with a series of gestures that suggested 'Me? A race traitor? No. I'm Irish' (cited in Renton 2006: 129). More broadly, it is perhaps no coincidence that the biggest contingents that attended the ANL carnivals in London came from Glasgow, Manchester and Liverpool (Widgery 1986: 84) – three of the main areas of Irish Catholic settlement where sectarianism and discrimination continued to structure their local employment opportunities (Neal 1988; Devine 2000). Significantly, this Irish Catholic solidarity with the ANL in Britain was reciprocated in 1979 and 1980 when the ANL led by Fitzpatrick arranged – with John Dennis and John Ellis – a Rock Against Racism Tour to Belfast and Derry in support of the H-block prisoners on hunger strike for political status (Renton 2006).

It is important to remember however that the Irish Catholic population in Britain were not immune to the politics of the National Front. Mickey Fenn – docker and ANL activist – observed how he was forced into regularly challenging the racism of Irish Catholic skinheads:

...what was so disturbing about these kids, you know, these skins out in Barking and Becontree and Dagenham way when you talk to them. Half of them have families from Ireland anyway. They've got some ideas about what's wrong with the world. But their only way of explaining anything is the easy one...black. Because they can see them.

(Widgery 1986: 14–16)

Ignatiev (1995), Roediger (1991, 1994) and others have also convincingly demonstrated how in the US, Irish Catholics embraced a white identification as a way of securing a pathway to upward social mobility. In Britain however, their incorporation into a racializing British nationalism underpinned by a shared whiteness was always more problematic because of the ongoing troubles in Northern Ireland, and the longer history of colonial subjugation. Only by collectively forgetting this centuries long history of colonial oppression by the British state could they be drawn to such politics.

What remains decisive in comprehending the formation, and subsequent success of the ANL, is the contribution made by a multi-ethnic group of social-ist activists. It was as Walter Benjamin (2006) reminds us, the resurrection of the 'picture of enslaved forbears' that stimulated such people into collective action, and led them to forge one of the most influential progressive social movements in British history.

8

Municipal Anti-Racism and Black Self-Organization

There really is no alternative.
> (Margaret Thatcher, Press Conference for American Correspondents, London, 25 June 1980)

None so fit to break the chains than those that bear them.
> (NALGO National Black Members Co-ordinating Committee, London, no date)

Introduction

Looking back at the 1980s from the vantage point of the present, it would be easy to represent the period as one characterized by uninterrupted working class defeat. In May 1979, Margaret Thatcher led the Conservatives to victory, promising to cure 'the sick man of Europe' by defeating the power of the organized working class and unleashing the potential of free market capitalism. By 1987, she and the Conservatives had inflicted a third consecutive defeat on the Labour Party, confirming in the minds of many – including within the Labour Party itself – that 'there really is no alternative'. The co-ordinates of the political settlement in Britain were undoubtedly re-set. The bipartisan consensus built around the welfare settlement was replaced by a commitment to individualism and the free market heralding the era of neoliberalism.

However, there are dangers in flattening history. It is sometimes easy to forget how divisive a figure Margaret Thatcher was during the 1980s. Even in the landslide victory at the 1983 general election, she secured just over the two-fifths of the popular vote. In particular, what such a broad-brush narrative masks is the scale and scope of the opposition that the Conservatives faced from workers, racialized minorities and other sections of society. Many will be familiar with the numerous set-piece confrontations, involving the carworkers,

145

miners and the dockers, as well as the seismic defeats they eventually suffered. However, other forms of collective resistance to the Thatcher juggernaut, particularly within the public sector and the local state, including against racism, have been the subject of far less attention and debate.

This chapter focuses on four questions. First, what were the economic and political consequences of the Conservative victory for black and Asian Britons? Second, what kinds of political strategies were employed to challenge racism in an era of consolidating neoliberalism? Third, and relatedly, what was the constellation of social forces that underpinned such resistance? And fourth, to what extent were these anti-racist social forces able to achieve their political objectives of combating racism and improving the lot of racialized minorities in a conjuncture characterized by working class defeat?

It demonstrates how black and Asian workers were disproportionately affected by the re-structuring of the British social formation. Rising levels of unemployment combined with increasing state harassment of black youth contributed to the urban unrest that unfolded in Britain in the early 1980s. However, socialist regroupment in the Labour Party – particularly in the South-East of England – followed by the conquest of local state power in multiple local authorities enabled the Labour Party to introduce policies that helped increase the numbers of minorities employed in non-manual local state work. This process was consolidated and arguably accelerated with the establishment of black self-organization in NALGO. These developments proved to be a catalyst, triggering similar trends throughout much of the public sector in the 1980s, as well as establishing the principle of black self-organization in the British trade union movement. Ultimately, they were responsible for an unprecedented transformation in the social and economic position of racialized minorities in British society, opening up key sectors of working class employment that had previously been closed to them. Given the adverse political conditions under which such social change was secured, it was nothing short of remarkable that the returns of 1970s anti-racism were actually consolidated in the 1980s.

Conservative victory, de-industrialization and the urban unrest

The Conservative victory at the May 1979 general election marked a decisive turning point in British history. Although they secured just over two-fifths of the popular vote (43.9 per cent), the Conservatives interpreted their electoral success as a mandate to rescue British capitalism and instantly initiated a series of radical policy initiatives ideologically informed by a new right perspective, known today as neoliberalism (Hall and Massey 2010). One of the most significant moves was to curb the power of trade unions who they alleged were the primary agents of economic inefficiency in the British economy (Marsh

1992; Taylor 1994). In particular, job protection and restrictive practices – born from union power – were highlighted as distorting the operation of the market economy (Dickens and Hall 1995).

The proposals contained in the 1977 Ridley Plan revealed Conservative intentions to wage a series of carefully orchestrated set-piece confrontations that would break the power of key unions, beginning with industries in which the unions were thought to be weak, leaving the most powerful groups of workers like the miners and dockers until last (Sked and Cook 1993). Within the first two years of its rule, the employers, aided by the Conservative administration, had successfully defeated different sections of the working class in bitter, drawn-out disputes, including most significantly the steel workers, and those employed in the West Midlands car plants.

By 1981, a distinctive pattern was unfolding that would increasingly define the character of industrial relations throughout the 1980s: rank and file anger at the new managerial practices provoking explosive bouts of strike action that would fail to generate the necessary solidarity action from workers in other industries; a vacillating trade union leadership split between those who were unable to face up to the changed relations of force – characterized by an increasingly aggressive employing class, and an unsympathetic government – and others who wished to negotiate and accommodate to these changing relations of force.

Accompanying the macho-management holding out against strikes was 'the systematic removal of collective and individual employment rights and the impositions of restrictions on various forms of unionised political activity' including the 1980 Employment Act which made picketing away from the picket's own workplace unlawful (Eldridge et al. 1991: 86). Further, the Conservatives' rejection of incomes policies and government intervention in the economy and the increased emphasis placed on the need for strict monetarist measures to control the rate of inflation went hand in hand with a major programme of public spending cuts and privatization of state-held assets (Colling and Ferner 1995; Winchester and Bach 1995). It was these policies that were to contribute to the recession of 1979–1981 when unemployment doubled from 1.14 million (4.7 per cent of civil employment) in June 1979 to 2.3 million (9.4 per cent of the labour force) in June 1981 (Kessler and Bayliss 1995: 42). Manufacturing employment was particularly adversely affected with a quarter of all jobs being lost between 1979 and 1983 (Eldridge et al. 1991: 32).

Significantly, the Conservatives undertook these initiatives comfortable in the knowledge that they had secured the consent of a stratum of the working class – one that was atomized, individualistically oriented, and averse to socialist politics (Hall 1983). This stratum had been successfully mobilized around an 'authoritarian populist' agenda (Hall 1983) whose distinctive elements emphasized self-reliance over government intervention, of individualism over collectivism, and a racializing nationalism underpinned by a shared allegiance to cultural homogeneity. This vision was counterposed by Thatcher to the unassimilable, the enemy within, made up variously of racialized minorities, trade unions, socialists, feminists and other alleged 'social deviants'.

Thatcherism had a devastating impact on the collective psyche of the working class, including the not insignificant minority that had continued to collectively resist such changes between 1976 and 1979. Successive defeats coupled with an increasingly adverse economic and political climate had undermined the efficacy of collective action. From now on, workers would be less confident about taking collective action, and when they did, they did so reluctantly and with less confidence than ever before. The wave of industrial action that had engulfed the country since the late 1960s began to slowly subside as the employing class, ably supported by the Conservative government, began to carry through 'a decisive shift in the balance of class forces such as had not been seen since the defeat of the General Strike in the 1920s' (Harman 1985: 73).

How did this process of industrial restructuring that followed the Thatcherite reforms impact on the racialized minority fraction of the working class? What is often presented by sociologists as a race-neutral class-based process of industrial re-structuring (see for example Eldridge et al. 1991) was in actual fact deeply racialized. The over-representation of racialized minorities in the manufacturing sector of British industry in 1980 and 1981 (Brown 1982) was the product of the deeply embedded racism and discrimination that scarred the post-war era of the welfare settlement when they had been denied skilled manual work and white collar jobs. Thus, racism and disadvantage were inscribed into the contemporary class structure of British society, and it was this relationship of racism to class that helps us to understand why black and Asian minorities were disproportionately affected by the re-structuring of the British social formation (Virdee 2006, 2010). Alongside the devastating impact of job losses in manufacturing industry on minorities in general, black youth in particular found themselves increasingly unable to secure jobs in the remaining sectors of manufacturing employment due to the widespread operation of racist discriminatory practices (Wrench 1986). The resultant rising levels of black youth unemployment (Brown 1982) accompanied by their systematic harassment by the police combined to create a kind of tipping point (Solomos 1988).

In April 1981, in Brixton, South London, a riot broke out a week after the local police launched Swamp 81 – an operation designed to combat an alleged increase in muggings and street crime: 'For a week 120 officers, working in plainclothes, walked the streets, with specific instructions to stop and question "persistently and accurately" anyone who looked suspect' (Race and Class 1981: 224). The police had focused their attention overwhelmingly on black youth who in turn accused them of treating 'us like dirt' (cited in Race and Class 1981: 225). Such state racism was a crucial ingredient in the toxic cocktail that Thatcherism was constructing around its authoritarian populist

agenda, a racism where blackness and Britishness were re-produced as mutually exclusive categories (Gilroy 1987). However, such state racism also served
to legitimize and embolden the National Front as the events in Southall in
July 1981 testify when coachloads of skinheads gathered at the Hambrough
Tavern, shouting racist abuse and attacking Asian residents. It was in response
to such provocation that hundreds of Asian youth came on to the streets and
besieged the pub until it was eventually set ablaze with petrol bombs (Race
and Class 1981: 225).

While The Specials' *Ghost Town* – aptly reflecting on the industrial and
social malaise in Thatcher's Britain – topped the UK pop charts, the Brixton
and Southall riots were quickly followed by riots in over 30 towns and cities
throughout July 1981 reflecting the more general feelings of anger and loss of
hope within black, Asian and white working class communities under threat of
annihilation by the neoliberal Thatcherite juggernaut. In Toxteth, Liverpool,
Moss Side in Manchester and many other small towns and cities, working class
youth took to the streets refusing to accept the dystopian future that lay ahead
for them, collectively resisting any attempts by the police to restore 'law and
order'. By the end of the summer of 1981, more than 3,000 people had been
arrested (cited in Race and Class 1981: 229).

The Scarman Inquiry (1981) into the Brixton disorder strongly rejected the
existence of institutional racism within British society generally, and the police
force more specifically. Instead, it recommended a number of positive action
measures to address the scourge of what it termed 'racial disadvantage', which
reconceived the 'problem' as one of creating a black middle class while at the
same time leaving the racialized class inequalities facing black working class
people untouched. Apart from offering some qualified support to the findings contained in the Report (see Raison 1984: 244–257), the Conservative
government remained resolutely averse to introducing even these mildly ame-
liorative reforms. Such aversion was probably strengthened by the fact that
much of the tabloid press forcefully denied the roots of the unrest as being the
result of racism and discrimination; instead, they tried to criminalize the events
by claiming they were the product of a black criminal underbelly within society (Solomos 1988). The Labour Party in opposition, whilst acknowledging
the material roots of the unrest, offered little in the way of practical support
to the rioters other than renewing their call for the re-election of a Labour
government (Ball and Solomos 1990).

Drawing inferences from previous instances of large-scale working class
defeat – such as that which occurred in the aftermath of the new unionism
in the mid-1890s – one might have predicted that Britain would see a consolidation in racist sentiment – not just emanating from the state and employers,
but also parts of the working class, as attempts were made to reintegrate the
population around an imagined national interest. While there is little doubt
that racism was a crucial element to the Thatcherite political project throughout much of the 1980s, including most importantly in terms of policing and

immigration legislation (Gilroy 1987; Solomos 1988), what has been little
commented upon is the fact that significant parts of the working class, and
activist base of the organized labour movement, did not retreat into racism.
That is, participation in social movements like RAR and the ANL alongside the
important anti-racist transformations within the labour movement appear to
have consolidated a durable anti-racist consciousness within significant layers
of white youth and organized workers. Further, such anti-racist gains, particularly in the aftermath of the urban unrest of 1981, were extended into the
1980s.

Socialist regroupment in the Labour Party and municipal anti-racism

Paradoxically, running parallel to the urban unrest and the series of defeats
inflicted on the working class in the industrial sphere in the early 1980s was the
marked upturn in the fortunes of the socialist left in the Labour Party. Disappointed by the Labour government under Callaghan, particularly its attempts
to make the working class pay for the economic crisis under the terms of the
Social Contract, many party activists had shifted their allegiance to the socialist left by the mid-1970s. Their active participation in the large anti-racist and
anti-fascist social movements of that period was one indication of this radicalization in political consciousness. The Conservative general election victory of
May 1979 further bolstered their strength, confirming in their eyes that the
Labour government had lost because it had failed to implement the socialist policies contained in its manifesto of October 1974. From May 1979, the
Labour left focused its energies on democratizing the Labour Party constitution, believing that making the leadership more accountable to the rank and
file activist would ensure the implementation of socialist policies, especially
those contained in the package of measures known as the 'alternative strategy'.

   This socialist left was made up of diverse and sometimes conflicting currents,
and included such prominent 'class struggle' socialists such as Arthur Scargill,
Dennis Skinner, and Eric Heffer along with the Trotskyist formation, Militant.
Further, there was a growing New Left influence within Labour, particularly
in the Greater London area, represented by such figures as Ken Livingstone,
Linda Bellos and Ted Knight.

   Their attempts to break out of the traditional Labour Party concern for class
and its understanding that 'the only oppression is economic oppression' was
decisive in helping to draw into their orbit many activists from the new social
movements including feminist, peace and antiracist activists. It was around the
totemic figure of Tony Benn – the former Labour Cabinet minister – that this
constellation of socialist forces rallied in their quest to find the best political solutions to defend the diverse but complementary concerns of workers,
racialized minorities, women, gays and peace activists against the ravages of an
unrestrained capitalist and conservative offensive.

Important successes were achieved including in 1980 when the Labour Party conference agreed to support its demands for the mandatory reselection of MPs once in every parliament, and an electoral college comprising all sections of the Labour Party (including the Constituency Labour Parties (CLP's)) when electing the party leader. In the summer of 1981, at a special Labour Party conference, Tony Benn narrowly missed securing the deputy leadership of the Party. Significantly, amid the wider crisis on the left resulting from the major defeats of the organized working class in the industrial sphere, such successes, however modest, instilled a sense of hope among socialist activists that the Labour Party might yet become a vehicle for collective working class resistance, and perhaps even socialism. Such hopes and aspirations would be immediately put to the test, first in London, and then in other local authorities, throughout many of the main conurbations of Britain.

Just weeks before the Brixton riot in April 1981, the London Labour Party had launched its manifesto for the forthcoming GLC elections in which it declared its commitment to making services and resources accessible and relevant to minority needs; providing an equal and fair share of jobs and training opportunities; creating a public image embracing all of London's racialized minority groups, and establishing new initiatives to combat racism (cited in Ouseley 1990: 139). In May 1981, the London Labour Party won the GLC elections, and the day after, Ken Livingstone challenged Andrew McIntosh for the leadership and defeated him. Livingstone (1984: 17–18), like much of the London Labour left, had been shaped by the politics of the New Left and was a committed anti-racist who recognized that the Labour Party had to 'articulate the needs of minorities and the dispossessed in a way that Labour governments and the Labour Party never have in the past ... and really make the Labour Party represent the working class living in inner London.' Further, he was determined to use the GLC – a large local authority with a high public profile and significant material resources and power – to rectify the historical failure of the Labour Party to combat racism and the inequalities that arose from it: 'we can't underestimate the fact that more than any other institution the Left has ever got its hands on, the GLC is a mechanism for the redistribution of wealth on a grand scale' (Livingstone 1984: 19).

As part of its municipal anti-racist strategy, the GLC under Livingstone's leadership launched a number of initiatives using the full powers given to local authorities by Section 71 of the 1976 Race Relations Act and related legislation. The most significant of these included:

(a) positive action measures designed to remove discriminatory barriers to full equality of opportunity (for example rethinking job application requirements, placing jobs advertisements in the minority press) and to encourage minority group participation in education and the labour force by providing additional training and education (by using section 11 of the 1966 Local Government Act to create new posts);

(b) contract compliance programmes that required companies tendering for contracts from the GLC to adhere to an equal opportunities policy and develop strategies for implementing it;
(c) training strategies designed to increase awareness of processes of discrimination and to encourage the implementation of equality policies (Solomos and Ball 1990: 211).

Significantly, such anti-discriminatory measures were underpinned by support for the principle of black self-organization where minorities were encouraged to come together 'free of the influence of white people, discuss the discrimination they feel, decide how to articulate their demands and then come forward to the movement with proposals for change' (Livingstone 1984: 22). This deliberately more inclusive approach was part of a broader strategy adopted by the London Labour Party that aimed to empower all oppressed groups, including women and gay and lesbian people, by providing a political space in which to frame and articulate their concerns in a way that was acceptable to them. Alongside the establishment of an Ethnic Minorities Unit, the GLC also established 'consultation networks with the black communities of London' thereby enabling them to feed in directly to the policy formation process (Livingstone 1984: 22).

These were dramatic changes introduced by the ruling Labour Party under Livingstone, particularly given that in 'its pre-1981 existence', it 'had made no positive impact on black people's lives' having a reputation instead 'for channeling black households into the most deficient and least desirable public housing accommodation' and having 'very few black people on the payroll, the vast majority of whom were in low grade and low status occupations' (Ouseley 1990: 139). Herman Ouseley (1990: 140) – a leading race relations adviser at the GLC at the time – recalls how County Hall suddenly became 'vibrant with excitement because of its new-found openness and sudden attractiveness for large numbers of people from the local communities. A previously uninviting building came to be dubbed the "People's Palace"'.

With the socialist left strengthening its position within the Labour Party during the early 1980s, many Labour-run local councils including Lambeth, Brent, Hackney, Haringey as well as Bradford, Manchester, Birmingham and ILEA followed the lead given by the GLC, and introduced important policy initiatives to combat racism and discrimination in the areas of employment, social services, education, housing and policing (see Ball and Solomos 1990). These changes in policy and practice not only allowed the Labour left to consolidate its support base within the black and Asian communities during the early 1980s, but also served to draw in much of the remaining activist base that had remained outside the Labour Party. Tariq Ali of the International Marxist Group (IMG) justified this volte-face by contending that under the influence of Bennism and municipal socialists like Livingstone 'a new socialist party could be seen struggling to emerge from the shell of Labourism' and a genuine possibility existed of 'turning the entire organization into a gigantic lever of popular political mobilizations, championing the causes of all sectors of the oppressed and offering a governmental perspective of real change' (Ali cited in *Socialist Review* 1981).

At the same time, there were others like Ambalavanar Sivanandan – black Marxist and Director of the Institute of Race Relations (IRR) – who were more skeptical. He wrote a withering critique of municipal socialism's anti-racism strategy alleging that because 'the white Left had no socialist frame of reference to fight racism' (Sivanandan 1990: 149), in the aftermath of the urban rebellions they turned to the liberal recommendations contained in the Scarman Report (1981) to combat 'racial disadvantage' through the promotion of equality of opportunity and the distribution of local authority funding on the basis of 'ethnic need'. The latter was to prove especially disastrous he charged because

> The fight against racism became a fight for culture, and culture itself was evacuated of its economic and political significance to mean lifestyle, language, custom, artifact. And black, from being a 'political colour', was broken down into its cultural parts of West Indian, Asian, African – and these in turn reduced to their ethnic constituents... there was a sudden flowering of a thousand ethnic groups. Everybody was ethnic now – Irish, Italians, Rastas, Sikhs, Chinese, Jews, Bengalis, Gypsies – and they all vied with each other for 'ethnic handouts' and 'ethnic positions' and set themselves against each other, politiking for 'ethnic power'.
>
> (Sivanandan 1990: 147–148)

In a speech made to the GLC EM Unit in 1983 – the citadel of municipal anti-racism – Sivanandan (1990: 63) continued that

> I come as a heretic, as a disbeliever in the efficacy of ethnic policies and programmes to alter by one iota, the monumental and endemic racism of this society... On the contrary. What ethnicity has done is to mask the problem of racism and weaken the struggle against it.

Further, he claimed that while the intention may have been to help minorities overcome their 'specific disadvantages', what such policies effectively did was absolve the 'state and its institutions of racism', with the burden of 'racial disadvantage' passed on to the minorities themselves 'as though it were they who were wanting in something' (Sivanandan 1990: 148). Consequently, Sivanandan contended that the only beneficiaries of the urban unrest were the black petit-bourgeoisie who in a number of social spaces (media, police consultancy, the Labour Party and so on) were able to appropriate the politics of blackness, create self-organized structures to further their own specific class interests, and in the process, wrench apart a more authentic political blackness based on the living, organic connections that had been forged in the course of the struggles of the 1960s and 1970s involving themselves and 'ordinary black people' (Sivanandan 1990):

> They do not come out of the struggles of ordinary black people in the inner-cities – and they do not relate to them – but they have attached themselves to black struggles, like limpets, the more readily to gain office.... There is no such thing as a black-qua-black movement any more. There are middle class blacks fighting for a place in the (white) middle-class sun and there are workless and working-class blacks fighting for survival and basic freedoms.
>
> (Sivanandan 1990: 124–126)

Although there is much of value in Sivanandan's analysis, particularly his observation about the creation of a class of black professionals occupying a contradictory class position (Wright 1985, 1997), there is little evidence of a systematic assessment of the relative effectiveness of the wide range of policies introduced by local councils to curb the racist discrimination and inequality faced by working class black and Asian people in important areas of social life including housing, employment and social services.

One major site which illustrates the scale and scope of the transformation effected by many radical Labour councils is employment. Prior to the urban rebellions of the early 1980s, most local authorities throughout Britain, including those led by Labour, had singularly failed to open up local state work to black workers to any significant extent. In areas of significant minority concentration such as Greater London, black and Asian workers remained substantially under-represented in such work. In Lambeth, only 4 per cent of the workforce were black and Asian in the late 1970s while black and Asian employment in the GLC was minimal (Mayet 1986: 58; Ouseley 1990). In Hackney – a long-established area of minority settlement – only 11 per cent of the council workforce was black and Asian (Ouseley 1990: 151, table 8.1). However, between 1981 and 1986, the GLC 'more than trebled the number of black staff, many of whom obtained middle-ranking positions and raised consciousness about racism' (Ouseley 1990: 141). The GLC acted as a catalyst encouraging other local authorities to launch similar anti-racist initiatives resulting in further increases in representation of black staff in local state work. In Lambeth, black employment in such work rose from 4 per cent in the late 1970s to nearly 20 per cent in 1986 (Mayet 1986: 58), while in north-east London in Hackney, it rose from 11 per cent in 1981 to 27 per cent in 1986, and then 35 per cent in 1988 (Ouseley 1990: 151, table 8.1). In Ealing, only 3 per cent of the workforce were of Caribbean or South Asian descent in 1986 whereas by 1989 this had increased to 20 per cent (London Borough of Ealing 1990: 7–8). Similar changes were seen in other radical-run Labour authorities like Camden such that by the late 1980s, 26 per cent of its workforce was made up of black and Asian workers (London Borough of Camden

1996: 22). Most Greater London local authorities followed suit and increased the numbers of black and Asian workers employed in their offices over the course of the 1980s, and similar developments unfolded in some of the other urban local authorities throughout Britain such as Birmingham, Manchester and Bradford (Ball and Solomos 1990).

As can be seen, the scale and scope of the transformation in employment within local authorities extended far beyond the creation of a small elite of 'race-wallahs' or a black petit-bourgeois class of race professionals that Sivanandan refers to. The full significance of these social changes can only be grasped when they are set against the backdrop of the neo-liberal restructuring of manufacturing employment, and its disproportionately adverse impact on racialized minorities. The opening up of local state employment in radical Labour-run local authorities in the aftermath of the urban unrest helped protect parts of the minority population from an impending catastrophe. Through such employment, it gave them a degree of economic and psychic security that would otherwise have been unimaginable in Thatcher's Britain. Further, what radical critics of municipal anti-racism ignored was the part played by black self-organization in effecting such a transformation. The increased availability of such employment opportunities wasn't a gift bestowed on minorities by radical Labour-run authorities, but something which that early cohort of black and Asian workers entering local state employment actively pressed for through black self-organization in the local state unions (see Virdee and Grint 1994). This was one of the unintended consequences of municipal socialism's anti-racist strategy, and its ripple effects were to eventually transform large parts of the British trade union movement.

'Don't discuss blacks behind our backs': Black workers' groups from NALGO to the TUC

That cohort of black and Asian workers that entered local state employment in the early 1980s joined the National and Local Government Officers' Association (NALGO). NALGO had a reasonable record in combatting racism having passed its first anti-racist motion at its national conference in 1968 (NBMCC no date: 6). Further, it played an influential role in challenging the National Front, particularly through its participation in the activities of the Anti-Nazi League (*Public Service* July/August 1978: 9). Significantly, and unlike many of the manual trades unions that were being defeated in set-piece confrontations against the employers and the state leading to large losses in membership, NALGO avoided such a fate, and retained a significantly large membership throughout the 1980s.

Many of the black and Asian workers who joined NALGO in the early 1980s had actively participated in the campaigns against racism and fascism during the 1970s, and they were determined to continue this campaign in local government and beyond. Their preferred strategy of organizing was black self-organization which presumed that those who were the subject of racism should have the primary voice in determining how the union challenged it. Or as one document produced by their national body put it there are 'none so fit to break their chains as those that bear them' (National Black Members' Co-ordinating Committee (NBMCC) no date). By 1982, black workers' groups had been 'formed all over Britain at break-neck speed' (NBMCC no date: 7). Significantly, they acknowledged the political debt owed to those who had participated in the urban unrest in forcing open non-manual local state work for those like themselves, as well as their responsibility to further anti-racist initiatives from within local government (NBMCC no date: 7). An organic connection between these anti-racist struggles was consciously constructed:

> ...this was 1982. The summer before had been the long hot one of the uprisings. Things would never be quite the same for NALGO again ... Black action had arrived.
>
> (NBMCC no date: 6)

These workers were determined to ensure that through self-organization, the union would be moved to mobilize its resources to challenge racism. However, the first step in achieving this goal was to secure the formal recognition of the principle of black self-organization within NALGO itself. Karen Chouhan – secretary of the NBMCC established within NALGO in 1983 – symbolically inaugurated this campaign with a forceful statement:

> As black trade unionists we must force the union to recognise the vital role it must play in fighting against exploitation and for equal rights. The 1980s, however, have been witness to an increased urgency for consolidation and action on equality. The black perspective is vital in the analysis, the policies and action of NALGO, and is the only thing which can hope to change the structures and services of the union so that black people are no longer an itch on someone's back but the very spine for solidarity, the first principle of trade unionism... It is not self-organisation for the sake of being separate. It is to ensure exactly the opposite that black issues and rights are addressed by the trade unions to which we belong in a way acceptable to black members. As black trade unionists we believe in the principles of solidarity and support but these can never happen if the union works only for some.
>
> (First Official National Black Members Conference 1986: 6)

Chouhan helped clarify that the intention behind the demand for black self-organization was not a desire for separatism, but rather that racism would be more effectively tackled if black trade unionists were able to define the problem first, on their own terms. However, this demand for self-organization was almost immediately opposed by some white members of NALGO who interpreted it as a form of special treatment. One member writing into the main newspaper of the union alleged:

> To me it is appalling that any people's organisation should have a sepa-
> rate section exclusive to those of a certain skin colour. Surely it is time we
> recognised that all people have the same needs and to sectionalise them
> according to skin colour merely weakens the power to influence national
> decisions.
>
> (*Public Service* June 1986: 6)

Such members advocated a 'colour-blind' approach that held strongly to the view that 'everybody ought to be treated the same'. However, it was also a view that allowed little space to acknowledge the existence of racism, its ability to adversely structure the lives of black workers, or the need for the union to challenge it. At the same time, another member objected to the demands of black activists to have a national black members' conference on the grounds that

> A conference restricted to black members sounds to me like the most bla-
> tant racism and apartheid. Whatever would your black members say if we
> insisted on having a conference restricted only to whites? Whatever they
> said would be well justified. The best way of combatting racism is to treat
> everyone alike and make no distinctions whatever based on a person's skin
> colour. And that will have to go for everyone.
>
> (*Public Service* June 1986: 6)

Such rank and file intransigence helped strengthen the position of NALGO's national leadership, the majority of whom refused to sanction black self-organization as the core principle informing the formation of a national strategy against racism. One leading NALGO executive member argued:

> I've got personal reservations about the policy of self-organization. The rise
> of self-organization has actually diverted energy to the sidelines...I think
> the principle of self-organization is not a way forward...I want a broad-
> based union...I don't want a little gay bit, a little black bit, a little
> disabled bit, and a little women's bit...The more we have of this sep-
> aratism...where you say you can't come to this meeting because you're
> white, the more I find it abhorrent.
>
> (cited in Virdee and Grint 1994: 208–209)

Instead, the counter-claim was advanced that 'because unity is strength and most NALGO members are white...any organization and structure devised by the union should ensure all members are involved, and white members are not "let off the hook" ' (NALGO 1984: 4). Furthermore,

All races should be involved in this work . . . It is important that [we] win the confidence of ethnic minority members, but also engage the full support of the white majority within the branches.

(NALGO 1984: 15)

However, the advocacy of a colour-blind, class-based approach to combating racism in a political context of generalized working class defeat, and one where the current of mass mobilizations against racism had largely disintegrated, would have effectively limited the scale and scope of anti-racist action the union took. The deadlock was broken by two developments. First, the numbers of black and Asian workers entering local state employment, and then joining NALGO, accelerated throughout the mid-1980s (Ball and Solomos 1990). The NALGO national executive found itself unable to prevent the establishment of a growing network of informal black workers' groups throughout the country. Second, black activists forged an alliance with the socialist left in NALGO comprising in particular members of the Labour Party, the SWP and other smaller socialist formations. These socialist activists had seen first-hand how such groups had not only succeeded in maintaining pressure on the union leadership to combat racism, but had helped to increase the participation of black workers in the union thereby making it more representative: 'until self-organisation developed . . . there were no black workers involved in any level of the union.' What was particularly noteworthy was the significance attached to the learning process. Such autonomously organized groups were not self-evidently advantageous to trade unions but their actions had demonstrated their utility to such activists:

I've seen a lot of activists who were in the black NALGO groups who are now active in the mainstream of the union. That's very important to me . . . I feel I should support them in their battles.

(Virdee and Grint 1994: 217)

It was this coalition between the black workers' groups and the socialist left that ensured the principle of black self-organization was ratified at the 1985 NALGO annual conference. Two motions were passed which committed the NALGO NEC to developing and promoting a positive action programme for the black members' groups at all levels of the union (NALGO 1986: 43). Further confirmation of union recognition for black self-organization followed when the NEC agreed to fund the next national black members' conference with each NALGO branch able to send up to six delegates to the conference of whom half were expected to be women (see NALGO 1986: 77–78; *Public Service* May 1986: 9). Black members hoped that the sanctioning of the conference would allow black members to voice their demands

...which NALGO must accede to, if it is serious about joining us in our fight to wipe out racism at all levels within its own structures and outside. These changes are long over-due.

(cited in *Public Service* May 1986: 9)

The first officially approved National Black Members' Conference was held in Leeds in May 1986 with more than '400 delegates and observers from all parts of the country, representing all NALGO services' attending (NALGO 1987: 79). By the mid-1980s then, one of the largest trade unions in Britain had officially committed itself to the principle of black self-organization allowing black and Asian workers to collectively determine and formulate the most appropriate strategy to combat racism. This was a historic achievement and one that would have repercussions throughout the public sector and the British trade union movement in the 1980s.

Pressed by the on-going transformations in local government, other large public sector employers, including most notably the Civil Service, the National Health Service as well as many government quangos, were forced to follow suit and introduce a raft of measures under the rubric of equal opportunities that attempted to create a more level playing field when it came to questions of recruitment and selection. Of course, employers like the NHS had long employed doctors and nurses of Caribbean and Asian descent, but most had been confined to the least desirable parts of their professions – the intention now became to challenge the representations and procedures that sustained such structural racialized inequalities (Beishon et al. 1995; Kyriakides and Virdee 2003).

The machinery of appointment in the Civil Service, the NHS and elsewhere was not as politicized as in local government, where radical Labour administrations had been elected on a firm commitment to transform the employment position of minorities in the aftermath of the urban unrest. Consequently, the danger remained that such commitments to alter recruitment and employment practices would be largely symbolic in nature. However, many of the racialized minorities that were already employed in such workplaces had themselves been radicalized by the urban unrest, and then by the developments in local government. As a result, they too began to self-organize within their unions, including most prominently, the NUCPS, CPSA, NUPE and COHSE.

Throughout the mid-1980s, the demand for black self-organization or some configuration thereof was secured – often in opposition to the union leaderships – across most large unions organizing within the public sector. It allowed black and Asian members to collectively feed into, and determine, official union responses to combating racism in the workplace and beyond. And through such self-organized structures, racialized minorities became a kind of catalytic agent that collectively brought its weight to bear on their unions, and through them, forced employers to further democratize the recruitment and selection process, contributing eventually to the significantly increased levels of black and Asian employment in these sectors during the 1980s and 1990s (Virdee 2006, 2010).

The ripples generated by the urban unrest, municipal anti-racism and black self-organization were eventually to reach the Trade Union Congress (TUC) itself. We saw previously how under pressure from socialist activists, and a series of strikes against racism by black workers, the TUC had finally moved to a position committing itself to challenging racism and fascism in the working class, and beyond. Such progress had continued throughout the 1980s, although perhaps more at a symbolic and ideological level. A number of policy documents had been introduced to undercut racism within its own ranks (e.g. TUC 1981, 1983, 1987, 1989), and in 1989, a rule had been passed at the annual conference allowing for the expulsion of union members for 'deliberate acts of unlawful discrimination'. Alongside this, the TUC had made efforts to create a layer of black and white lay stewards and full-time officials who were more capable of tackling racism in the workplace. Regular training courses for shop stewards and full-time officials were held at the TUC National Education Centre in North London and several documents were produced for use in such courses (TUC 1990a, 1990b). Finally, in 1990, and in the face of the creation of black self-organized structures in most public sector unions, the TUC itself endorsed the establishment of self-organized structures to facilitate the participation and representation of black members. The following year, the first annual TUC black workers conference was held with affiliated unions sending delegates in proportion to the size of their membership (Virdee 2000: 221–222).

This shift on the part of the TUC to a position of anti-racism, and now support for black self-organization did not go unchallenged by those remaining conservative elements within the leadership of the trade union movement. Active attempts were made by the right-wing to divide the working class along the fault-line of race. When Bill Morris – a trade unionist of Caribbean descent – stood for the position of general secretary of the Transport and General Workers Union (TGWU) in April 1992, he faced considerable racism from within his own union, and an evident lack of enthusiasm from some other union leaders, including Eric Hammond (then leader of the EETPU), who said it was 'not the best thing for the country or the TGWU' (*The Observer*, 9 June 1991 cited in Virdee and Grint 1994: 206). Unlike in the 1960s and 1970s however, such expressions of racism were actively challenged by the TGWU leadership including by Morris's predecessor, Ron Todd, and rejected by the vast majority of the TGWU membership who went on to elect Bill Morris as general secretary. Further, while the current of large-scale white opposition to racism that had briefly flourished in the late 1970s was far less in evidence in the 1980s, echoes of it could still be discerned in the working class solidarity extended to black and Asian workers on strike, most notably in the case of the Burnsall workers in the West Midlands (see Buyum 1993; Wrench and Virdee 1996), the Hillingdon hospital workers in west London (Lalkar 1998) and the local strike against racism by NALGO workers in Islington Council in 1985 (see Miller 1996).

By the close of the 1980s, an important transformation in the occupational position of black and Asian workers in British society was clearly discernible. Triggered by the urban unrest, the experiment in municipal anti-racism in radical Labour-run local authorities had decisively opened up areas of non-manual local state employment. Further, through black self-organization and the alliance with the socialist left in trade unions such changes were consolidated throughout the public sector. However, contrary to liberal explanations that interpret the increased representation in such work as evidence of upward social mobility (e.g. Iganski and Payne 1996), I contend that it marked the growing representation of minorities in the new state working class (Fairbrother 1989: 188). By the 1980s such work was increasingly proletarian in nature, characterized by growing routinization and de-skilling (Hyman and Price 1983; Crompton and Jones 1984). Nevertheless, black and Asian workers were now no longer overwhelmingly restricted to largely unskilled and semi-skilled manual work – irrespective of their qualifications – as they had been in the 1960s and 1970s (Virdee 2006, 2010).

What is remarkable about these developments – and a testament to the action taken by black and Asian workers and their socialist allies – is that this social change took place in an era of consolidating neoliberalism. Racism did not disappear in the late 1980s – neither in the trade union movement, nor more widely in society. As we have already seen, a racializing nationalism formed a crucial component of the authoritarian populist agenda around which the Conservatives secured consent for their policies (Hall 1983). However, what was also evident by the close of the 1980s was the existence of a durable current of anti-racism in British society, one that had emerged over the course of the black struggles against racism in the 1960s, the growth of the anti-racist and anti-fascist social movements in the 1970s, and which by the 1980s, had become institutionalized in key sectors of the organized labour movement, and the public sector.

9

Conclusions

The enduring significance of racism

We have long known that the British state strategically positioned itself at the epicentre of a vast array of social, political and economic networks which enabled it to move commodities and humans across continents and oceans, and ultimately facilitated its rise as the undisputed hegemon of the modern world-system until superseded, in its turn, by the United States. Yet, somehow the impression has lingered that such large-scale global social change had left Britain itself largely untouched until the *Empire Windrush* docked at Tilbury in 1948. This study has demonstrated how accompanying the large-scale importation into Britain of goods such as tea, coffee and sugar from its colonial lands went the settling of migrants – Irish Catholics, freed African and African-American slaves, and Indian, Arab and African labourers. The English working class in particular was a heterogeneous, multi-ethnic formation from the moment of its inception. By lifting the veil that has hidden this history from view, we are better able to demonstrate the influential role that such migrants played both as subjects of history and as objects of antipathy within English society.

From the time when the English elites learnt to rule in a more consensual manner in the mid-Victorian period to the bipartisan consolidation of the welfare settlement in the 1940s, a series of influential social and political reforms, accompanied by the delivery of sustained periods of economic security, facilitated the incorporation of ever larger components of the working class into the imagined nation as active members of an imperial state. Significantly, racism – in all its variegated forms – accompanied this process of working class integration. Already, by the 1850s and 1860s, the inclusion of the respectable working class of craft workers and others went hand in hand with the consolidation of racism against Irish Catholics. The even earlier association of the English with Protestantism was over-determined by an increasingly influential understanding of themselves as members of the Anglo-Saxon race. Irish Catholics – long excluded from the nation as a result of their Catholic faith – now found themselves doubly disadvantaged as a result of their alleged membership of the Celtic race. Similarly, in the 1950s and 1960s, amid the consolidation of the welfare settlement, the English re-imagined themselves again, this time as members of the white race in opposition to the migration from the Caribbean and the Indian subcontinent. The content of race-making changed over the course of this century of working class integration but the idea of race itself remained constant.

Significantly, large parts of the working class and its institutions were active agents in the production of such racialized difference. From the late nineteenth century, successive waves of socialist-led industrial and political action in pursuit of economic and social justice for those parts of the working class excluded from the earlier reforms justified such claims with reference to a racializing nationalism. While their conception of national belonging was undoubtedly broader than that of the elites of the time, and their intention was to democratize English society, they did so by portraying elite conceptions of national belonging as unjust due to the exclusion of those like themselves who were of the same race and British, and therefore deserving of fair and equal treatment. Thus as the boundary of the nation was expanded to include ever-increasing numbers of the working class, it was simultaneously racialized, forcing the most recently arrived migrant group to serve as the exclusionary foil to enhanced working class inclusion.

The identification of this deeply contradictory process reminds one of Nairn's observation that nationalism is 'like the old Roman god, Janus, who stood above gateways with one face looking forward and one backwards' (1975: 18). By developing a greater sensitivity and acuity to questions of racism and nationalism and their articulation to working class politics, this study has drawn attention to the Janus-like character of such politics, particularly how deeply nationalism – a racializing nationalism – shaped the socialist movement in the nineteenth century and beyond.

Such racism and nationalism profoundly scarred English society, and the working class within it. Its effects can be traced throughout the political and cultural spheres as well as the economic. From the creation and consolidation of a stratified division of labour in the workplace to the informal regulation of intimate social relations in the community, racism's reach was all-encompassing. And over time, such racism became institutionalized and no longer always required active enforcement because the structures and institutions of society came to reflect its distorted understanding of the world. It became, in Bourdieusian terms, an integral component of the English habitus – those sets of resilient and unconscious dispositions acquired by social groups over time. And alongside this, the working class re-imagined itself as a racialized class such that race became 'the modality in which class [was] lived, the medium through which class relations [were] experienced, the form in which it [was] appropriated and "fought through"' (Hall 1980: 341).

The durability of such racism in every sphere of social life has important implications for any political projects that identify the working class as the primary agent in progressive social transformation. It has led some to conclude that '[t]he Proletariat of yesterday, classically conceived or otherwise, now has rather more to lose than its chains' (Gilroy 1987: 246), while others have identified racialized minorities as the primary agent in any attempt to challenge racism (Sivanandan 1982, 1990). While the significance of the autonomous agency of racialized minorities in combating racism is unquestionable, as this study has also demonstrated, I want to draw attention to a further social actor – that of racialized minorities in socialist movements who played an instrumental role in trying to align struggles against racism with those against class exploitation.

From racial formation to working class formation: The racialized outsider as linchpin

Throughout the period under investigation, there were moments when the working class collectively suppressed expressions of racism and, on occasion, actively rejected it. Central to the formation of such multi-ethnic class solidarity were those socialist men and women I have described as racialized outsiders. Belonging to minority groups in Britain – Irish Catholic, Jewish, Indian, Caribbean and African – against whom the dominant conception of British nationalism was constructed at different moments in its history, their attachment to the British nation tended to be less firm, whilst their participation in subaltern conflicts gave them a unique capacity to see through the fog of blood, soil and belonging so as to universalize the militant yet often particularistic fights of the working class. In this sense, they acted as a leavening agent nourishing the struggles of all, informed by their unique perspective on society.

As we have seen, numerous case studies or vignettes of English, Irish and African solidarity have been identified during the heroic age of the proletariat where such minorities played a formative role in its development. However, such multi-ethnic working class solidarity became less evident after the catastrophic defeat of Chartism, and the consolidation of racist, nationalist and imperialist ideas within the working class. Between 1848 and 1973, the current of proletarian internationalism largely became the preserve of socialists who were racialized minorities. Apart from some notable exceptions like William Morris, Belfort Bax, Sylvia Pankhurst and John Maclean – it was men and women like Eleanor Marx, James Connolly, Zelda Kahan, Theodore Rothstein, Shapurji Saklatvala and Arthur MacManus who attempted against great odds to challenge racist divisions within the working class. Significantly, in the course of the new unionism in the 1880s and 1890s, they were able, albeit briefly, to broaden the development of the emergent English–Irish working class solidarity such that it also encompassed the newly arrived Jewish migrants. Similarly, in the 1920s and 1930s, racialized minorities within the CPGB attempted to challenge the hold of racist, anti-semitic and imperialist ideas within the working class, culminating in the solidarity action in support of Arab seamen in the North-East of England, as well as the defence of the Jewish community in the East End of London.

However, it was in the aftermath of the world revolution of 1968 that the working class finally began to bifurcate on the question of racism within a world now shaped, on the one hand, by decolonization in Asia, Africa and the Caribbean; the political struggle for civil rights in the United States; and black resistance at home and, on the other, by the organic crisis of British capitalism, the collapsing welfare settlement and the intensification of the class struggle. By the 1970s, the organized labour movement shifted from their long-held position of indifference towards racism to one of actively challenging it, including most notably in support of Asian women workers on strike at Grunwick. Alongside such anti-racist action in the workplace, parts of organized labour and youth helped fashion anti-racist and anti-fascist social movements of a scale unprecedented in Britain to this day.

The part played by socialist internationalists, particularly those of racialized minority descent was decisive. They proved to be the conduit through which anti-racist ideas, consciousness and political practice – until then, narrowly confined to the minority communities – came to be transmitted to the left wing of the organized labour movement and beyond. In that moment when the class struggles were brought into alignment with those against racism, an organic fusion of social forces took place in which, to paraphrase Sivanandan (1982: 17), racialized minority workers 'through a consciousness of their colour . . . arrive[d] at a consciousness of class' and in which the white working class 'in recovering its class instinct . . . arrive[d] at a consciousness of racial oppression'.

The experiment in municipal anti-racism in radical Labour-run local authorities further extended such anti-racist sentiment within society opening up areas of non-manual local state employment to racialized minorities. And through black self-organization and the alliance with the socialist left in trade unions such changes were consolidated throughout the public sector. While racism remained a powerful structuring force throughout the 1980s, the outcome of such collective action was the consolidation of a more durable current of anti-racism in British society, one that had been facilitated over the course of the black struggles against racism in the 1960s, the growth of the anti-racist and anti-fascist social movements in the 1970s and which, by the 1980s had become institutionalized in key sectors of the organized labour movement and the public sector. Such anti-racism was the legacy bequeathed to English society by the racialized outsiders of Irish Catholic, Jewish, African and Asian descent. During the period of imperial ascendency and scientific racism, this current was almost extinguished alongside that of socialist internationalism. Without it, English society would have been comprised of two communities stratified by racism.

Underpinning this study philosophically has been the understanding that intellectual renewal is bound up with the process of political renewal.

Influential intellectuals such as Immanuel Wallerstein (2004: 77) have warned of the final, impending crisis of the capitalist world-economy, even going so far as to predict its demise sometime in the middle of the twenty-first century. Yet, the elaboration and support for emancipatory projects that seek to transform our existing social relations and free us from exploitation and oppression remain marginal, especially in the West. Indeed, Gramsci's (1971: 276) observation remains pertinent, namely that while '[t]he old is dying...the new cannot be born; in this interregnum a great variety of morbid symptoms appear' – including, we might add, manifestations of racist absolutism. By reassessing our past, as well as reminding many individuals of their own histories of 'enslaved forbears' (Benjamin 2006), I hope this volume makes a small contribution towards encouraging them to step forward and collectively challenge manifestations of racist oppression today, and the structural foundations that sustain it.

Bibliography

Adi, H. 1998. *West Africans in Britain: 1900–1960.* London: Lawrence and Wishart.

Allen, T.W. 1994. *The Invention of the White Race.* Vol. 2. London: Verso.

Anderson, P. 1964. 'Origins of the Present Crisis' *New Left Review* 1: 23: 26–53.

Anderson, P. 1977. 'The Limits and Possibilities of Trade Union Action' in T. Clarke and T. Clements (eds.) *Trade Unions Under Capitalism.* London: Fontana.

Aptheker, H. 1943. *American Negro Slave Revolts.* New York: Columbia University Press.

Armitage, D. 2007. *The Declaration of Independence: a global history.* Cambridge, MA: Harvard University Press.

Armstrong, A. 2013. *The Ghost of James Connolly.* Edinburgh: Introfobel Publications.

Attridge, S. 2003. *Nationalism, Imperialism and Identity in Late Victorian Culture.* Basingstoke: Palgrave Macmillan.

Baldwin, L.V. and Al-Hadid, A.Y. 2002. *Between Cross and Crescent.* Gainesville: University of Florida Press.

Ball, W. and Solomos, J. 1990. 'Racial Equality and Local Politics' in W. Ball and J. Solomos (eds.) *Race and Local Politics.* Basingstoke: Macmillan Education.

Banton, M. 1987. *Racial Theories.* Cambridge: Cambridge University Press.

Barkan, E. 1993. *The Retreat of Scientific Racism.* Cambridge: Cambridge University Press.

Beauchamp, K. no date. *Black Citizens.* London: CPGB.

Beaver, P. 1985. *The Match Makers.* London: Henry Melland Limited.

Beishon, S., Virdee, S. and Hagell, A. 1995. *Nursing in a Multi-Ethnic NHS.* London: Policy Studies Institute.

Belchem, J. 1985. 'English Working-Class Radicalism and the Irish, 1815–50' in R. Swift and S. Gilley (eds.) *The Irish in the Victorian City.* London: Croom Helm.

Bellamy, J. 1968. *Homes, Jobs, Immigration – the facts.* London: CPGB.

Ben-Tovim, G. 1978. 'The Struggle Against Racism: theoretical and strategic perspectives' *Marxism Today*, July, pp. 203–213.

Benjamin, W. 1940/2006. 'On the Concept of History' in H. Eiland and M.W. Jennings (eds.) *Selected Writings of Walter Benjamin.* Vol. 4. Cambridge, MA: Harvard University Press.

Benn, T. 1982. *Parliament, People and Power.* London: Verso.

Bevir, M. 2000. 'Republicanism, Socialism, and Democracy in Britain: the origins of the radical left' *Journal of Social History* 34: 2: 351–368.

Bhambra, G. 2011. 'Historical Sociology, Modernity and Postcolonial Critique' *American Historical Review* 116: 3: 653–662.

Billig, M. 1995. *Banal Nationalism.* London: Sage.

Birchall, I. 1981. *The Smallest Mass Party in the World.* London: SWP.

Blackburn, R. 1988. *The Overthrow of Colonial Slavery.* London: Verso.

Bourke, J. 1994. *Working Class Cultures in Britain, 1890–1960.* London: Routledge.

Bourne, J. 2007. *Lewisham '77: success or failure?* http://www.irr.org.uk/news/lewisham-77-success-or-failure/ Accessed 24 November 2012.

Branson, N. 1997. *History of the CPGB, 1941–1951.* London: Lawrence and Wishart.

Brockway, F. 1942. *Inside the Left.* London: Allen Unwin.

Brown, C. 1982. *Black and White Britain: the third PSI survey.* London: Heinemann Educational Books.

Brown, J. 1998. *The Oxford History of the British Empire, the Twentieth Century.* Vol. IV. Oxford: Oxford University Press.

Buckley, D. 2005. *Strange Fascination – David Bowie: the definitive story.* London: Virgin.

Buckman, J. 1980. 'Alien Working-Class Response: the Leeds Jewish tailors, 1880–1914' in K. Lunn (ed.) *Hosts, Immigrants and Minorities: historical responses to newcomers in British society, 1870–1914.* Folkestone: Dawson.

Buyum, M. 1993. *The Burnsall Strike: account of a struggle.* Unpublished M.A. thesis, University of Warwick.

Byrne, D. 1977. 'The 1930 "Arab Riot" in South Shields: a race riot that never was' *Race and Class* 18: 3: 261–277.

Calhoun, C. 1982. *The Question of Class Struggle.* Oxford: Blackwell.

Callaghan, J. 1995. 'The Communists and the Colonies: anti-imperialism between the wars' in G. Andrews, N. Fishman and K. Morgan (eds.) *Opening the Books: essays on the social and cultural history of the British Communist Party.* London: Pluto Press.

Callaghan, J. 2003. *Cold War, Crisis and Conflict: the CPGB 1951–1968.* London: Lawrence and Wishart.

Callinicos, A. 1993. *Race and Class.* London: Bookmarks.

Cannadine, D. 2002. *Ornamentalism: how the British saw their empire.* Oxford: Oxford University Press.

Carretta, V. 2005. *Equiano, the African.* London: Penguin.

Carter, R., Joshi, S. and Harris, C. 1987. 'The 1951–55 Conservative Government and the Racialisation of Black Immigration' *Policy Papers in Ethnic Relations No.11.* Coventry: CRER, University of Warwick.

Centre for Contemporary Cultural Studies (CCCS). 1982. *The Empire Strikes Back.* London: Hutchinson.

Cesarani, D. 1994. 'The Study of Anti-Semitism in Britain: trends and perspectives' in M. Brown (ed.) *Approaches to Antisemitism.* New York: International Centre for the University Teaching of Jewish Civilization.

Challinor, R. 1977. *The Origins of British Bolshevism.* London: Croom Helm.

Coats, A.V. 2011. 'Spithead Mutiny: introduction' in A.V. Coats and P. MacDougall (eds.) *The Naval Mutinies of 1797.* Woodbridge: The Boydell Press.

Cohen, S. 1984. *That's Funny You Don't Look Anti-Semitic: an anti-racist analysis of left anti-semitism.* London: Beyond the Pale Collective.

Colley, L. 1986. 'Whose Nation? class and national consciousness in Britain 1750–1830' *Past and Present* 113: 1: 97–117.

Colley, L. 1996. *Britons.* London: Vintage.

Colling, T. and Ferner, A. 1995. 'Privatization and Marketization' in P. Edwards (ed.) *Industrial Relations: Theory and Practice in Britain.* Oxford: Blackwell.

Communist Party of Great Britain (CPGB). 1951. *The British Road to Socialism.* London: CPGB.

Communist Party of Great Britain (CPGB). 1975. *The Fight against Racialism in Britain*. London: CP Education Department.

Communist Party of Great Britain (CPGB). no date. *Racism Action Guide: how to combat it*. London: CP National Race Relations Committee.

Connolly, J. 1903. *The Socialist Labour Party of America and the London SDF*. http://www.marxists.org/archive/connolly/1903/06/slpsdf.htm Accessed 24 November 2012.

Cowden, M. 1963. 'Early Marxist Views on British Labor, 1837–1937' *Western Political Quarterly* 16: 1: 34–52.

Crick, M. 1994. *The History of the Social Democratic Federation*. Bodmin: Ryburn Publishing.

Crompton, R., Devine, F., Savage, M. and Scott, J. 2000. *Renewing Class Analysis*. Oxford: Blackwell.

Crompton, R. and Jones, G. 1984. *White-Collar Proletariat: deskilling and gender in the clerical labour process*. Basingstoke: Macmillan Press.

Curtis, L. 1968. *Anglo-Saxons and Celts: a study of anti-Irish prejudice in Victorian England*. New York: New York University Press.

Curtis, L. 1971. *Apes and Angels: The Irishman in Victorian caricature*. Washington, DC: Smithsonian Institution Press.

Daniel, W.W. 1968. *Racial Discrimination in England*. London: Penguin Books.

Darlington, R. 1994. *The Dynamics of Workplace Unionism*. London: Mansell.

Davidson, N. 2006. 'Carnival, March, Riot' *International Socialism* 112: 209–215.

De Beauvoir, S. 1948/1976. *The Ethics of Ambiguity*. New York: Citadel Press.

Denselow, R. 1989. *When the Music Stopped: the story of political pop*. London: Faber and Faber.

Deutscher, I. 1968. *The Non-Jewish Jew and Other Essays*. London: Oxford University Press.

Devine, F., Savage, M., Crompton, R. and Scott, J. (eds.) 2005. *Re-Thinking Class*. London: Palgrave Macmillan.

Devine, T. 2000. *Scotland's Shame: bigotry and sectarianism in modern Scotland*. Edinburgh: Mainstream Publishing.

Dickens, L. and Hall, M. 1995. 'The State: labour law and industrial relations' in P. Edwards (ed.) *Industrial Relations: theory and practice in Britain*. Oxford: Blackwell.

Draper, H. 1978. *Karl Marx's Theory of Revolution: the politics of social classes*. Vol. 2. New York: Monthly Review Press.

Dresser, M. 1986. *Black and White on the Buses: the 1963 colour bar dispute in Bristol*. Bristol: Bristol Broadsides.

Driver, F. and Gilbert, D. (eds.) 2003. *Imperial Cities*. Manchester: Manchester University Press.

Du Bois, W.E.B. 1903/1994. *The Souls of Black Folk*. New York: Dover Publications.

Duffield, M. 1988. *Black Radicalism and the Politics of De-Industrialisation: the hidden history of Indian foundry workers*. Aldershot: Avebury.

Duffy, A.E.P. 1961. 'New Unionism in Britain, 1889–90: a reappraisal' *The Economic History Review* 14: 2: 306–319.

Edwards, P. and Dabydeen, D. 1991. *Black Writers in Britain, 1760–1890*. Edinburgh: Edinburgh University Press.

Eldridge, J., Cressey, P. and MacInnes, J. 1991. *Industrial Sociology and Economic Crisis*. Hemel Hempstead: Harvester Wheatsheaf.

Eley, G. 2002. *Forging Democracy*. Oxford: Oxford University Press.

Ellis, P.B. 1997. *Selected Writings of James Connolly*. London: Pluto Press.

Engels, F. 1845/1987. *The Conditions of the Working Class in England*. London: Penguin Books.

Engels, F. 1894. *Engels to Eduard Bernstein in Zurich*, London, 29 December. http://www.marxists.org/archive/marx/works/1884/letters/84_12_29.htm Accessed 24 November 2012.

Fairbrother, P. 1989. 'State Workers: class position and collective action' in G. Duncan (ed.) *Democracy and the Capitalist State*. Cambridge: Cambridge University Press.

Fanon, F. 1961/2001. *The Wretched of the Earth*. London: Penguin Books.

Ferro. M. 1973. *The Great War, 1914–1918*. London: Routledge and Kegan Paul.

Fishman, N. 1995. 'No Home but the Trade Union Movement: communist activists and "reformist" leaders: 1925–1956' in G. Andrews, N. Fishman and K. Morgan (eds.) *Opening the Books: essays on the social and cultural history of the British Communist Party*. London: Pluto Press.

Foot, P. 1965a. 'Immigration and the British Labour Movement' *International Socialism* 1: 22: 8–13.

Foot, P. 1965b. 'The Strike at Courtaulds, Preston: 24 May to 12 June 1965' *IRR Newsletter Supplement*.

Foot, P. 1969. *The Rise of Enoch Powell*. London: Penguin.

Foot, P. no date. *Workers Against Racism*. London: International Socialists.

Foster, J. 1977. *Class Struggle and the Industrial Revolution*. London: Routledge.

Foster, J. 1990. 'Strike Action and Working Class Politics on Clydeside, 1914–1919' *International Review of Social History* 35: 1: 33–70.

Fryer, P. 1984. *Staying Power: the history of black people in Britain*. London: Pluto Press.

Gallacher, W. 1936. *Revolt on the Clyde*. London: Lawrence and Wishart.

Giddens, A. 1987. *A Contemporary Critique of Historical Materialism: the nation-state and violence*. Berkeley: University of California Press.

Gidley, B. 2003. *Citizenship and Belonging: East London Jewish radicals, 1903–1918*. Unpublished Ph.D. dissertation, London: Goldsmiths College, University of London.

Gilmour, I. 1977. *Inside Right*. London: Hutchinson.

Gilroy, P. 1987. *There Ain't No Black in the Union Jack*. London: Hutchinson.

Gilroy, P. 2000. *Between Camps:* London: Allen Lane.

Glasgow Labour History Workshop (GLHW). 1970. *Glasgow 1919: the story of the 40 hours strike*. Glasgow: Molendinar Press.

Glasgow Labour History Workshop (GLHW). 1989. *The Singer Strike Clydebank, 1911*. Clydebank: Clydebank District Library.

Goodhart, D. 2013. *The British Dream*. London: Atlantic Books.

Goodyer, I. 2009. *Crisis Music: the cultural politics of Rock Against Racism*. Manchester: Manchester University Press.

Gordon, P. 1990. 'A Dirty War: the new right and local authority anti-racism' in W. Ball and J. Solomos (eds.) *Race and Local Politics*. Basingstoke: Macmillan.

Gordon, P. and Reilly, D. 1986. 'Guestworkers of the Sea: racism in British shipping' *Race and Class* 28: 2: 73–82.

Gramsci, A. 1971. *Selections from the Prison Notebooks*. London: Lawrence and Wishart.

Gray, B. 1999. 'Ben Tillet and the Rise of the Labour Movement in Britain' *History Review*. September.

Green, J. 1990. 'Some Findings on Britain's Black Working Class, 1900–1914' *Immigrants and Minorities* 19: 2: 168–177.

Gregg, R. 1998. 'Class, Culture and Empire' *Journal of Historical Sociology* 11: 4: 419–460.

Gregory, A. 2007. *The Last Great War*. Cambridge: Cambridge University Press.

Grint, K. 1991. *The Sociology of Work*. London: Polity Press.

Gupta, P.S. 1975. *Imperialism and the British Labour Movement, 1914–1964*. New York: Holmes and Meier Publishers.

Hall, C. 1992. *White, Male and Middle Class*. Oxford: Polity Press.

Hall, C. 2002. *Civilising Subjects*. Oxford: Polity Press.

Hall, C., McClelland, K. and Rendell, J. 2000. *Defining the Victorian Nation*. Cambridge: Cambridge University Press.

Hall, C. and Rose, S. (eds.) 2006. *At Home with the Empire*. Cambridge: Cambridge University Press.

Hall, S. 1980. 'Race, Articulation and Societies Structured in Dominance' in UNESCO (ed.) *Sociological Theories: race and colonialism*. Paris: UNESCO.

Hall, S. 1983. 'The Great Moving Right Show' in S. Hall and M. Jacques (eds.) *The Politics of Thatcherism*. London: Lawrence and Wishart.

Hall, S., Critcher, C., Jefferson, T., Clarke, J. and Roberts, B. 1978. *Policing the Crisis*. Basingstoke: Macmillan Press.

Hall, S. and Massey, D. 2010. 'Interpreting the Crisis' *Soundings* 44: 57–71.

Hargreaves, J. 1993. 'The Comintern and Anti-Colonialism: new research opportunities' *African Affairs* 92: 367: 255–261.

Harman, C. 1985. '1984 and the Shape of Things to Come' *International Socialism* 2: 29: 62–127.

Harris, N. 1968. 'Race and Nation' *International Socialism* 1: 34: 22–27.

Hatton, T., Boyer, G. and Bailey, R. 1994. 'The Union Wage Effect in Late Nineteenth Century Britain' *Economica* 61: 435–456.

Hay, J.R. 1983. *The Origins of the Liberal Welfare Reforms, 1906–14*. Basingstoke: Macmillan.

Heathorn, S. 2000. *For Home, Country and Race: constructing gender, class and Englishness in the elementary school, 1880–1914*. Toronto: University of Toronto Press.

Heffer, S. 1998. *Like the Roman: the life of Enoch Powell*. London: Weidenfeld and Nicolson.

Hennessy, P. 2001. *Prime Minister: the office and its holders since 1945*. London: Penguin.

Hickman, M. 1995. *Religion, Class and Identity*. Aldershot: Avebury.

Hickman, M. 1998. 'Reconstructing Deconstructing "Race": British political discourses about the Irish in Britain' *Ethnic and Racial Studies* 21: 2: 288–307.

Hier, S. 2001. 'The Forgotten Architect: Cox, Wallerstein and world-system theory' *Race and Class* 42: 3: 69–86.

Hill, C. 1968. *Puritanism and Revolution*. Manchester: Panther Books.

Hillman, N. 2001. ' "Tell Me Chum, In Case I Got It Wrong. What Was It We Were Fighting During the War?" the re-emergence of British Fascism, 1945–58' *Contemporary British History* 15: 4: 1–34.

Hinton, J. 1973. *The First Shop Stewards' Movement*. London: Allen Unwin.

Hinton, J. and Hyman, R. 1975. *Trade Unions and Revolution: the industrial politics of the early British Communist Party*. London: Pluto Press.

Hobsbawm, E. 1949. 'General Labour Unions in Britain, 1889–1914' *Economic History Review* 1: 2/3: 123–142.

Hobsbawm, E. 1964. *Labouring Men*. London: Weidenfeld and Nicholson.

Hobsbawm, E. 1967. 'Trade Union History' *Economic History Review* 20: 2: 358–364.

Hobsbawm, E. 1968/1990. *Industry and Empire*. London: Penguin Books.

Hobsbawm, E. 1978. 'The Forward March of Labour Halted?' *Marxism Today*, September, pp. 279–286.

Hobsbawm, E. 1983. 'Mass Producing Traditions: Europe, 1870–1914' in E. Hobsbawm and T. Ranger (eds.) *The Invention of Tradition*. Cambridge: Cambridge University Press.

Hobsbawm, E. 1984a. *Worlds of Labour*. London: Weidenfeld and Nicholson.

Hobsbawm, E. 1984b. 'Artisan or Labour Aristocrat?' *Economic History Review* 37: 3: 355–372.

Hobsbawm, E. 1997. *The Age of Capital, 1848–1875*. London: Abacus.

Hofstadter, R. 1967. *Social Darwinism in American Thought*. Boston: Beacon Press.

Holmes, C. 1988. *John Bull's Island*. Basingstoke: Macmillan.

Home Office. 1977. *A Guide to the Race Relations Act 1976*. London: Home Office.

Hyman, R. 1972. *Marxism and the Sociology of Trade Unionism*. London: Pluto Press.

Hyman, R. and Price, R. 1983. *The New Working Class?* Basingstoke: Macmillan Press.

Hyndman, H. 1881/1973. *England for All*. Brighton: Harvester Press.

Iganski, P. and Payne, G. 1996. 'Declining Racial Disadvantage in the British Labour Market' *Ethnic and Racial Studies* 19: 1: 113–133.

Ignatiev, N. 1995. *How the Irish Became White*. New York: Routledge.

International Socialists. 1974. *The Black Worker in Britain*. London: International Socialists.

James, C.L.R. 1938/1991. *The Black Jacobins*. London: Allison and Busby.

Jenkinson, J. 1996. 'The 1919 Riots' in P. Panikos (ed.) *Racial Violence in Britain in the 19th and 20th Centuries*. Leicester: Leicester University Press.

Jenkinson, J. 2008. 'Black Sailors on Red Clydeside: rioting, reactionary trade unionism and conflicting notions of Britishness following the First World War' *Twentieth Century British History* 19: 1: 29–60.

Jenkinson, J. 2009. *Black 1919: riots, racism and resistance in Imperial Britain*. Liverpool: Liverpool University Press.

Josephides, S. 1990. 'Principles, Strategies and Anti-racist Campaigns: the case of the Indian Worker's Association' in H. Goulbourne (ed.) *Black Politics in Britain*. Aldershot: Avebury.

Joshi, S. and Carter, R. 1984. 'The Role of Labour in the Creation of a Racist Britain' *Race and Class* 25: 3: 53–71.

Joyce, P. 1991. *Visions of the People*. Cambridge: Cambridge University Press.

Kapp, Y. 1976. *Eleanor Marx: the crowded years, 1884–1898*. Vol. 2. London: Lawrence and Wishart.

Kay, D. and Miles, R. 1992. *Refugees or Migrant Workers? European volunteer workers, 1946–51*. London: Routledge.

Kaye, H.J. and McClelland, K. 1990. *EP Thompson: critical debates*. London: Polity.

Kelly, J. 1988. *Trade Unions and Socialist Politics*. London: Verso.

Kendall, W. 1969. *The Revolutionary Movement in Britain, 1900–1921*. London: Weidenfeld and Nicholson.

Kessler, S. and Bayliss, F. 1995. *Contemporary British Industrial Relations*. Basingstoke: Macmillan Press.

Kirk, N. 1985. *The Growth of Working Class Reformism in Mid-Victorian England*. London: Croom Helm.

Klugman, J. 1960. 'The Foundation of the Communist Party of Great Britain' *Marxism Today* 4: 1: 1–11.

Knowles, C. 2003. *Race and Social Analysis*. London: Sage.

Knox, W.W. 1988. 'Religion and the Scottish Labour Movement, c.1900–1939' *Journal of Contemporary History* 23: 4: 609–630.

Kyriakides, C. and Virdee, S. 2003. 'Migrant Labour, Racism and the British National Health Service' *Ethnicity and Health* 8: 4: 283–305.

Lalkar. 1998. 'Hillingdon Hospital Strikers: their fight is our fight' *Lalkar*. March.

Laybourn, K. 1994. 'The Failure of Socialist Unity in Britain c.1893–1914' *Transactions of the Royal Historical Society* 4: 153–175.

Leed, E.J. 1981. *No Man's Land: combat and identity in World War One*. Cambridge: Cambridge University Press.

Lees, L.H. 1979. *Exiles of Erin*. Manchester: Manchester University Press.

Lenin, V. 1914/1983. *The Right of Nations to Self-Determination*. Moscow: Progress Publishers.

Lindop, F. 2001. 'Racism and the Working Class: strikes in support of Enoch Powell in 1968' *Labour History Review* 66: 1: 79–100.

Linebaugh, P. and Rediker, M. 2001. *The Many-Headed Hydra*. Boston: Beacon Press.

Livingstone, K. 1984. 'Renaissance Labour Style' *Marxism Today*, December, pp. 19–22.

Lunn, K. 1985. 'Race Relations or Industrial Relations? race and labour in Britain, 1880–1950' *Immigrants and Minorities* 4: 2: 1–29.

Mac an Ghaill, M. 2000. 'The Irish in Britain: the invisibility of ethnicity and anti-Irish racism' *Journal of Ethnic and Migration Studies* 26: 1: 137–147.

MacCarthy, F. 2010. *William Morris*. London: Faber and Faber.

MacDonald, R. 1994. *The Language of Empire*. Manchester: Manchester University Press.

Mackenzie, J. (ed.) 1986. *Imperialism and Popular Culture*. Manchester: Manchester University Press.

Mackenzie, J. 1999. 'Empire and Metropolitan Cultures' in A. Porter (ed.) *The Oxford History of the British Empire, The Nineteenth Century*. Oxford: Oxford University Press.

MacRaid, D. 1999. *Irish Migrants in Modern Britain*. Basingstoke: Palgrave Macmillan.

McBriar, A.M. 1963. *Fabian Socialism and English Politics*. Cambridge: Cambridge University Press.

McCalman, I. (ed.) 1991. *The Horrors of Slavery and Other Writings by Robert Wedderburn*. Princeton: Markus Weiner Publishers.

McClintock, A. 1995. *Imperial Leather*. London: Routledge.

McCrudden, C., Smith, D.J. and Brown, C. 1991. *Racial Justice at Work*. London: Policy Studies Institute.

McDermott, M. 1979. *Irish Catholics and the British Labour Movement: a study with particular reference to London, 1918–1970.* Unpublished M.A. thesis, University of Kent.

McIlroy, J. 1995. *Trade Unions in Britain Today.* Manchester: Manchester University Press.

Manwaring, G. and Dobree, B. 1935. *The Floating Republic: an account of the mutinies at Spithead and the Nore in 1797.* London: Penguin.

Marsh, D. 1992. *The New Politics of British Trade Unionism.* Basingstoke: Macmillan Press.

May, R. and Cohen, R. 1974. 'The Interaction Between Race and Colonialism: a case study of the Liverpool race riots of 1919' *Race and Class* 16: 111–126.

Mayet, G. 1986. *Race and Trade Unions.* Unpublished document.

Messina, A.M. 1989. *Race and Party Competition in Britain.* Oxford: Clarendon Press.

Meth, M. 1972. *Brothers to All Men?* London: Runnymede Trust.

Miles, R. 1982. *Racism and Migrant Labour.* London: Routledge and Kegan Paul.

Miles, R. 1984. 'Marxism Versus the Sociology of Race Relations' *Ethnic and Racial Studies* 7: 2: 217–237.

Miles, R. 1993. *Racism after 'Race Relations'.* London: Routledge.

Miles, R. and Kay, D. 1990. 'The TUC, Foreign Labour and the Labour Government: 1945–51' *Immigrants and Minorities* 9: 1: 85–108.

Miles, R. and Phizacklea, A. 1977. *The TUC, Black Workers and New Commonwealth Immigration, 1954–1973.* Working Paper No.6. Birmingham: University of Aston.

Miles, R. and Phizacklea, A. 1978. 'The TUC and Black Workers, 1974–1976' *British Journal of Industrial Relations* 16: 2: 195–207.

Miles, R. and Phizacklea, A. 1984. *White Man's Country: racism and British politics.* London: Pluto Press.

Miliband, R. 1987. *Parliamentary Socialism.* London: Merlin Press.

Miller, C. 1996. *Public Sector Trade Unionism and Radical Politics.* Aldershot: Dartmouth Publishing Company.

Millward, P. 1985. 'The Stockport Riots of 1852' in R. Swift and S. Gilley (eds.) *The Irish in the Victorian City.* London: Croom Helm.

Moran. M. 1980. *The Politics of Industrial Relations.* London: Macmillan Press.

Morgan, K., Cohen, G. and Flinn, A. 2007. *Communists and British Society, 1920–1991.* London: Rivers Oram Press.

Morton, A.L. 1994. *A People's History of England.* London: Lawrence and Wishart.

Nairn, T. 1964. 'The English Working Class' *New Left Review* 1: 24: 43–57.

Nairn, T. 1970. 'Enoch Powell: the new right' *New Left Review* 1: 61: 3–27.

Nairn, T. 1975. 'The Modern Janus' *New Left Review* 94: 3–29.

Nairn, T. 1982. *The Break-up of Britain.* London: Verso.

Neal, F. 1988. *Sectarian Violence: the Liverpool Experience, 1819–1914.* New York: St. Martin's Press.

Newman, G. 1996. 'Nationalism Revisited' *Journal of British Studies* 35: 1: 118–127.

Nicholson, B. 1974. *Racialism, Fascism and the Trade Unions.* London: TGWU Region No.1.

O'Higgins, R. 1961. 'The Irish Influence in the Chartist Movement' *Past and Present* 20: 83–96.

Omi, M. and Winant, H. 1994. *Racial Formation in the United States.* London: Routledge.

O'Murchadha, C. 2011. *The Great Famine*. London: Continuum.

O'Riordan, M. 1988. 'Connolly, Socialism and the Jewish Worker' *Saothar: Journal of the Irish Labour History Society* 13: 120–130.

Ouseley, H. 1990. 'Resisting Institutional Change' in W. Ball and J. Solomos (eds.) *Race and Local Politics*. Basingstoke: Macmillan Press.

Owen, N. 1999. 'Critics of Empire in Britain' in J.M. Brown and L. Roger (eds.) *The Oxford History of the British Empire: the twentieth century*. Vol. 4. Oxford: Oxford University Press.

Panayi, P. 1993. *Racial Violence in Britain, 1840–1950*. Leicester: Leicester University Press.

Panayi, P. 1994. *Immigration, Ethnicity and Racism in Britain: 1815–1945*. Manchester: Manchester University Press.

Park, R. 1950. *Race and Culture*. C. Everett Hughes (ed.). New York: Free Press.

Parmar, P. 1990. 'Black Feminism: the politics of articulation' in J. Rutherford (ed.) *Identity: Community, Culture, Difference*. London: Lawrence and Wishart.

Pearson, R., Anitha, S. and McDowell, L. 2010. 'Striking Issues: from labour process to industrial dispute at Grunwick and Gate Gourmet' *Industrial Relations Journal* 41: 5: 408–428.

Pelling, H. 1958. 'The Early History of the Communist Party of Great Britain, 1920–29' *Transactions of the Royal Historical Society* 5: 8: 41–57.

Pelling, H. 1987. *A History of British Trade Unionism*. London: Penguin.

Phizacklea, A. and Miles, R. 1978. 'The Strike at Grunwick' *New Community* 6: 3: 268–278.

Phizacklea, A. and Miles, R. 1980. *Labour and Racism*. London: Routledge and Kegan Paul.

Pinder, B. 1961. 'Trade Unions and Coloured Workers' *Marxism Today*, September, pp. 282–286.

Piratin, P. 1978. *Our Flag Stays Red*. London: Lawrence and Wishart.

Porter, A. 1999. 'Introduction: Britain and the empire in the nineteenth century' in A. Porter (ed.) *The Oxford History of the British Empire*. Oxford: Oxford University Press.

Quail, J. 1978. *The Slow Burning Fuse: the lost history of the British anarchists*. London: Paladin.

Race and Class. 1981. 'The Riots' *Race and Class* 23: 2–3: 223–232.

Raison, T. 1984. 'The View from the Government' in J. Benyon (ed.) *Scarman and After*. Oxford: Pergamon Press.

Ramdin, R. 1987. *The Making of the Black Working Class in Britain*. London: Gower Publishing Company.

Raw, L. 2009. *Striking a Light*. London: Continuum.

Renton, D. 2005. 'Guarding the Barricades' in N. Copsey and D. Renton (eds.) *British Fascism, the Labour Movement and the State*. Basingstoke: Macmillan.

Renton, D. 2006. *When We Touched The Sky: the Anti-Nazi League, 1977–1981*. London: New Clarion Press.

Rex, J. and Tomlinson, S. 1979. *Colonial Immigrants in a British City*. London: Routledge and Kegan Paul.

Riga, L. 2008. 'The Ethnic Roots of Class Universalism: rethinking the "Russian" revolutionary elite' *American Journal of Sociology* 114: 3: 649–705.

Robinson, C. 1983. *Black Marxism: the making of the black radical tradition*. London: Zed Books.

Rodney, W. 1981. *A History of the Guyanese People.* Baltimore: John Hopkins University Press.

Roediger, D. 1991. *The Wages of Whiteness.* London: Verso.

Roediger, D. 1994. *Towards the Abolition of Whiteness.* London: Verso.

Rogaly, J. 1977. *Grunwick.* London: Penguin.

Rose, J. 2002. *The Intellectual Life of the British Working Classes.* New Haven: Yale University Press.

Rosenberg, C. 1987. *Britain on the Brink of Revolution.* London: Bookmarks.

Roth, A. 1970. *Enoch Powell: Tory tribune.* London: Macdonald and Co.

Rudé, G. 1956. 'The Gordon Riots' *Transactions of the Royal Historical Society* 6: 93–114.

Said, E. 1978. *Orientalism.* London: Vintage.

Savage, M. and Miles, A. 1994. *The Re-Making of the British Working Class, 1840–1940.* London: Routledge.

Saville, J. 1987. *1848: the British State and the Chartist movement.* Cambridge: Cambridge University Press.

Scarman, Lord. 1981. *The Brixton Disorders 10–12 April 1981: report of an Inquiry by the Rt Hon. the Lord Scarman OBE.* London: HMSO.

Schwarz, B. 1996. ' "The Only White Man In There": the re-racialization of England, 1956–1968' *Race and Class* 38: 1: 65–78.

Scott, J. 1986. 'Gender: a useful category of historical analysis' *American Historical Review* 91: 5: 1053–1075.

Scott, J. 1988. *Gender and the Politics of History.* New York: Columbia University Press.

Serge, V. 1939/1982. *Midnight in the Century.* London: Writers and Readers.

Sheldrake, J. 1991. *Industrial Relations and Politics in Britain: 1880–1989.* London: Pinter Publishers.

Sherwood, M. 1999. *Claudia Jones: a life in exile.* London: Lawrence and Wishart.

Shukra, K. 1996. 'A Scramble for the British Pie' *Patterns of Prejudice* 30: 1: 28–35.

Sivanandan, A. 1977. 'The Liberation of the Black Intellectual' *Race and Class* 18: 4: 329–344.

Sivanandan, A. 1982. *A Different Hunger.* London: Pluto Press.

Sivanandan, A. 1990. *Communities of Resistance.* London: Verso.

Sked, A. and Cook, C. 1993. *A Post-War Britain: a political history, 1945–1992.* London: Penguin.

Skidelsky, R. 1975. *Oswald Mosley.* Basingstoke: MacMillan.

Smith, E. 2008. ' "Class Before Race": British communism and the place of empire in postwar race relations' *Science and Society* 72: 4: 455–481.

Solomos, J. 1988. *Black Youth, Racism and the State.* Cambridge: Cambridge University Press.

Solomos, J. 1993. *Race and Racism in Britain.* Basingstoke: Macmillan.

Solomos, J. 2003. *Race and Racism in Contemporary Britain,* 3rd ed. Basingstoke: Palgrave Macmillan.

Solomos, J. and Back, L. 1995. *Race, Politics and Social Change.* London: Routledge.

Solomos, J. and Ball, W. 1990. 'New Initiatives and the Possibilities of Reform' in W. Ball and J. Solomos (eds.) *Race and Local Politics.* Basingstoke: Macmillan Education.

Solomos, J., Findlay, B., Jones, S. and Gilroy, P. 1982. 'The Organic Crisis of British Capitalism and Race' in CCCS (ed.) *The Empire Strikes Back*. London: Hutchinson.

Sooben, P. 1990. *The Origins of the Race Relations Act*. Research Papers in Ethnic Relations No.12. Warwick: Warwick University.

Squires, M. 1990. *Saklatvala: a political biography*. London: Lawrence and Wishart.

Stedman Jones, G. 1983. *Languages of Class*. Cambridge: Cambridge University Press.

Stephens, L. 1956. *Employment of Coloured Workers in the Birmingham Area*. London: Institute of Personnel Management.

Street, J. 1986. *Rebel Rock*, 1st ed. Oxford: Blackwell.

Swift, R. 2002. *Irish Migrants in Britain, 1815–1914*. Cork: Cork University Press.

Tabili, L. 1994. *We Ask for British Justice: workers and racial difference in late imperial Britain*. Ithaca: Cornell University Press.

Tarbuck, K. 1991. 'Obituary of Tamara Deutscher' *Revolutionary History* 3: 3: 43.

Tarrow, S. 1998. *Power in Movement*. Cambridge: Cambridge University Press.

Taylor, B. 1991. *Eve and the New Jerusalem*. London: Virago.

Taylor, R. 1994. *The Future of the Trade Unions*. London: Andre Deutsch.

Taylor, S. 1979. 'The National Front' in R. Miles and A. Phizacklea (eds.) *Racism and Political Action in Britain*. London: Routledge Kegan Paul.

Taylor, S. 1982. *The National Front in English Politics*. Basingstoke: Macmillan.

Thale, M. (ed.) 1983. *Selections from the Papers of the London Corresponding Society, 1792–1799*. Cambridge: Cambridge University Press.

Thompson, D. 1982. 'Ireland and the Irish in English Radicalism Before 1850' in J. Epstein and D. Thompson (eds.) *The Chartist Experience*. London: Macmillan.

Thompson, E.P. 1963/1991. *The Making of the English Working Class*. London: Penguin.

Thompson, E.P. 1965. 'The Peculiarities of the English' *Socialist Register* 2: 311–362.

Thompson, E.P. 2009. *Customs in Common*. London: Merlin Press.

Thorpe, A. 2000. 'The Membership of the Communist Party of Great Britain, 1920–1945' *Historical Journal* 43: 3: 777–800.

Thurlow, R. 1987. 'Jew Wise: dimensions of British political anti-semitism, 1918–1939' *Immigrants and Minorities* 6: 1: 44–65.

Thurlow, R. 1998. *Fascism in Britain*. London: IB Tauris.

Tilly, C. 2005. *Popular Contention in Great Britain, 1758–1834*. New York: Paradigm Publishers.

Tinker, H. 1974. *A New System of Slavery*. Oxford: Oxford University Press.

Torr, D. (ed.) 1942. *Karl Marx and Frederick Engels: correspondence, 1846–1895*. New York: International Publishers.

Trades Union Congress. 1981. *Black Workers: a TUC charter for equality of opportunity*. London: TUC.

Trades Union Congress. 1983. *TUC Workbook on Racism*. London: TUC.

Trades Union Congress. 1987. *Black and Ethnic Minority Women in Employment and Trades Unions*. London: TUC.

Trades Union Congress. 1988. *Meeting the Challenge: first report of the special review body*. London: TUC.

Trades Union Congress. 1989. *Tackling Racism: a TUC workbook*. London: TUC.

Trades Union Congress. 1990a. *Racial Harassment at Work*. London: TUC.

Trades Union Congress. 1990b. *Race Discrimination at Work*. London: TUC.

Trades Union Congress. 1991. *Involvement of Black Workers in Trade Unions*. London: TUC.

Travis, A. 2009. 'After 44 Years Secret Papers Reveal Truth about Five Nights of Violence in Notting Hill' *The Guardian*, 24 August 2002. http://www.guardian.co.uk/uk/2002/aug/24/artsandhumanities.nottinghillcarnival2002   Accessed 9 May 2009.

Tuathaigh, M.A.G.O. 1981. 'The Irish in Nineteenth-Century Britain: problems of integration' *Transactions of the Royal Historical Society* 5: 31: 149–173.

Van der Linden, M. 2003. *Transnational Labour History*. Aldershot: Avebury.

Verberckmoes, J. 1996. 'The United Kingdom: between policy and party' in P. Pasture, J. Verberckmoes and H. De Witte (eds.) *The Lost Perspective? trade unions between ideology and social action in the new Europe*. Vol. 1. Aldershot: Avebury.

Virdee, S. 2000. 'A Marxist Critique of Black Radical Theories of Trade-union Racism' *Sociology* 34: 3: 545–565.

Virdee, S. 2006. '"Race", Employment and Social Change: a critique of current theoretical orthodoxies' *Ethnic and Racial Studies* 29: 4: 605–628.

Virdee, S. 2010. 'Racism, Class and the Dialectics of Social Transformation' in P. Hill-Collins and J. Solomos (eds.) *Handbook of Race and Ethnic Studies*. London and New York: Sage, pp. 135–165.

Virdee, S. and Grint, K. 1994. 'Black Self-Organisation in Trade Unions' *Sociological Review* 42: 2: 202–226.

Visram, R. 2002. *Asians in Britain*. London: Pluto Press.

Walker, M. 1977. *The National Front*. London: Harper Collins.

Wallerstein, I. 2004. *World-Systems Analysis*. Durham: Duke University Press.

Watson, D. 1996. 'Black Workers in London in the 1940s' *Historical Studies in Industrial Relations* 1: 1: 149–158.

Webb, S. and Webb, B. 1919. *The History of Trade Unionism, 1666–1920*. London: Webb and Webb.

White, S. 1974. 'Soviets in Britain' *International Review of Social History* 19: 2: 165–193.

Widgery, D. 1976. *The Left in Britain, 1956–1968*. London: Penguin.

Widgery, D. 1986. *Beating Time*. London: Chatto and Windus.

Widgery, D. 1989. *Preserving Disorder*. London: Pluto Press.

Wilkinson, G.T. 1972. *An Authentic History of the Cato Street Conspiracy 1820*. New York: Arno Press.

Williams, B. 1980. 'The Beginnings of Jewish Trade Unionism in Manchester, 1889–1891' in K. Lunn (ed.) *Hosts, Immigrants and Minorities: historical responses to newcomers in British society, 1870–1914*. Folkestone: Dawson.

Wilson, A. 1978. *Finding a Voice*. London: Virago.

Wilson, T. 2010. *The Myriad Faces of War*. London: Faber and Faber.

Winchester, D. and Bach, S. 1995. 'The State: the public sector' in P. Edwards (ed.) *Industrial Relations: theory and practice in Britain*. Oxford: Blackwell.

Wrench, J. 1986. *YTS, Racial Equality and the Trade Unions*. Coventry: CRER, University of Warwick.

Wrench, J. 1987. 'Unequal Comrades: trade unions, equal opportunity and racism' in R. Jenkins and J. Solomos (eds.) *Racism and Equal Opportunity Policies in the 1980s*. Cambridge: Cambridge University Press.

Wrench, J. and Virdee, S. 1996. 'Organising the Unorganised: "race", poor work and trade unions' in P. Ackers, C. Smith and P. Smith (eds.) *The New Workplace and Trade Unionism*. London: Routledge.
Wright, E.O. 1985. *Classes*. London: Verso.
Wright, E.O. 1997. *Class Counts*. Cambridge: Cambridge University Press.
Wright, P. 1968. *The Coloured Worker in British Industry*. London: Oxford University Press.
Young, R. 2001. *Postcolonialism*. Oxford: Blackwell Publishing.

Periodicals

Black Action. 1989a. *Issue 2*. London: NALGO Black Action.
Black Action. 1989b. *Annual Conference Pack 1989*. London: NALGO Black Action, p. 14.
Camden Black Workers Group. 1984. 'Lucille Guichard – 15 Years' *Black Eye*, May, pp. 5–6.
Camden Black Workers Group. no date. *Camden Black Workers Group: 1982–1986*. London: Camden Black Workers Group.
CPSA. 1980. *National Annual Report 1979*. London: CPSA.
CPSA. 1981. *National Annual Report 1980*. London: CPSA.
First Official National Black Members Conference. 1986. *Transcript of Proceedings*. Leeds, 31 May.
Lambeth NALGO. 1981. *Race and Racism*. London: Lambeth NALGO.
London Borough of Camden. 1996. *Annual Report*. London: Camden Council.
London Borough of Ealing. 1990. *Annual Report*. London: Ealing Council.
Metropolitan District Council and Tower Hamlets Branch of NALGO. 1984. *Motion on Self-Organisation*. London: Metropolitan District Council and Tower Hamlets Branch of NALGO.
NALGO. 1975. *NALGO Annual Report 1974*. London: NALGO.
NALGO. 1977. *NALGO Annual Report 1976*. London: NALGO.
NALGO. 1979. *NALGO Annual Report 1978*. London: NALGO.
NALGO. 1980. *NALGO Annual Report 1979*. London: NALGO.
NALGO. 1981. *NALGO Annual Report 1980*. London: NALGO.
NALGO. 1982. *NALGO Annual Report 1981*. London: NALGO.
NALGO. 1983. *NALGO Annual Report 1982*. London: NALGO.
NALGO. 1984. *Race Equality*. London: NALGO.
NALGO. 1986. *NALGO Annual Report 1985*. London: NALGO.
NALGO. 1987. *NALGO Annual Report 1986*. London: NALGO.
National Black Members Conference. 1986. *Transcript of Proceedings of the First Official National Black Members Conference*. London: NBMCC.
National Black Members Co-ordinating Committee (NBMCC). no date. *None So Fit to Break Their Chains as Those That Bear Them*. London: NBMCC.
National Executive Council NALGO. 1988. *The National Executive Council's Report on Positive Action*. London: NALGO.
Positive Action Working Party. 1987. *Positive Action in NALGO*. London: NALGO.
Sawyer, P. 2007. 'Redemption Songs' *New Statesman*, 23 April 2007.

SCPS. 1983. *SCPS Annual Report 1982.* London: SCPS.
SCPS. 1984. *SCPS Annual Report 1983.* London: SCPS.
The Marxist. 1996. 'Saklatvala and the Fight against Racism and Imperialism 1921–28'
    The Marxist 13: 1.

NALGO Newspaper

Public Service July/August 1978.
Public Service November 1982, p. 16.
Public Service Mid-March 1983, p. 13.
Public Service July/August 1983, p. 5.
Public Service June 1984.
Public Service May 1986, p. 9.
Public Service June 1986, p. 6.
Public Service July 1987, p. 8.
Public Service July 1988, p. 3.
Public Service November 1988, p. 2.
Public Service July 1989, p. 5.
Public Service July 1990, p. 6.

Index

181